PUBLISHED

Jane Austen: *Emma* DAVID LODGE
Jane Austen: *'Northanger Abbey' and 'Persuasion'* B. C. SOUTHAM
Jane Austen: *'Sense and Sensibility', 'Pride and Prejudice' and 'Mansfield Park'*
  B. C. SOUTHAM
William Blake: *Songs of Innocence and Experience* MARGARET BOTTRALL
Charlotte Brontë: *'Jane Eyre' and 'Villette'* MIRIAM ALLOTT
Emily Brontë: *Wuthering Heights* MIRIAM ALLOTT
Browning: *'Men and Women' and Other Poems* J. R. WATSON
Bunyan: *The Pilgrim's Progress* ROGER SHARROCK
Byron: *'Childe Harold's Pilgrimage' and 'Don Juan'* JOHN JUMP
Chaucer: *Canterbury Tales* J. J. ANDERSON
Coleridge: *'The Ancient Mariner' and other Poems* ALUN R. JONES AND
  WILLIAM TYDEMAN
Conrad: *The Secret Agent* IAN WATT
Dickens: *Bleak House* A. E. DYSON
Donne: *Songs and Sonets* JULIAN LOVELOCK
George Eliot: *Middlemarch* PATRICK SWINDEN
T. S. Eliot: *Four Quartets* BERNARD BERGONZI
T. S. Eliot: *The Waste Land* C. B. COX AND ARNOLD P. HINCHLIFFE
Henry Fielding: *Tom Jones* NEIL COMPTON
E. M. Forster: *A Passage to India* MALCOLM BRADBURY
Hardy: *The Tragic Novels* R. P. DRAPER
Gerard Manley Hopkins: *Poems* MARGARET BOTTRALL
Jonson: *Volpone* JONAS A. BARISH
James Joyce: *'Dubliners' and 'A Portrait of the Artist as a Young Man'*
  MORRIS BEJA
John Keats: *Odes* G. S. FRASER
D. H. Lawrence: *Sons and Lovers* GĀMINI SALGĀDO
D. H. Lawrence: *'The Rainbow' and 'Women in Love'* COLIN CLARKE
Marlowe: *Doctor Faustus* JOHN JUMP
The Metaphysical Poets GERALD HAMMOND
Milton: *'Comus' and 'Samson Agonistes'* JULIAN LOVELOCK
Milton: *Paradise Lost* A. E. DYSON AND JULIAN LOVELOCK
John Osborne: *Look Back in Anger* JOHN RUSSELL TAYLOR
Peacock: *The Satirical Novels* LORNA SAGE
Pope: *The Rape of the Lock* JOHN DIXON HUNT
Shakespeare: *Antony and Cleopatra* JOHN RUSSELL BROWN
Shakespeare: *Hamlet* JOHN JUMP
Shakespeare: *Henry IV Parts I and II* G. K. HUNTER
Shakespeare: *Henry V* MICHAEL QUINN
Shakespeare: *Julius Caesar* PETER URE
Shakespeare: *King Lear* FRANK KERMODE
Shakespeare: *Macbeth* JOHN WAIN
Shakespeare: *Measure for Measure* G. K. STEAD
Shakespeare: *The Merchant of Venice* JOHN WILDERS
Shakespeare: *Othello* JOHN WAIN
Shakespeare: *Richard II* NICHOLAS BROOKE

Shakespeare: *The Tempest* D. J. PALMER
Shakespeare: *Troilus and Cressida* PRISCILLA MARTIN
Shakespeare: *Twelfth Night* D. J. PALMER
Shakespeare: *The Winter's Tale* KENNETH MUIR
Shelley: *Shorter Poems and Lyrics* PATRICK SWINDEN
Spenser: *The Faerie Queene* PETER BAYLEY
Swift: *Gulliver's Travels* RICHARD GRAVIL
Tennyson: *In Memoriam* JOHN DIXON HUNT
Webster: '*The White Devil*' and '*The Duchess of Malfi*'
R. V. HOLDSWORTH
Virginia Woolf: *To the Lighthouse* MORRIS BEJA
Wordsworth: *Lyrical Ballads* ALUN R. JONES AND WILLIAM
TYDEMAN
Wordsworth: *The Prelude* W. J. HARVEY AND RICHARD GRAVIL
Yeats: *Last Poems* JON STALLWORTHY

TITLES IN PREPARATION INCLUDE

George Eliot: '*The Mill on the Floss*' and '*Silas Marner*' R. P. DRAPER
T. S. Eliot: '*Prufrock*', '*Gerontion*', '*Ash Wednesday*' and Other Shorter Poems
B. C. SOUTHAM
Farquhar: '*The Beaux' Stratagem*' and '*The Recruiting Officer*'
RAY ANSELMENT
Jonson: '*Every Man in His Humour*' and '*The Alchemist*'
R. V. HOLDSWORTH
Shakespeare: *Coriolanus* B. A. BROCKMAN
Shakespeare: '*Much Ado about Nothing*' and '*As You Like It*'
JENNIFER SEARLE
Shakespeare: *Sonnets* PETER JONES
Sheridan: '*The Rivals*', '*The School for Scandal*' and '*The Critic*'
WILLIAM RUDDICK
Thackeray: *Vanity Fair* ARTHUR POLLARD

The Evolution of Novel Criticism STEPHEN HAZELL
The Romantic Imagination JOHN S. HILL

CONTENTS

Acknowledgements   7

General Editor's Preface   9

Introduction   11

Note on Verse Citation and References   20

Part One: *Eighteenth- and Nineteenth-century Criticism*

JOHN HUGHES (1715), p. 23 – WILLIAM HAZLITT (1818),
p. 34 – EDWARD DOWDEN (1882), p. 40.

Part Two: *Introducing the Poem*

1. Sources and Influences

   H. G. LOTSPEICH: Classical Mythology in Spenser's
   Poetry (1932)   49

   H. H. BLANCHARD: Spenser and Boiardo (1925)   58

   R. E. NEIL DODGE: Spenser's Imitations from Ariosto
   (1897)   66

   P. J. ALPERS: Spenser's Use of Ariosto (1967)   69

   ROSEMOND TUVE: Spenser and Medieval Romances
   (1966)   74

2. Allegory

   GRAHAM HOUGH: Allegory in *The Faerie Queene* (1962)   101

   MAURICE EVANS: Spenserean Allegory (1970)   107

3. Rhetoric, Language, Versification

   P. J. ALPERS: The Rhetorical Mode of Spenser's
   Narrative (1967)   118

   MARTHA CRAIG: The Secret Wit of Spenser's Language
   (1967)   127

WILLIAM EMPSON: Spenser's Rhythm (1930)   142

NORTHROP FRYE: Verbal *Opsis* in Spenser (1957)   144

HARRY S. BERGER, JR: Conspicuous Irrelevance (1957)   147

Part Three: *General Twentieth-century Studies*

C. S. LEWIS: 'To Read him is to Grow in Mental Health'
(1936)   161

A. C. HAMILTON: The *Architectonike* of the Poem (1961)   170

WILLIAM NELSON: That True Glorious Type (1963)   179

FRANK KERMODE: 'The Element of Historical Allegory'
(1964)   197

PETER BAYLEY: The Poetic Achievement (1971)   211

ALASTAIR FOWLER: Neoplatonic Order in *The Faerie
Queen* (1973)   224

A. KENT HIEATT: A Spenser to Structure our Myths (1975)   240

Select Bibliography   247

Notes on Contributors   249

Index   251

ACKNOWLEDGEMENTS

The editor and publishers wish to thank the following who have kindly given permission for the use of copyright material: P. J. Alpers, selections from *The Poetry of 'The Faerie Queen'*; copyright 1967 by Princeton University Press, reprinted by permission of the publishers. Peter Bayley, extracts from *Edmund Spenser, Prince of Poets* (1971) by permission of the author and Hutchinson Publishing Group Ltd. H. Berger, extracts from *The Allegorical Temper: Vision and Reality in Book II of Spenser's 'Faerie Queene'* (1957) by permission of Yale University Press. Harold Hooper Blanchard, extracts from 'Spenser and Boiardo', *PMLA*, XL (1925) reprinted by permission of the Modern Language Association of America. Martha A. Craig, extracts from 'The Secret Wit of Spenser's Language' from *Elizabethan Poetry: Modern Essays in Criticism* ed. Paul J. Alpers; copyright 1967 by Oxford University Press Inc., reprinted by permission. R. E. Neil Dodge, extract from 'Spenser's Imitations from Ariosto', *PMLA*, XII (1897) reprinted by permission of the Modern Language Association of America. William Empson, extract from *Seven Types of Ambiguity* (1930) by permission of the author and Chatto and Windus Ltd. Maurice Evans, extracts from *Spenser's Anatomy of Heroism* (1970) by permission of the author and Cambridge University Press. Alastair Fowler, extract from 'Emanations of Glory: Neoplatonic Order in *The Faerie Queen*' from *A Theatre for Spenserians*, ed. Kennedy and Reither (1973), by permission of the author. Northrop Frye, extracts from *The Anatomy of Criticism: Four Essays*; copyright 1957 by Princeton University Press (Princeton Paperback 1971), reprinted by permission of the publishers. A. C. Hamilton, extract from *The Structure of Allegory in the 'Faerie Queene'*; copyright 1961 by Oxford University Press, reprinted by permission of the publishers. A. Kent Hieatt, extracts from 'A Spenser to Structure our Myths' from *Contemporary Thoughts on Edmund Spenser*, ed. Frushell and Vandersmith (1975), by permission of the author. Graham Hough, extract from *A Preface to 'The Faerie Queen'* (1962) by permission of Gerald Duckworth & Co. Ltd. Frank Kermode, extracts from *Shakespeare, Spenser, Donne* (1971) by permission of Routledge & Kegan Paul Ltd. C. S. Lewis, extracts from *The Allegory of Love* (1936) by permission of Oxford University Press. H. G. Lotspeich, extracts from *Classical Mythology in the Poetry of Edmund Spenser*; copyright 1932 by Princeton University Press. William Nelson, extracts from *The Poetry of Edmund Spenser* (1963) by permission of the author and Columbia University Press. Rosemond Tuve, extracts from *Allegorical Imagery: Some Mediaeval Books and Their Posterity*; copyright 1966 by Princeton University Press, reprinted by permission of the publishers.

GENERAL EDITOR'S PREFACE

Each of this series of Casebooks concerns either one well-known and influential work of literature or two or three closely linked works. The main section consists of critical readings, mostly modern, brought together from journals and books. A selection of reviews and comments by the author's contemporaries is also included, and sometimes comments from the author himself. The Editor's Introduction charts the reputation of the work from its first appearance until the present time.

The critical forum is a place of vigorous conflict and disagreement, but there is nothing in this to cause dismay. What is attested is the complexity of human experience and the richness of literature, not any chaos or relativity of taste. A critic is better seen, no doubt, as an explorer than as an 'authority', but explorers ought to be, and usually are, well equipped. The effect of good criticism is to convince us of what C. S. Lewis called 'the enormous extension of our being which we owe to authors'. A Casebook will be justified if it helps to promote the same end.

A single volume can represent no more than a small selection of critical opinions. Some critics have been excluded for reasons of space, and it is hoped that readers will follow up the further suggestions in the Select Bibliography. Other contributions have been severed from their original context, to which some readers may wish to return. Indeed, if they take a hint from the critics represented here, they certainly will.

A. E. DYSON

INTRODUCTION

Although in recent years *The Faerie Queene* has attracted much attention from critics and scholars, it has had only a minority of readers for the last hundred years. Yet it is a poem which, once read and known, no reader ever loses his affection and admiration for. A part of the problem has always been worry about what sort of a poem it is, and therefore about how to approach it. Gabriel Harvey, to whom his friend Spenser had sent a draft of some part of *The Faerie Queene* in 1580, called it, with jocose belittlement, '*that Elvish Queene*', and 'sent her home at the last, neither in better nor worse case' than he found her. He was reluctant to comment ('. . . must you of necessity have my judgement of her?') but when he did comment, thought reprovingly that *Hobgoblin* had 'run away with the garland from *Apollo*', and concluded: 'Mark what I say, and yet I will not say that I thought, but there an end for this once, and fare you well, till God or some good angel put you in a better mind.' Harvey was the first to be perplexed or in some way not altogether satisfied with the poem. It is likely, because of other references in the Spenser–Harvey correspondence,[1] that what he had seen was writing influenced by Ariosto, perhaps some of the love and romance material which eventually appeared in Books III and IV, or the Braggadocchio or Acrasia episodes of the present Book II. He seems to have thought the 'Elvish Queene' too Ariostan, or perhaps too local and demotic (no epic is so much concerned with the activities of ordinary life); he almost certainly wished it were more exalted and Virgilian. The vital cause of much perplexity about *The Faerie Queene* may lie here. Was there ever such a Hobgoblin epic, such an Apollonian romance?

So from the beginning readers have been puzzled and often dissatisfied. Even the greatest admirers have been confused about its form, its tone, or its significance and direction, none of which is simple or unchallengeably clear. What sort of a poem is it? Romantic or epic? Original or very derivative? Up-to-the-minute or anachronistic? Is it didactic or too romantically entertaining, too serious or not serious enough? Does it express vital truths of great moment to men, or is it an escapist work? The truth is it is an exceedingly complex poem, with a complicated family tree, and it exercises in its course a large number of different functions – poetic, religious, didactic, philosophical, historical – some of which would seem to cancel others out at times. Often, because of its allegorical basis and its use of symbolism, it exercises more than one of these functions at the same time; but sometimes it behaves straightforwardly as a simple narrative. Readers have always been baffled by this, and I think it is the chief factor in the relative neglect of one of the world's great works of literature. Of course, from the beginning readers have found what they wanted or what they liked in the poem, and have placed their emphasis, of praise or dis-esteem, in different places. Those who have found it heroic have tended to describe it in terms of Homer and Virgil; others have liked it for being heroic in the romance way of Ariosto and Tasso; some have liked it for its resemblance to medieval romance; some have found and liked reference to contemporary personalities and consistent historical allegory; some for being Christian and moral, concerned to present and promote the moral virtues; some have picked out the praise and honouring of the Queen, some the skilful iconography; and have singled out for special commendation his verse, his use of language – archaic and inventive – and his power in poetic description and in engendering atmosphere.

Many-sided Spenser has continued and indeed continues to be seen in different ways, but it is possible to chart some changes in depth and area of critical response.

Early writers on Spenser and editors of the late seventeenth century and the eighteenth century, proficient in the classics and well versed in Italian literature, admired Spenser's nobility and his fancy almost equally. What troubled them was the fact that this heroic poem, as they saw it, lacked the classical unity they deemed appropriate. Thomas Rymer (1674) felt he must 'blame the Italians for debauching great Spenser's judgment . . . he suffered himself to be misled by *Ariosto*; with whom blindly rambling on *marvellous* adventures, he makes no conscience of *Probability*'. John Hughes, Spenser's first editor, (in 1715) criticised the lack of inter-dependence between the separate books and thought Prince Arthur not a major enough figure to be considered the central hero. John Upton (1758)

had no difficulty here, finding, against the evidence, a 'beginning
. . . the British Prince saw in a vision the Fairy Queen, and fell in
love with her: The middle, his search after her . . . : The end, his
finding whom he sought': a strangely false account of the facts from
one whose notes and comments were so accurate and excellent. But
Hughes's admiration for the poem led him to see beyond reverence
for neo-classical rigidity, and he found a way out. To compare *The
Faerie Queene* with the 'models of antiquity would be like drawing a
parallel between the *Roman* and the *Gothic* architecture. In the first
there is doubtless a more natural grandeur and simplicity; in the
latter we find great mixtures of beauty and barbarism.' Thomas
Warton (1762) shared in all the neo-classical doubts, but was
equally sure that *The Faerie Queene* was a great poem, and saw the
absurdity of 'judging either Ariosto or Spenser by precepts which
they did not attend to. We who live in the days of writing by rule,
are apt to try every composition by those laws which we have been
taught to think the sole criterion of excellence.' 'Epic severity' had
been replaced 'by something which more powerfully attracts us:
something which engages the affections and the feelings of the heart,
rather than the cold approbation of the head . . .'. Richard Hurd
(1762) picked up Hughes's warning not to expect *The Faerie Queene*
to be like the models of antiquity, developing the idea that the poem
was 'not of a classical but Gothic composition', and drawing bizarre
parallels between classical heroes and Gothic knights and their
respective doings. So the neo-classical age, although worried about
the obvious lack of unity of the poem, happily excused it on other
grounds. Neither the critics of that age, nor the Romantic and
Victorian critics who followed, were much worried by the fact that
the poem is unfinished, and, like most critics up to the present,
tended rather to excuse defects they found in the poem on the
grounds of its incompleteness.

The critics of the nineteenth century did not worry much about
unity and design, nor about the other preoccupation of earlier or
later critics, the allegory and the meaning. Hazlitt (1818) did not
intend readers to ignore the allegory when he advised them that, if
they didn't meddle with it, it wouldn't meddle with them. He meant
that it was not usually obtrusive, or recondite, and that they should
not be frightened of it: 'It might as well be pretended that we
cannot see Poussin's pictures for the allegory, as that the allegory

prevents us understanding Spenser.' James Russell Lowell (1875) found fault with the historical allegory and the method whereby 'all his characters double their parts, and appear in his allegory as the impersonations of abstract moral qualities' (not that this is strictly true) and decided: 'We may fairly leave the allegory on one side, for perhaps, after all, he adopted it only for the reason that it was in fashion, and put it on as he did his ruff, not because it was becoming, but because it was the only wear.' He failed to see that what he admired in Homer is largely true of Spenser: 'The true type of the allegory is the Odyssey, which we read without suspicion as pure poem, and then find a new pleasure in divining its double meaning.' Yet one sees what he means, and he frankly admits to being bored by the allegory, which 'is too often forced upon us against our will'. No one would deny that there are flat and dull patches of elementary personification and allegory in *The Faerie Queene* but Lowell went further, and found himself disliking the moral purpose: 'whenever . . . you come suddenly on the moral, it gives you a shock of unpleasant surprise, a kind of grit, as when one's teeth close on a bit of gravel in a dish of strawberries and cream'. What he wanted was escapism, and it was Lowell more than anyone else, more even than Leigh Hunt (1844) – 'Spenser's great characteristic is poetic luxury' – who was responsible for a sickly-sweet view of Spenser's 'endless grace and dreaming pleasure' which has persisted until today. Between them, too, they put about the idea that 'Spenser is the farthest removed from the ordinary cares and haunts of the world' (Hunt); and Lowell advised: 'whoever wishes to be rid of thought and to let the busy anvils of the brain be silent for a time, let him read in the "Faery Queene". There is the land of pure heart's ease where no ache or sorrow of spirit can enter.' Edward Dowden (1884) strongly refuted Lowell's soporifics within a decade, to give the first reading of the poem which encompassed (briefly though it was done) its seriousness of purpose, its Christian basis, its 'moral breadth' and 'noble sanity', 'its conciliation of what is earthly and what is divine' as well as its romantic imaginative appeal and its sense of humanity. But at least the nineteenth-century critics, like those of the eighteenth, recognised that above all it was romantic narrative they were reading and enjoying. This is generally true, too, of the critics of the first half of the twentieth

century, before the era of the professional academic critic had
replaced that of the civilising scholarly appreciator.

It is only since the completion of the great Variorum edition in
1949 that criticism of Spenser has become specialised and recondite.
This is not to deny the subtlety and scholarship of writers like de
Selincourt, Cory, Osgood, Renwick, Janet Spens, Josephine Bennett
and C. S. Lewis, but, in their different ways, they all belonged to an
older literary and critical tradition, which some call humane and
others might call old-fashioned or even amateur. Whether the severe
professionalism of recent scholarship and criticism has really added
as much as is claimed to the true understanding of Spenser, and
whether it has contributed at all to our enjoyment of him, is an
open question. We understand him better for our newish knowledge
of Alciati and other emblematists, new insights into mythography
and iconography, and from the extended inquiries into theology,
and legal philosophy and history, and our new awareness of his
lively use of language and rhetoric. But Spenser's profundities and
complexities of knowledge, intuition, understanding and purpose are
so great that we are still making discoveries: in the last twenty or
thirty years, more than ever before has been discovered about the
background and sources of his thought and vision. Naturally there
is danger of imbalance. Iconographers and numerologists may
exaggerate the significance of their findings, indeed may over-
estimate Spenser's subtlety here. The rhetoricists may – I think they
do – over-state their claims of the importance of elaborate concern
for the poet's manipulation of the reader's response. Historians may
know too much about the Elizabethan age, far more than Spenser
did, and may consequently over-subtilise or complicate his intention;
as may theologians and philosophers, not to mention linguisticians
and other minute scrutineers of the text. Ignorance has no monopoly
of the power to blind or distort; knowledge can have the same
power. In any case, time is needed for the assimilation of this remarkable recent extension of our knowledge about Spenser, which
has promoted a great increase in professional academic preoccupation with *The Faerie Queene* but not, alas, made it any more
popular with students and the general reader.

I have included less specialised and 'hard'-line criticism than is
usual in this series, partly for this reason, partly because in some
ways criticism of Spenser, in the modern sense, is still uncertain of its

steps. The older controversies – about Aristotelianism and neo-
Platonism, about Spenser's alleged perversity (he lusted after the
girls in the fountain or longed for the amenities of Castle Joyous
while seeming to deplore them), about 'the two orders of nature and
of grace', about his supposed Calvinism or Puritanism, even Lewis's
canard about his 'being the instrument of a detestable policy in
Ireland, and . . . the wickedness he had shared begins to corrupt
his imagination' – have all been resolved or died down. It is just
possible that Spenser will escape 'hard' critical defoliation. The
scale of the poem, the extent and variety of its detail, its synoptic
width, its depth of focus and the universality of its concern, make it
extremely difficult to 'process'. It is always moving on. To those who
think of it as only half a poem (but they are few nowadays), it is
open-ended. To others, who detect a sense of completeness, or at
least the sense of an ending, there is still something circular and
unending about it, like the serpent with its tail in its mouth. One
has always to be looking forward as one goes and to be looking
back when going forward.

When all is said and done *The Faerie Queene* is many poems, and
large poems at that. The other great poems of the western world,
*Odyssey, Iliad, Aeneid, The Divine Comedy, Orlando Furioso, Gerusalemme
Liberata, Paradise Lost*, are clear, simple, *manageable* beside it. You
can summarise their fable or message in ten or twelve sentences or
less; you can put them on the table, as it were, and concentrate
your gaze and mind upon them; you can turn them round, appraise
their shape, realise them in three dimensions. Even their subtleties
shine forth, are quickly recognisable, and can be *handled*. *The Faerie
Queene* eludes the grasp, and this is not only because its shape is less
perfect. Its message is more multifold. It is more various and complex
in conception. While it treats of remote times (its flavour of 'Once
upon a time' is peculiarly strong) it yet constantly reminds us of
Spenser's own age, and at the same time of our own. This is not true
of most epics. Furthermore, not being limited to one or two *actions*,
its referential power is extremely wide and so is the range of human
activity it presents. And unlike the other great epics it leans heavily
on the contemporary and has strong foundations deep in popular
culture. These balance the learned inspiration of its message and
much of its detail, and the literary inspiration revealed in the many
forms pressed into service. Medieval romance, romantic epic,

classical epic details, legend, saints' legend, pageant, folk-tale, parable, fable, myth: all may be discerned in its unparalleled abundancy. Naturally, it is difficult to criticise. It is not easy to write about a long work (it is longer than all of the epics I have mentioned except Ariosto's); all the more difficult if, like *The Faerie Queene*, it consists of many actions, with an enormous and changing company of characters, and, while telling a succession of clear romantic narratives, is also concerned to present and discuss profound human problems, and questions of both public and private morality.

Critical differences arise naturally from disagreement about which of the *Faerie Queenes* has primacy – the epic, the romantic, the medieval, the moralistic, the Christian, the neo-Platonic. In his Letter to Sir Walter Raleigh, which was printed in 1590 with the first three books, Spenser himself made epic claims, citing classical and romantic models. He also wrote of the poem's distinct moral purpose and of his method of promoting this, the allegorical; the 'continued Allegory, or darke conceit'. But the most extended reference is to romance, and when we read the poem we find that it is first and foremost a romantic narrative. This was what above all he had resolved to write. It is avowed in the Letter, and apparent in the work within a few stanzas of the beginning. This is where I have placed the emphasis in my selection, for I think a new reader should come to *The Faerie Queene* expecting to read a romance or chain of romances. This would be to begin in the right way. He should not approach it expecting either an epic or an allegory. As he reads, he will not be able to ignore the elements of epic – great contests, heroic actions, visits to the underworld, supernatural forces, epic similes – nor the Renaissance materials – masques, pageants, processions, symbolic actions, classical figures and scenes – but he will see them in proportion. In Books III and IV he will find the medieval romance vivified by characters now more typical or representative and more 'Elizabethan', and will find the narrative method diversified from a simple pattern of quest or journey into a more sophisticated pattern by complex interlacing of sub-plots. But it is still primarily a romance world, though nearer the world of epic than of Arthurian romance.

Two other problems may trouble him, the question of allegory and symbolism and the poem's incompleteness. The question of allegory and symbolism is not in fact a difficult one, though many writers on the topic have made it seem so, even that fine scholar and critic C. S. Lewis. The purpose of allegory is to reveal and not to conceal; or rather, it is to reveal while seeming to conceal. The Elizabethan writer, Sir John Harington, in the preface to his English version of Ariosto's *Orlando Furioso* (1591), referred to the allegory 'which *Plutarch* defineth to be when one thing is told, and by that another is understood'. It is a gross but sublime simplification, which I commend to new readers of Spenser worried by the term 'allegory'. In *The Faerie Queene* it covers a wide range from the most rudimentary to the fairly complex; from the presentation of the monster Error (Book I, Canto 1) whose vomit of books and papers represents Catholic propaganda and erroneous theology, or of the House of Temperance in Book II, Canto 9, a tediously explicit presentation of the human body in ingenious and sometimes comic detail, to characters like Ignaro (Book I, Canto 8) or Despair (Book I, Canto 9) whose vigorous life in the narrative is not limited by their allegorical function, and to characters like Malbecco (Book III, Canto 10) who turn into allegories as we watch them.[2] At the higher end, allegory becomes so subtle as to verge upon symbol. The reader of *The Faerie Queene* should not be anxiously on the alert for allegory; it is unlikely that he will miss it even at the first reading, even if he is following the advice to embark upon the poem as a romance or collection of romances. Nor should he expect the poem to be continuously allegorical. It is basically romantic narrative. From time to time a special significance or meaning is intended, and is pointed up in an allegorical sequence or character, but then the poem reverts to romantic narrative again and we follow further knightly, courtly or heroic adventures. This is not to deny a subliminal layer of significance: the journeys, quests, combats, mistakes and perils of the knights and ladies are themselves part of a protracted metaphor, for the poem is a protracted metaphor of human life. Yet another strand of allegorical significance, the contemporary and historical reference to Elizabeth's court and courtiers and to Roman Catholicism is even less consistently maintained. Hazlitt was right. You don't have to meddle with the allegory overmuch: it has its own effective insistency. But it cannot be ignored, as Lowell wished. The moral significance of the poem is chiefly communicated by means of allegory, simple or complex, and of symbol.

The other problem, of the poem's incompleteness, has not in fact much troubled readers and critics. Most writers tacitly assume now that Spenser brought his poem to a sort of conclusion, and that he indirectly said so in the two Cantos of Mutabilitie and the two 'personal' stanzas at the very end. Certainly it is difficult to see what further development was possible. Courtesy, the virtue of Book VI, as it is presented and commented on seems to embrace most of the preceding ones. The last hero–knight, Sir Calidore, seems a more perfect knight (with the sole exception of Britomart) than any of his predecessors. Courtesy stands in Book VI almost as the equivalent of the loving generosity of Christ; Spenser was near enough to the Middle Ages to remember how 'courtesy' and 'courteous' were used then of God, of Christ and of the Virgin Mary. Yet this virtue is shown to be fragile and vulnerable. Spenser adjusted his focal depth, so to speak, in Books V and VI so that the hopes, struggles and virtues of the good knights exist not only in an ideal or never-never-land context, but are shown in implied apposition to the real world – Spenser's own sixteenth-century world – of evil and impermanence. That is also our world. This change towards the end of the poem, in Book V and VI, means that *The Faerie Queene* takes a great stride towards us, moves into a new dimension of relevance. Spenser makes his point emphatic at the end, first in an invented mythological sequence in the Mutabilitie Cantos, and then in specifically Christian terms in the final two stanzas, setting the fact of earthly deficiency and impermanence against the unchanging love of God.

I have stated this more clearly and definitely than others, but almost all writers on Spenser tacitly assume that they are dealing with a complete entity in the six books, two cantos 'of Mutabilitie: which . . . appeare to be parcell of some following Booke of the *Faerie Queene*' and the two stanzas of the so-called eighth canto 'unperfite' of that book.

There are several collections of essays on *The Faerie Queene*. I have tried to avoid duplicating their work, but one or two pieces I have felt compelled to use. I present more extracts from books than articles, partly because the latter tend to be detailed and particular and I want to give a comprehensive general introduction. What new readers of Spenser need is not high-powered academic controversy from learned periodicals, but wide perspectives. I think new readers need help over sources, influences and literary forms, so I have printed brief pieces on Spenser's use of Bioardo and Ariosto, as well as the long extracts on romance from Rosemond Tuve's great book. I have chosen pieces which illuminate important topics, like allegory, important elements in the poem like the Arthurian background, and significant themes, symbols and characters like mutability, the dance of the Graces, and Britomart. At the publishers' request, I have in general put emphasis on Books I, II, and III, and I have included a piece of my own, at the General Editor's kind insistence.

The Faerie Queene, daunting though it may sound to a new reader, is a remarkably enjoyable and moving narrative of extraordinary imaginative range, full of excitement, action and movement, and by no means without humour, and of significant human concern. I have remembered Warton, and present, as far as I can, that writing on Spenser which like the great work itself 'engages the affections and the feelings of the heart, rather than the cold approbation of the head'.

NOTES

1. Published in 1580. It is to be found in some complete editions of Spenser's work, e.g. the Variorum edition and the Oxford Standard Authors volume edited by E. de Selincourt.

2. See below, pp. 218–19.

NOTE ON VERSE CITATION AND REFERENCES

All quotations from *The Faerie Queene* and names of characters and places are printed as they appeared in the original books or articles. Most notes and references in the original material have been omitted, the exceptions being those which helpfully suggest further reading.

PART ONE

Eighteenth- and Nineteenth-century Criticism

John Hughes (1715)

An allegory is a fable or story in which under imaginary persons or things is shadowed some real action or instructive moral; or, as I think it is somewhere very shortly defined by Plutarch, it is that 'in which one thing is related and another thing is understood'. It is a kind of poetical picture, or hieroglyphic, which by its apt resemblance conveys instruction to the mind by an analogy to the senses and so amuses the fancy whilst it informs the understanding. Every allegory has therefore two senses, the literal and the mystical; the literal sense is like a dream or vision, of which the mystical sense is the true meaning or interpretation.

This will be more clearly apprehended by considering that as a simile is but a more extended metaphor, so an allegory is a kind of continued simile or an assemblage of similitudes drawn out at full length. Thus when it is said that 'Death is the offspring of Sin', this is a metaphor to signify that the former is produced by the latter as a child is brought into the world by its parent. Again, to compare death to a meagre and ghastly apparition starting out of the ground, moving towards the spectator with a menacing air and shaking in his hand a bloody dart is a representation of the terrors which attend that great enemy to human nature. But let the reader observe in Milton's *Paradise Lost* with what exquisite fancy and skill this common metaphor and simile, and the moral contained in them, are extended and wrought up into one of the most beautiful allegories in our language.

The resemblance which has been so often observed in general between poetry and painting is yet more particular in allegory, which, as I said before, is a kind of picture in poetry. Horace has in one of his odes pathetically described the ruinous condition of his country after the civil wars and the hazard of its being involved in new dissensions, by the emblem of a ship shattered with storms and driven into port with broken masts, torn sails and disabled rigging and in danger of being forced by new storms out to sea again. There is nothing said in the whole ode but what is literally applicable to a ship, but it is generally agreed that the thing signified is the Roman State. Thus Rubens, who had a good allegorical genius in painting, has in his famous work of the Luxembourg Gallery figured the government of France, on Louis the Thirteenth's arriving at age, by a galley. The king stands at the helm; Mary of Medicis, the queen mother and regent, puts the rudder in his hand; Justice, Fortitude, Religion and Public Faith are seated at the oars; and other Virtues have their proper employments in managing the sails and tackle.

By this general description of allegory it may easily be conceived that in works of this kind there is a large field open to invention, which among the ancients was universally looked upon to be the principal part of poetry. The power of raising images or resemblances of things, giving them life and action and presenting them as it were before the eyes was thought to have something in it like creation. And it was probably for this fabling part that the first authors of such works were called 'poets', or 'makers' as the word signifies and as it is literally translated and used by Spenser. . . . However, by this art of fiction or allegory more than by the structure of their numbers, or what we now call 'versification', the poets were distinguished from historians and philosophers, though the latter sometimes invaded the province of the poet and delivered their doctrines likewise in allegories or parables. And this, when they did not purposely make them obscure in order to conceal them from the common people, was a plain indication that they thought there was an advantage in such methods of conveying instruction to the mind and that they served for the more effectual engaging the attention of the hearers and for leaving deeper impressions on their memories.

Plutarch, in one of his discourses, gives a very good reason for the use of fiction in poetry: because Truth of itself is rigid and austere and cannot be moulded into such agreeable forms as fiction can. 'For neither the numbers,' says he, 'nor the ranging of the words, nor the elevation and elegance of the style have so many graces as the artful contrivance and disposition of the fable.' For this reason, as he relates it after Plato, when the wise Socrates himself was prompted by a particular impulse to the writing of verses, being by his constant employment in the study of truth a stranger to the art of inventing, he chose for his subject the fables of Aesop, 'not thinking,' says Plutarch, 'that anything could be poetry which was void of fiction'. The same author makes use of a comparison in another place which I think may be most properly applied to allegorical poetry in particular: that as grapes on a vine are covered by the leaves which grow about them, so under the pleasant narrations and fictions of the poets there are couched many useful morals and doctrines.

It is for this reason – that is to say, in regard to the moral sense – that allegory has a liberty indulged to it beyond any other sort of writing whatsoever; that it often assembles things of the most contrary kinds in nature and supposes even impossibilities – as that a golden bough should grow among the common branches of a tree, as Virgil has described it in the Sixth Book of his *Aeneis*. Allegory is indeed the fairyland of poetry, peopled by imagination; its inhabitants are so many apparitions; its woods, caves, wild beasts, rivers, mountains and palaces are produced by a kind of magical power and are all visionary and typical; and it abounds in such licenses as would be shocking and monstrous if the mind did not attend to the mystic sense contained under them. . . .

I am not insensible that the word 'allegory' has been sometimes used in a larger sense than that to which I may seem here to have restrained it and has been applied indifferently to any poem which contains a covered moral, though the story or fable carries nothing in it that appears visionary or romantic. It may be necessary, therefore, to distinguish allegory into the two following kinds.

The first is that in which the story is framed of real or historical persons and probable or possible actions, by which however some other persons and actions are typified or represented. In this sense the whole *Aeneis* of Virgil may be said to be an allegory, if we consider Aeneas as representing Augustus Caesar and his conducting the remains of his countrymen from the ruins of Troy to a new settlement in Italy as emblematical of Augustus' modelling a new government out of the ruins of the aristocracy and establishing the Romans, after the confusion of the civil war, in a peaceable and flourishing condition. It does not, I think, appear that Homer had any such design in his poems or that he meant to delineate his contemporaries or their actions under the chief characters and adventures of the Trojan War. And though the allusion I have mentioned in Virgil is a circumstance which the author has finely contrived to be coincident to the general frame of his story, yet he has avoided the making it plain and particular and has thrown it off in so many instances from a direct application that his poem is perfect without it. This then, for distinction, should I think, rather be called a parallel than an allegory; at least, in allegories framed after this manner, the literal sense is sufficient to satisfy the reader, though he should look no further, and without being considered as emblematical of some other persons or action, may of itself exhibit very useful morals and instructions. Thus the morals which may be drawn from the *Aeneis* are equally noble and instructive whether we suppose the real hero to be Aeneas or Augustus Caesar.

The second kind of allegory, and which I think may more properly challenge the name, is that in which the fable or story consists for the most part of fictitious persons or beings, creatures of the poet's brain, and actions surprising and without the bounds of probability or nature. In works of this kind it is impossible for the reader to rest in the literal sense, but he is of necessity driven to seek for another meaning under these wild types and shadows. This grotesque invention claims, as I have observed, a licence peculiar to itself and is what I would be understood in this discourse more particularly to mean by the word 'allegory'. . . . It may be proper to give an instance or two, by which the distinction of this last kind of allegory may more plainly appear.

The story of Circe in the *Odysses* is an allegorical fable of which there are perhaps more copies and imitations than of any other what-ever. Her offering a cup filled with intoxicating liquor to her guests, her mingling poison with their food and then by magical arts turning them into the shapes of swine, and Ulysses resisting her charms by the virtue of an herb called moly, which he had received from the God Mercury, and restoring his companions to their true persons are all fictions of the last kind I have mentioned. The person of the goddess is likewise fictitious and out of the circle of the Grecian divinities, and the adventures are not to be understood but in a mystical sense. The episode of Calypso, though somewhat of the same kind, approaches nearer to nature and probability. But the story of Dido in the *Aeneis*, though copied from the Circe and Calypso and formed on the same moral – namely, to represent a hero obstructed by the allurements of pleasure and at last breaking from them – and though Mercury likewise assists in it to dissolve the charm, yet is not necessarily to be looked upon as an allegory. The fable does not appear merely imaginary or emblematical; the persons are natural; and excepting the distance of time which the critics have noted between the real Aeneas and Dido (a circumstance which Virgil, not being bound to historical truth, wilfully neglected), there is nothing which might not really have happened. Ariosto's Alcina and the Armida of Tasso are copies from the same original. These again are plainly allegorical: the whole literal sense of the latter is a kind of vision, or scene of imagination, and is everywhere transparent, to show the moral sense which is under it. The Bower of Bliss, in the Second Book of *The Faerie Queene*, is in like manner a copy from Tasso; but the ornaments of description, which Spenser has transplanted out of the Italian poem, are more proper in his work, which was designed to be wholly allegorical, than in an epic poem, which is superior in its nature to such lavish embellishments. There is another copy of the Circe in the dramatic way in a masque by our famous Milton, the whole plan of which is allegorical and is written with a very poetical spirit on the same moral, though with different characters.

I have here instanced in one of the most ancient and best-imagined allegories extant. Scylla, Charybdis and the Sirens in the same poem are of the same nature and are creatures purely allegorical. But the Harpies in Virgil, which disturbed Aeneas and his followers at their banquet, as they do not seem to exhibit any certain moral, may probably have been thrown in by the poet only as an omen and to raise what is commonly called 'the wonderful', which is a property as essential to epic poetry as probability. Homer's giving speech to the River Xanthus in the *Iliad* and to the horses of Achilles seem to be inventions of the same kind, and might be designed to fill the reader with astonishment and concern and with an apprehension of the greatness of an occasion which, by a bold fiction of the poet, is supposed to have produced such extraordinary effects.

As allegory sometimes, for the sake of the moral sense couched under its fictions, gives speech to brutes and sometimes introduces creatures which are out of nature – as goblins, chimeras, fairies and the like – so it frequently gives life to virtues and vices, passions and diseases, to natural and moral qualities and represents them acting as divine, human or infernal persons. A very ingenious writer calls these characters 'shadowy Beings'[1] and has with good reason censured the employing them in just epic poems. Of this kind are Sin and Death, which I mentioned before, in Milton and Fame in Virgil. We find likewise a large group of these shadowy figures placed, in the Sixth Book of the *Aeneis*, at the entrance into the infernal regions; but as they are only shown there and have no share in the action of the poem, the description of them is a fine allegory and extremely proper to the place where they appear. . . .

Every book of *The Faerie Queene* is fruitful of these visionary beings, which are invented and drawn with a surprising strength of imagination. I shall produce but one instance here, which the reader may compare with that just mentioned in Virgil, to which it is no way inferior. It is in the Second Book where Mammon conducts Guyon through a cave underground to show him his treasure:

> At length they came into a larger space,
>> That stretcht it selfe into an ample plaine,
>> Through which a beaten broad high way did trace,
>> That streight did lead to *Plutoes* griesly raine:
>> By that wayes side, there sat infernall Payne,
>> And fast beside him sat tumultuous Strife:
>> The one in hand an yron whip did straine,
>> The other brandished a bloudy knife,
> And both did gnash their teeth, and both did threaten life.
>
> On thother side in one consort there sate
>> Cruell Reuenge, and rancorous Despight,
>> Disloyall Treason, and hart-burning Hate,
>> But gnawing Gealosie out of their sight
>> Sitting alone, his bitter lips did bight,
>> And trembling Feare still to and fro did fly,
>> And found no place, where safe he shroud him might,
>> Lamenting Sorrow did in darknesse lye,
> And Shame his vgly face did hide from liuing eye.
>
> And ouer them sad Horrour with grim hew,
>> Did alwayes sore, beating his yron wings;
>> And after him Owles and Night-rauens flew,
>> The hatefull messengers of heauy things,
>> Of death and dolour telling sad tidings;

> Whiles sad *Celeno*, sitting on a clift,
> A song of bale and bitter sorrow sings,
> That hart of flint a sunder could haue rift:
> Which hauing ended, after him she flyeth swift. (11, 7, 21–3)

The posture of Jealousy and the motion of Fear in this description are particularly fine. These are instances of allegorical persons which are shown only in one transient view. The reader will everywhere meet with others in this author which are employed in the action of the poem and which need not be mentioned here.

Having thus endeavoured to give a general idea of what is meant by allegory in poetry and shown what kinds of persons are frequently employed in it, I shall proceed to mention some properties which seem requisite in all well-invented fables of this kind. . . .

The first is that it be lively and surprising. The fable, or literal sense, being that which most immediately offers itself to the reader's observation, must have this property in order to raise and entertain his curiosity. As there is, therefore, more invention employed in a work of this kind than in mere narration or description or in general amplifications on any subject, it consequently requires a more than ordinary heat of fancy in its first production. If the fable, on the contrary, is flat, spiritless or barren of invention, the reader's imagination is not affected nor his attention engaged, though the instruction conveyed under it be ever so useful or important.

The second qualification I shall mention is elegance, or a beautiful propriety and aptness in the fable to the subject on which it is employed. By this quality the invention of the poet is restrained from taking too great a compass or losing itself in a confusion of ill-sorted ideas, such representations as that mentioned by Horace of 'dolphins in a wood' or 'boars in the sea' being fit only to surprise the imagination without pleasing the judgement. The same moral may likewise be expressed in different fables, all of which may be lively and full of spirit yet not equally elegant – as various dresses may be made for the same body, yet not equally becoming. As it therefore requires a heat of fancy to raise images and resemblances, it requires a good taste to distinguish and range them and to choose the most proper and beautiful where there appears an almost distracting variety. I may compare this to Aeneas searching in the wood for the golden bough: he was at a loss where to lay his hand till his mother's doves, descending in his sight, flew before him and perched on the tree where it was to be found.

Another essential property is that the fable be everywhere consistent with itself. As licentious as allegorical fiction may seem in some respects, it is nevertheless subject to this restraint. The poet is indeed at liberty in choosing his story and inventing his persons, but after he has introduced them, he is obliged to sustain them in their proper characters as well as in more regular kinds of writing. It is difficult to give particular rules under this head; it may suffice to say that this wild nature is, however, subject to an economy proper to itself, and though it may sometimes seem extravagant, ought never to be absurd. Most of the allegories in *The Faerie Queene* are agreeable to this rule. . . .

The last property I shall mention is that the allegory be clear and intelligible. The fable, being designed only to clothe and adorn the moral but not to hide it, should methinks resemble the draperies we admire in some of the ancient statues, in which the folds are not too many nor too thick, but so judiciously ordered that the shape and beauty of the limbs may be seen through them.

. . . An allegory which is not clear is a riddle, and the sense of it lies at the mercy of every fanciful interpreter.

Though the epic poets, as I have shown, have sprinkled some allegories through their poems, yet it would be absurd to endeavour to understand them everywhere in a mystical sense. We are told of one Metrodorus Lampsacenus, whose works are lost, that turned the whole writings of Homer into an allegory. It was doubtless by some such means that the principles of all arts and sciences whatever were discovered in that single author, for nothing can escape an expositor who proceeds in his operations like a Rosicrucian and brings with him the gold he pretends to find.

It is surprising that Tasso, whose *Jerusalem* was, at the time when he wrote it, the best plan of an epic poem after Virgil, should be possessed with this affectation and should not believe his work perfect till he had turned it into a mystery. I cannot help thinking that the 'Allegory', as it is called, which he has printed with it, looks as if it were invented after the poem was finished. He tells us that the Christian army represents Man; the City of Jerusalem, Civil Happiness; Godfrey, the Understanding; Rinaldo and Tancred, the other Powers of the Soul; and that the Body is typified by the common soldiers – with a great deal more that carries in it a strong cast of enthusiasm. He is indeed much more intelligible when he explains the flowers, the fountains, the nymphs and the musical instruments to figure to us Sensual Pleasures under the false appearance of Good. But for the rest, I appeal to anyone who is acquainted with that poem whether he would ever have discovered these mysteries if the poet had not let him into them or whether, even after this, he can keep them long in his mind while he is reading it.

Spenser's conduct is much more reasonable: as he designed his poem upon the plan of the virtues by which he has entitled his several books, he scarce ever loses sight of this design, but has almost everywhere taken care to let it appear. Sir William Temple, indeed, censures this as a fault and says that though his flights of fancy were very noble and high, yet his moral lay so bare that it lost the effect. But I confess I do not understand this. A moral which is not clear is in my apprehension next to no moral at all.

It would be easy to enumerate other properties which are various according to the different kinds of allegory or its different degrees of perfection. Sometimes we are surprised with an uncommon moral which ennobles the fable that conveys it, and at other times we meet with a known and obvious truth placed in some new and beautiful point of light and made surprising by the fiction under which it is exhibited. I have thought it sufficient to touch upon such properties only as seem to be the most essential, and perhaps many more might be reduced under one or other of these general heads. . . .

By what has been offered in the foregoing discourse on allegorical poetry we may be able, not only to discover many beauties in *The Faerie Queene*, but likewise to excuse some of its irregularities. The chief merit of this poem consists in that surprising vein of fabulous invention which runs through it and enriches it everywhere with imagery and descriptions more than we meet with in any other modern poem. The author seems to be possessed of a kind of poetical magic; and the figures he calls up to our view rise so thick upon us that we are at once pleased and distracted by the exhaustless variety of them, so that his faults may in a manner be imputed to his excellencies. His abundance betrays him into excess, and his judgement is overborne by the torrent of his imagination.

That which seems the most liable to exception in this work is the model of it and the choice the author has made of so romantic a story. The several books appear rather like so many several poems than one entire fable; each of them has its peculiar knight and is independent of the rest, and though some of the persons make their appearance in different books, yet this has very little effect in connecting them. Prince Arthur is, indeed, the principal person and has, therefore, a share given him in every legend, but his part is not considerable enough in any one of them. He appears and vanishes again like a spirit, and we lose sight of him too soon to consider him as the hero of the poem.

These are the most obvious defects in the fable of *The Faerie Queene*. The want of unity in the story makes it difficult for the reader to carry it in his mind and distracts too much his attention to the several parts of it; and indeed the whole frame of it would appear monstrous if it were to be examined by the rules of epic poetry as they have been drawn from the practice of Homer and Virgil. But as it is plain the author never designed it by those rules, I think it ought rather to be considered as a poem of a particular kind, describing in a series of allegorical adventures or episodes the most noted virtues and vices. To compare it, therefore, with the models of antiquity would be like drawing a parallel between the Roman and the Gothic architecture. In the first there is doubtless a more natural grandeur and simplicity; in the latter we find great mixtures of beauty and barbarism, yet assisted by the invention of a variety of inferior ornaments. And though the former is more majestic in the whole, the latter may be very surprising and agreeable in its parts.

It may seem strange indeed, since Spenser appears to have been well acquainted with the best writers of antiquity, that he has not imitated them in the structure of his story. Two reasons may be given for this: the first is that at the time when he wrote the Italian poets, whom he has chiefly imitated and who were the first revivers of this art among the moderns, were in the highest vogue and were universally read and admired. But the chief reason was probably that he chose to frame his fable after a model which might give the greatest scope to that range of fancy which was so remarkably his talent. There is a bent in nature which is apt to determine men that particular way in which they are most capable of excelling, and though it is certain he might have formed a better plan, it is to be questioned whether he could have executed any other so well.

It is probably for the same reason that among the Italian poets he rather followed Ariosto, whom he found more agreeable to his genius, than Tasso, who had formed a better plan and from whom he has only borrowed some particular ornaments. Yet it is but justice to say that his plan is much more regular than that of Ariosto. In the *Orlando Furioso* we everywhere meet with an exuberant invention joined with great liveliness and facility of description, yet debased by frequent mixtures of the comic genius as well as many shocking indecorums. Besides, in the huddle and distraction of the adventures, we are for the most part only amused with extravagant stories without being instructed in any moral. On the other hand, Spenser's fable, though often wild, is, as I have observed, always emblematical; and this may very much excuse likewise that air of romance in which he has followed the Italian author. The perpetual stories of knights, giants, castles, and enchantments and all that train of legendary adventures would indeed appear very trifling if Spenser had not found a way to turn them all into allegory or if a less masterly hand had filled up his draught. But it is surprising to observe how much the strength of the painting is superior to the design. It ought to be considered too that at the time when our author wrote the remains of the old gothic chivalry were not quite abolished. It was not many years before that the famous Earl of Surrey, remarkable for his wit and poetry in the reign of King Henry the Eighth, took a romantic journey to Florence, the place of his mistress's birth, and published there a challenge against all nations in defence of her beauty. Jousts and tournaments were held in England in the time of Queen Elizabeth. Sir Philip Sidney tilted at one of these entertainments, which was made for the French ambassador when the treaty of marriage was on foot with the Duke of Anjou. And some of our historians have given us a very particular and formal account of preparations, by marking out lists and appointing judges, for a trial by combat in the same reign which was to have decided the title to a considerable estate, and in which the whole ceremony was perfectly agreeable to the fabulous descriptions in books of knight-errantry. This might render his story more familiar to his first readers, though knights in armour and ladies errant are as antiquated figures to us as the court of that time would appear if we could see them now in their ruffs and farthingales.

Source: extract from 'An Essay on Allegorical Poetry' and 'Remarks on *The Faerie Queene*', in Hughes's edition of Spenser's works (1715).

NOTE

1. *Spectator*, no. 273 (of 12 January 1712).

William Hazlitt (1818)

Spenser, as well as Chaucer, was engaged in active life; but the genius of his poetry was not active; it is inspired by the love of ease, and relaxation from all the cares and business of life. Of all the poets, he is the most poetical. Though much later than Chaucer, his obligations to preceding writers were less. He has in some measure borrowed the plan of his poem (as a number of distinct narratives) from Ariosto; but he has engrafted upon it an exuberance of fancy, and an endless voluptuousness of sentiment, which are not to be found in the Italian writer. Further, Spenser is even more of an inventor in the subject-matter. There is an originality, richness, and variety in his allegorical personages and fictions, which almost vies with the splendour of the ancient mythology. If Ariosto transports us into the regions of romance, Spenser's poetry is all fairy-land. In Ariosto, we walk upon the ground, in a company, gay, fantastic, and adventurous enough. In Spenser, we wander in another world, among ideal beings. The poet takes and lays us in the lap of a lovelier nature, by the sound of softer streams, among greener hills and fairer valleys. He paints nature, not as we find it, but as we expected to find it; and fulfils the delightful promise of our youth. He waves his wand of enchantment – and at once embodies airy beings, and throws a delicious veil over all actual objects. The two worlds of reality and of fiction are poised on the wings of his imagination. His ideas, indeed, seem more distinct than his perceptions. He is the painter of abstractions, and describes them with dazzling minuteness. In the Mask of Cupid he makes the God of Love 'clap on high his coloured winges *twain*'; and it is said of Gluttony, in the Procession of the Passions, 'In greene vine leaues he was right fitly clad.' At times he becomes picturesque from his intense love of beauty; as where he compares Prince Arthur's crest to the appearance of the almond tree: [quotes 1, 7, 32]. . . . The love of beauty, however, and not of truth, is the moving principle of his mind; and he is guided in his fantastic delineations by no rule but the impulse of an inexhaustible imagination. He luxuriates equally in scenes of Eastern magnificence; or the still solitude of a hermit's cell – in the extremes of sensuality or refinement.

In reading *The Faerie Queene*, you see a little withered old man by a wood-side opening a wicket, a giant, and a dwarf lagging far behind, a damsel in a boat upon an enchanted lake, wood-nymphs, and satyrs; and all of a sudden you are transported into a lofty palace, with tapers burning, amidst knights and ladies, with dance and revelry, and song, 'and mask, and antique pageantry'. What can be more solitary, more shut up in itself, than his description of the house of Sleep, to which Archimago sends for a dream:

> And more, to lulle him in his slumber soft,
>> A trickling streame from high rocke tumbling downe
>> And euer-drizling raine vpon the loft,
>> Mixt with a murmuring winde, much like the sowne
>> Of swarming Bees, did cast him in a swowne:
>> No other noyse, nor peoples troublous cryes,
>> As still are wont t'annoy the walled towne,
>> Might there be heard: but carelesse Quiet lyes,
> Wrapt in eternall silence farre from enemyes. (1, 1, 41)

It is as if 'the honey-heavy dew of slumber' had settled on his pen in writing these lines. How different in the subject (and yet how like in beauty) is the following description of the Bower of Bliss:

> Eftsoones they heard a most melodious sound,
>> Of all that mote delight a daintie eare,
>> Such as att once might not on liuing ground,
>> Saue in this Paradise, be heard elswhere:
>> Right hard it was, for wight, which did it heare,
>> To read, what manner musicke that mote bee:

> For all that pleasing is to liuing eare,
>   Was there consorted in one harmonee,
> Birdes, voyces, instruments, windes, waters, all agree.
>
> The ioyous birdes shrouded in chearefull shade,
>   Their notes vnto the voyce attempred sweet;
>   Th' Angelicall soft trembling voyces made
>   To th' instruments diuine respondence meet:
>   The siluer sounding instruments did meet
>   With the base murmure of the waters fall:
>   The waters fall with difference discreet,
>   Now soft, now loud, vnto the wind did call:
> The gentle warbling wind low answered to all. (ii, 12, 70–1)

The remainder of the passage has all that voluptuous pathos, and languid brilliancy of fancy, in which this writer excelled: [quotes ii, 12, 74–8].

The finest things in Spenser are, the character of Una, in the first book; the House of Pride; the Cave of Mammon, and the Cave of Despair; the account of Memory, of whom it is said, among other things,

> The warres he well remembred of king *Nine*,
>   Of old *Assaracus*, and *Inachus* diuine; (ii, 9, 56)

the description of Belphoebe; the story of Florimel and the Witch's son; the Gardens of Adonis, and the Bower of Bliss; the Mask of Cupid; and Colin Clout's vision, in the last book. But some people will say that all this may be very fine, but that they cannot understand it on account of the allegory. They are afraid of the allegory, as if they thought it would bite them; they look at it as a child looks at a painted dragon, and think it will strangle them in its shining folds. This is very idle. If they do not meddle with the allegory, the allegory will not meddle with them. Without minding it at all, the whole is as plain as a pike-staff. It might as well be pretended that, we cannot see Poussin's pictures for the allegory, as that the allegory prevents us from understanding Spenser. For instance, when Britomart, seated amidst the young warriors, lets fall her hair and discovers her sex, is it necessary to know the part she plays in the allegory, to understand the beauty of the following stanza?

And eke that straunger knight emongst the rest
  Was for like need enforst to disaray:
  Tho whenas vailed was her loftie crest,
  Her golden locks, that were in tramels gay
  Vpbounden, did them selues adowne display,
  And raught vnto her heeles; like sunny beames,
  That in a cloud their light did long time stay,
  Their vapour vaded, shew their golden gleames,
And through the persant aire shoote forth their azure streames.
                           (III, 9, 20)

Or is there any mystery in what is said of Belphoebe, that her hair was sprinkled with flowers and blossoms which had been entangled in it as she fled through the woods? Or is it necessary to have a more distinct idea of Proteus, than that which is given of him in his boat, with the frighted Florimel at his feet, while

    . . . the cold ysickles from his rough beard,
    Dropped adowne vpon her yuorie brest. (III, 8, 35)

Or is it not a sufficient account of one of the sea-gods that pass by them, to say –

    That was *Arion* crowned; . . .
    So went he playing on the watery plaine. (IV, 11, 23–4)

Or to take the Procession of the Passions that draw the coach of Pride, in which the figures of Idleness, of Gluttony, of Lechery, of Avarice, of Envy, and of Wrath speak, one should think, plain enough for themselves; such as this of Gluttony: [quotes I, 4, 21–2]. Or this of Lechery: [quotes I, 4, 24–5].

    Inconstant man, that loued all he saw,
    And lusted after all, that he did loue,
    Ne would his looser life be tide to law,
    But ioyd weake wemens hearts to tempt and proue
  If from their loyall loues he might them moue. (I, 4, 26)

This is pretty plain-spoken. Mr Southey says of Spenser:

    . . . Yet not more sweet
    Than pure was he, and not more pure than wise;
    High priest of all the Muses' mysteries!

On the contrary, no one was more apt to pry into mysteries which do not strictly belong to the Muses.

Of the same kind with the Procession of the Passions, as little obscure, and still more beautiful, is the Mask of Cupid, with his train of votaries: [quotes III, 7, 13, 22–3]. The description of Hope, in this series of historical portraits, is one of the most beautiful in Spenser: and the triumph of Cupid at the mischief he has made, is worthy of the malicious urchin deity. In reading these descriptions, one can hardly avoid being reminded of Ruben's allegorical pictures; but the account of Satyrane taming the lion's whelps and lugging the bear's cubs along in his arms while yet an infant, whom his mother so naturally advises to 'go seek some other play-fellows', has even more of this high picturesque character. Nobody but Rubens could have painted the fancy of Spenser; and he could not have given the sentiment, the airy dream that hovers over it!

With all this, Spenser neither makes us laugh nor weep. The only jest in his poem is an allegorical play upon words, where he describes Malbecco as escaping in the herd of goats, 'by the help of his fayre hornes on hight'. But he has been unjustly charged with a want of passion and of strength. He has both in an immense degree. He has not indeed the pathos of immediate action or suffering, which is more properly the dramatic; but he has all the pathos of sentiment and romance – all that belongs to distant objects of terror, and uncertain, imaginary distress. His strength, in like manner, is not strength of will or action, of bone and muscle, nor is it coarse and palpable – but it assumes a character of vastness and sublimity seen through the same visionary medium, and blended with the appalling associations of preternatural agency. We need only turn, in proof of this, to the Cave of Despair, or the Cave of Mammon, or to the account of the change of Malbecco into Jealousy. The following stanzas, in the description of the Cave of Mammon, the grisly house of Plutus, are unrivalled for the portentous massiness of the forms, the splendid chiaroscuro, and shadowy horror.

> That houses forme within was rude and strong,
>   Like an huge caue, hewne out of rocky clift,
>   From whose rough vaut the ragged breaches hong,
>   Embost with massy gold of glorious gift,
>   And with rich metall loaded euery rift,

    That heauy ruine they did seeme to threat;
    And ouer them *Arachne* high did lift
    Her cunning web, and spred her subtile net,
Enwrapped in fowle smoke and clouds more blacke then Iet.

Both roofe, and floore, and wals were all of gold,
    But ouergrowne with dust and old decay,
    And hid in darkenesse, that none could behold
    The hew thereof: for vew of chearefull day
    Did neuer in that house it selfe display,
    But a faint shadow of vncertain light;
    Such as a lamp, whose life does fade away:
    Or as the Moone cloathed with clowdy night,
Does shew to him, that walkes in feare and sad affright.

    .   .   .   .   .

And ouer them sad Horrour with grim hew,
    Did alwayes sore, beating his yron wings;
    And after him Owles and Night-rauens flew,
    The hatefull messengers of heauy things,
    Of death and dolour telling sad tidings;
    Whiles sad *Celeno*, sitting on a clift,
    A song of bale and bitter sorrow sings,
    That hart of flint a sunder could haue rift:
Which hauing ended, after him she flyeth swift. (II, 7, 28–9, 23)

The Cave of Despair is described with equal gloominess and power of fancy; and the fine moral declamation of the owner of it, on the evils of life, almost makes one in love with death. In the story of Malbecco, who is haunted by jealousy, and in vain strives to run away from his own thoughts –

    High ouer hilles and ouer dales he fled (III, 10, 55) –

the truth of human passion and the preternatural ending are equally striking. . . .

    The language of Spenser is full, and copious, to overflowing: it is less pure and idiomatic than Chaucer's, and is enriched and adorned with phrases borrowed from the different languages of Europe, both ancient and modern. He was, probably, seduced into a certain licence of expression by the difficulty of filling up the moulds of his complicated rhymed stanza from the limited resources of his native language. This stanza, with alternate and repeatedly recurring rhymes, is borrowed from the Italians. It was peculiarly fitted to their language, which abounds in similar vowel terminations, and is as little adapted to ours, from the stubborn, unaccommodating resistance which the consonant endings of the northern languages make to this sort of endless sing-song. – Not that I would, on that account, part with the stanza of Spenser. We are, perhaps, indebted to this very necessity of finding out new forms of expression, and to the occasional faults to which it led, for a poetical language rich and varied and magnificent beyond all former, and almost all later example. His versification is, at once, the most smooth and the most sounding in the language. It is a labyrinth of sweet sounds, 'in many a winding bout of linked sweetness long drawn out' – that would cloy by their very sweetness, but that the ear is constantly relieved and enchanted by their continued variety of modulation – dwelling on the pauses of the action, or flowing on in a fuller tide of harmony with the movement of the sentiment. It has not the bold dramatic transitions of Shakespeare's blank verse, nor the high-raised tone of Milton's; but it is the perfection of melting harmony, dissolving the soul in pleasure, or holding it captive in the chains of suspense. Spenser was the poet of our waking dreams; and he has invented not only a language, but a music of his own for them. The undulations are infinite, like those of the waves of the sea: but the effect is still the same, lulling the senses into a deep oblivion of the jarring noises of the world, from which we have no wish to be ever recalled.

SOURCE: extract from *Lectures on the English Poets* (1818).

Edward Dowden (*1882*)

Milton looks back and remembers his master, and he remembers him not as an idle singer, not as a dreamer of dreams, but as 'our sage and serious Spenser, whom I dare to name a better teacher than Scotus or Aquinas'.

A teacher, – what is the import of this? 'The true use of Spenser', says a poet of our own day, Mr J. R. Lowell, 'is a gallery of pictures which we visit as the mood takes us, and where we spend an hour or two at a time, long enough to sweeten our perceptions, not so long as to cloy them.' And again: 'Whenever in the *Faery Queen* you come suddenly on the moral, it gives you a shock of unpleasant surprise, a kind of grit, as when one's teeth close on a bit of gravel in a dish of strawberries and cream.' This, then, is the *Faery Queen* – a dish of strawberries and cream mixed up unfortunately with a good deal of grit. And as for the allegory, we may 'fairly leave it on one side';[1] Spenser employed it to 'convince the scorners that poetry might be seriously useful, and show Master Bull his new way of making fine words butter parsnips, in a rhymed moral primer'. Shall we accept this view or that of Milton – 'a better teacher than Scotus or Aquinas'? Was Spenser such a teacher 'sage and serious' to his own age? If so, does he remain such a teacher for this age of ours? . . .

In the spirit of Sidney's *Apologie for Poetry*, Spenser conceived and wrote the *Faery Queen*. It is an attempt to harmonise the three divisions of learning considered by Sidney – history, moral philosophy, poetry; and to make the first and second of these subserve the greatest of the three. The end of the whole is virtuous action; Spenser would set forth an ideal of human character and incite men to its attainment. He thought of his poem, while never ceasing to be a true poem, as if it were, in a certain sense, a study in ethics. One day Spenser's friend Bryskett, in his cottage near Dublin, gathered about him a circle of distinguished acquaintances; and conversing on the subject of ethics, which he wished were worthily handled in English, 'whereby our youth might speedily enter into the right course of vertuous life', he turned to Spenser with an embarrassing request – that Spenser should forthwith proceed to deliver a discourse on the virtues and vices and give the company a taste of true moral philosophy. Spenser naturally excused himself, and pleaded on his own behalf that, though he could not improvise a lecture on ethics, he had actually in hand a work which might in some sort satisfy his friend's desire:

For sure I am, that it is not unknowne unto you, that I have already under-taken a work tending to the same effect, which is in heroical verse under the title of a 'Faerie Queene' to represent all the moral vertues, assigning to every vertue a Knight to be the patron and defender of the same, in whose

actions and feats of arms and chivalry the operations of that vertue, whereof
he is the protector, are to be expressed, and the vices and unruly appetites
that oppose themselves against the same, to be beaten down and overcome.

'A poet at that time', says the Dean of St. Paul's,[2] commenting on
this passage, 'still had to justify his employment by presenting
himself in the character of a professed teacher of morality.' But this
is hardly in accordance with the facts. It was not as a professed
teacher of morality that Chaucer had told his *Canterbury Tales*; it
was not as a professed teacher of morality that Marlowe wrote his
Hero and Leander, or Shakspere his *Venus and Adonis*. 'Every great
poet', said Wordsworth, 'is a teacher: I wish either to be considered
as a teacher, or as nothing.' May it not be that Spenser had higher
thoughts than of justifying his employment? may not he, like
Wordsworth, but unlike Chaucer and Marlowe, have really aimed
at edification – such edification as is proper to a poet?

You have given me praise, [Wordsworth wrote to John Wilson] for having
reflected faithfully in my poems the feelings of human nature. I would fain
hope that I have done so. But a great poet ought to do more than this: he
ought, to a certain degree, to rectify men's feelings, to give them new
compositions of feeling, to render their feelings more sane, pure, and
permanent; in short, more consonant to nature and the great moving spirit
of things.

To render men's feelings more sane, pure, and permanent – this
surely was included in the great design of the *Faery Queen*; it was
deliberately kept before him as an object by Spenser – 'our sage and
serious Spenser, whom I dare to name a better teacher than Scotus
or Aquinas'.

How, then, should we read the *Faery Queen*? Is it poetry? or is it
philosophy? Are we merely to gaze on with wide-eyed expectancy
as at a marvellous pageant or procession, in which knights and ladies,
Saracens and wizards, anticks and wild men, pass before our eyes?
or are these visible shows only a rind or shell, which we must break
or strip away in order to get at that hidden wisdom which feeds the
spirit? Neither of these things are we to do. The mere visible
shows of Spenser's poem are indeed goodly enough to beguile a
summer's day in some old wood and to hold us from morning
to evening in a waking dream. The ethical teaching of Spenser
extracted from his poetry is worthy a careful study. Raphael
drew his fainting Virgin Mother as a skeleton in his preparatory

study, and the student of Raphael may well consider the anatomy of the figure, because whatever an artist has put into his work, that a critic may try to take out of it. So the moral philosophy of Spenser even apart from his poetry may rightly form a subject of study. But the special virtue of the *Faery Queen* will be found only by one who receives it neither as pageantry nor as philosophy, but in the way in which Spenser meant that it should be received – as a living creature of the imagination, a spirit incarnate, 'one altogether', 'of a reasonable soul and human flesh subsisting'.

There are, indeed, portions of the *Faery Queen* which are not vital – which are, so to speak, excrementitious. In a short poem – the expression of a moment of lyrical excitement – a single line, a single word which is not vital, destroys the integrity of the piece. But a poem which has taken into itself the writer's entire mind during long years cannot but be like a wide landscape that includes level with rise, and sandy patches with verdurous tracts. It seems inevitable that in such comprehensive works as the *Divine Comedy*, the *Paradise Lost*, the two parts of *Faust*, the *Faery Queen*, the stream of pure imagination should sometimes well out of rocky masses of intellectual argument or didactic meditation. The dullest portions of Spenser's poem are those in which he works with most self-consciousness, piecing together definite meanings to definite symbols; where his love of beauty slumbers and his spirit of ingenuity awakes; where his ideas do not play and part and gather themselves together and deploy themselves abroad, like the shifting and shredding of clouds blown by soft upper airs, but are rather cut out with hard edges by some process of mechanism. When in the 'Legende of Temperance' the poet allegorises Aristotle's doctrine that virtue is a mean betwixt the extremes of excess and of defect, our distaste for Elissa and Perissa would surely content the moralist, were it not that our feeling towards their virtuous sister is hardly less unfriendly. From the 'Castle of Alma' we should not be ill-pleased if the master-cook, Concoction, and the kitchen-clerk, Digestion, were themselves ignobly conveyed away (if allegory would permit such a departure) by that nether gate, the Port Esquiline. . . .

And so we are brought back to the statement that the high distinction of Spenser's poetry is to be found in the rare degree in which it unites sense and soul, moral seriousness and the Renaissance appetite for beauty. Herein lay his chief lesson for men of his own time. To incite and to conduct men to an active virtue is not only the express purpose of the *Faery Queen*, but as far as a poem can render such service, the *Faery Queen* doubtless has actually served to train knights of holiness, knights of temperance, knights of courtesy. Spenser, although an ardent patriot of the time of Elizabeth, or rather because he was an ardent patriot, did not flatter his own age. He believed that the world had declined from its high estate, and fearing that things might tend to worse, he observed anxiously the wrong-doings of the time. He speaks very plainly in 'Mother Hubberd's Tale' of vices in the court, the church, the army. He desired to serve his country and his age, as other great Englishmen were doing, and yet in his own proper way. . . .

With all its opulence of colour and melody, with all its imagery of delight, the *Faery Queen* has primarily a moral or spiritual intention. While Spenser sees the abundant beauty of the world, and the splendour of man and of the life of man, his vision of human life is grave and even stern. For life he regards as a warfare, a warfare needing all our foresight, strength, and skill. . . . Nor is the combat between good and evil in Spenser's poem one in which victory is lightly or speedily attainable; the sustaining thought is that victory is possible. . . .

Spenser's conception of life was Puritan in its seriousness; yet we think with wonder of the wide space that lies between the *Faery Queen* and our other great allegory, the *Pilgrim's Progress*. To escape from the City of Destruction and to reach the Celestial City is Christian's one concern; all his recompense for the countless trials of the way lies upon the other side of the river of death. His consuming thought is this: 'What must I do to be saved?' Spenser is spiritual, but he is also mundane; he thinks of the uses of noble human creatures to this world in which we move. His general end in the poem is 'to fashion a gentleman or noble person in virtuous and gentle discipline'.

A grand self-culture [I have elsewhere said] is that about which Spenser is concerned; not, as with Bunyan, the escape of the soul to heaven; not the attainment of supernatural grace through a point of mystical contact, like the vision which was granted to the virgin knight, Galahad, in the mediaeval allegory. Self-culture, the formation of a complete character for the uses of earth, and afterwards, if need be, for the uses of heaven, – this was subject sufficient for the twenty-four books designed to form the epic of the age of Elizabeth. And the means of that self-culture are of an active kind – namely, warfare, – warfare, not for its own sake, but for the generous accomplishments of unselfish ends.

Bunyan, with whom the visionary power was often involuntary, who would live for a day and a night in some metaphor that had attacked his imagination, transcribed into allegory his own wonderful experience of terrors and of comfort. Spenser is more impersonal: he can refashion Aristotle in a dream. But behind him lies all the sentiment of Christian chivalry, and around him all the life of Elizabethan England; and from these diverse elements arises a rich and manifold creation, which, if it lacks the personal, spiritual passion of Bunyan's allegory, compensates by its moral breadth, its noble sanity, its conciliation of what is earthly and what is divine.

SOURCE: extracts from 'Spenser, the Poet and Teacher', originally published in A. B. Grosart's edition of Spenser (1882); reprinted in Dowden's *Transcripts and Essays* (1888) pp. 270–1, 284–7, 294–5, 301–2.

NOTES

1. With which contrast Coleridge's words, 'No one can appreciate Spenser without some reflection on the nature of allegorical writing'; and Mr. Ruskin's painstaking attempt in *Stones of Venice* to interpret the allegory of Book I.

2. R. W. Church, in his *Spenser* (1879; English Men of Letters series).

PART TWO

Introducing the Poem

1. Sources and Influences
2. Allegory
3. Rhetoric, Language, Versification

1. SOURCES AND INFLUENCES

H. G. Lotspeich Classical Mythology in
Spenser's Poetry (1932)

Among Spenser's adaptations from classic myth, some may be
grouped together as, in a general way, Ovidian. Whether directly
inspired by passages in Ovid or not, they exhibit something of the
spirit of the 'tenerorum lusor amorum', to whom classic myth was
a plaything for his wit and a mine of pretty stories and pictures. In
several important instances, where Spenser is using myth almost
exclusively for its pictorial value, Ovid is his chief source; and in
nearly every case the picture which Spenser creates is more elaborate
and vivid than its Ovidian prototype. This is so in the passage on
the 'clothes of Arras and of Toure' which depict the love of Venus
and Adonis [III, 1, 34 ff.], in the more elaborate and splendid
tapestries in the hall of Busirane, of Cupid's wars and 'all of love
and all of lusty-head' [III, 11, 28 ff.], and perhaps most strikingly
in the adaptation from Ovid of Minerva's contest with Arachne, in
Muiopotmos. . . .

Spenser also shows himself completely at home in the Ovidian
technique of metamorphosis. Following a suggestion from Ovid, he
can make up his own, as in the case of Coronis. His manipulation of
changes is most skillful in *Muiopotmos*, where one metamorphosis,
that of Arachne, is from Ovid and the other, that of Astery, is his
own creation, developed from certain suggestions in the Psyche
myth. In *Muiopotmos* at least, Spenser is taking a holiday from the
serious business of the philosophic poet and is using myth as a
plaything. Like Ovid, he is seeing the world of mythology as 'a
free country, wherein the imagination can roam, forming and
transforming to suit its pleasure'.[1]

In this same lighter vein, and with a surer independence, is the
story of Faunus and Molanna, which comes as a pleasant interlude
in the midst of the more serious matter of the Mutability Cantos.

The story is an adaptation of the Actaeon myth, as Spenser found it in Ovid, but it becomes something essentially new. Spenser makes a serio-comic figure of his hero, Faunus, and does away with Ovid's tragic ending. The whole episode is in that vein of playful pleasantry, with just a touch of seriousness, which the Elizabethans controlled supremely well. Spenser's method here is somewhat like that of *Muiopotmos*, but his handling of myth is now more mature, easy, and confident.

Spenser's use of myth as source material for his own creations goes beyond the influence of Ovid or of any one poet. His ways of recreating the material of myth are of various kinds. A complete episode in his narrative may show significant points of similarity with a myth which is not embodied, in its entirety, in any one literary source. Thus the story of Marinell, of his birth and of the care with which he was sheltered by his mother, Cymodoce, has interesting parallels in the myth of Peleus and Thetis and Achilles. Describing the intrigues of Hellenore and Paridell, Spenser clearly has Helen and Paris in mind.

Myth has often helped him in his conception or elaboration of his own characters. . . . The most patent example is Geryoneo, who is simply a second edition of his father, Geryon. The process is usually more subtle and many-sided. Radigund seems to embody memories of Penthesilea, Diodorus' Myrina, and Ariosto's Marfisa, all shaped by Spenser's own ideas of the manly woman. In developing the character and rôle of Mutability, Spenser probably used what Natalis Comes had said about the goddess Fortuna. Sometimes the relationship consists only in a few stray hints. In the episode describing Scudamour in the House of Care [IV, 5, 33 ff.], we are now and then reminded of Vulcan and his smiths. We feel that Spenser wants us to think of the Cyclops when he says that the savage man, Lust, had the practice of rolling a stone over the mouth of his cave [IV, 7, 20].

In these various ways Spenser adapts and transforms classic myth in the creation of his narrative. He is using material which is an inseparable part of the large and ancient legacy of literary tradition. The poet who inherited this tradition and worked in its spirit might use it as he would, giving it new life in new settings and moulding it to his own purposes.

To the casual reader of Spenser, the uses which he makes of classic myth seem only to corroborate the traditional conception of him as 'the poets' poet', who, like his own creation, Clarion, lived among the flowers of the garden, enjoying 'delight with liberty'. Like any educated Renaissance poet, Spenser decorates his poetry with classical similes, invocations, and graceful allusions to the antique mythology. More than this, we find him turning myth into pictures, portraying the love of Venus and Adonis in 'costly clothes of Arras and of Toure', or weaving all the amours of the Olympians into the tapestries on the walls of Busirane's enchanted hall. In all this Spenser appears as the artist of sensuous things, the painter of pictures.

But Spenser did not intend that, in reading his poetry, we should stop with the shows of things. For better or worse, he sought

> to restraine
> The lust of lawlesse youth with good advice,

and he wrote a very long poem, which presents, as well as picture and fable, 'a continued allegory or darke conceit'. I do not propose here to take sides on the question as to whether Spenser was a poet, or a teacher, or both, or neither. A study of his classic myth can, however, be of some help toward an answer to that question. For, in addition to using myth for ornament and picture, Spenser also used it for allegory, especially for shadowing forth the moral doctrines which he considered of the first importance. Of the 'fierce warres and faithful loves' which moralize his song, not a little owes its being to the tradition of classic myth as it had been interpreted morally and allegorically by the poets and commentators before him. As an introduction to this part of our subject, we must consider Spenser's indebtedness to the two books which, for him, embodied the tradition of myth interpretation: the *Genealogia Deorum* of Boccaccio and the *Mythologiae* of Natalis Comes.

It has for some time been recognized that Spenser knew and used these two books, but the extent and nature of his indebtedness to them has not before been fully examined. The results of this study show, first of all, that Comes and Boccaccio gave Spenser enough, simply in the way of material, of narrative detail, to allow us to rank them among the poet's major sources. In numerous instances, when Spenser's version of a myth shows peculiarities which differentiate it from classical versions, authority for, or explanation of, such peculiarities has been found in Comes or Boccaccio. It appears also that some of the material, in its classical form, comes to Spenser, not from the classical texts themselves, but from quotations in these authorities, especially in Comes. We find Spenser, in a number of instances, writing with Comes open before him and following his comments and quotations from classical authors, often keeping the same sequence.

All this does not rule out the influence of the classics used at first hand. That he read much Greek is doubtful; but he does use the Latin poets extensively, especially Vergil and Ovid. What I wish to emphasize here is that the books of Comes and Boccaccio were of the first importance in the transmission of classic myth to Spenser, and that there is enough evidence of his use of them for external material alone to justify us in proceeding to enquire into their influence on his conception of what the ancient myths meant and how they could be used for the purposes of allegory.

Boccaccio and Comes regarded classic myth as a fundamental part of the great and venerable tradition of classical poetry. As such, they often treat it somewhat mystically, as containing hidden meanings of great import. Pagan and frivolous the ancient literature might appear on the surface, but studious insight would show that its creators, even Ovid and Apuleius, were profound speculative and moral philosophers, often inspired by the one God. Boccaccio and Comes did their work in the belief that they were providing keys to the understanding of these hidden meanings. They explain what lies beneath the veil of the fables: the accumulated wisdom of the ancients, their speculations on natural philosophy, their ethical teaching. 'This work of mine', says Boccaccio, 'removes the veil from these inventions, shows that poets were really men of wisdom, and renders their compositions full of profit and pleasure to the reader'. Every myth had a meaning, perhaps several; it was 'polyseme', as Boccaccio put it, of many meanings. According to Comes, 'the ancient makers of the myths' have given us, not only their speculations on natural philosophy, but also, and more important, 'the most useful precepts concerning the life of man'. They expressed these truths in the form of myth because they were more pleasant so, easier to remember, and because they were thus hidden from the vulgar and uneducated. . . .

That all this is quite in agreement with Spenser's own theory of poetry is fairly obvious. Mythology, as he found it interpreted, was allegorical. The emphasis was on its inner meaning, especially as that meaning had to do with morality. Mythology was 'polyseme' and so is Spenser's poetry, especially in such mythological passages as the Mammon episode, the vision of the Graces on Mount Acidale, and the Mutability Cantos. Specifically, he seems to have in mind Comes' idea that the sacred truths must be skillfully hidden and enshrined 'beneath the coverings of myth' when he addresses

> Ye sacred imps, that on Parnasso dwell,
> And there the keeping have of learnings threasures,
> Which doe all worldly riches far excell. . . .
> Ne none can find, but who was taught them by the Muse.
>
> Revele to me the sacred noursery
> Of Vertue, which with you doth there remaine. (VI, Pr. 2, 3)

These similarities between the general beliefs of the mythographers and of Spenser indicate that there is a real parallelism between the conception of myth in Boccaccio and Comes and the conception of epic poetry which appears in the Letter to Raleigh and underlies the whole *Faerie Queene*. Such agreement in fundamentals leads us to ask this question: can we say that this parallelism goes further and that Spenser believed this classical mythology to be the same kind of allegorical poetry as his own *Faerie Queene*? Did the myths seem to him to express truths allegorically, by fable, and character, and picture, in ways which were already his own? Was mythology really moral truth, 'coloured with an historicall fiction', 'good discipline, . . . clowdily enwrapped in allegorical devices', and therefore a convenient and worthy vehicle for the fashioning of 'a gentleman or noble person in vertuous and gentle discipline'? The answer will rest on a consideration of the nature and extent of Spenser's allegorical use of myth, in so far as it derives from these two books.

Of the traditional modes of interpreting myths, three are used most frequently by both Boccaccio and Comes: the physical, the euhemeristic, and the moral. These three modes are the ones distinguishable in Spenser. Discussion of Spenser's allegorical use of myth can, then, fall into three corresponding divisions, growing, in each instance, from a consideration of his indebtedness to Boccaccio and Comes.

Spenser's use of physical or naturalistic interpretations seems to be the least extensive. One idea, however, should be noticed, a poetic one which enlivens the poet's whole conception of the world of nature. It is the idea, or better, the feeling that there is one great cosmic principle of generation and growth and fertility in the world. This is a favorite with the mythographers and, while Spenser needed no single authority to convince him of its general truth, he does seem to be indebted to Boccaccio and Comes, in several instances, for his use of it. It is in his mind when he speaks of the Nymphs as

> The which in floods and fountaines doe appere,
> And all mankinde do nourish with their waters clere; (iv, 11, 52)

and when he speaks of the Ocean's 'fruitful froth', and when he says of Apollo,

> Great father he of generation
> Is rightly cald, th'authour of life and light. (iii, 6, 9)

The same idea controls most of his treatment of Venus, about whom we shall have something to say later.

Euhemerism, which originated as a way of explaining how human beings came, in various unenlightened ways, to be worshipped as gods, is used by Boccaccio and Comes with different effect. With them it is a way of making the gods seem more like real people. They show that the fables are real because in them lies historical truth. This conception of the historical nature of myth manifests itself in Spenser in several ways; and, in several cases, the influence of Boccaccio and Comes is demonstrable. For example, Comes gives a full and circumstantial account of Bacchus' human activities as a conqueror and a peace-maker. Bacchus appears in these capacities, along with Hercules and Artegal, at the beginning of Book Five. E. K. says that Atlas was a king who gained his reputation by his skill in finding out 'the hidden courses of the starres by an excellent imagination'. This interpretation is in Boccaccio and Comes and others. Boccaccio looks upon the whole Aeneas myth as the true history of the founding of Rome. The manner in which Spenser introduces the same story into one of his passages on the ancestry of Britomart and the origins of England shows that he also is con- sidering it as history. Perhaps the clearest case of euhemerism in Spenser is in what he says of Osiris:

> Well therefore did the antique world invent,
>   That Justice was a god of soveraine grace,
>   And altars unto him, and temples lent,
>   And heavenly honors in the highest place;
>   Calling him great Osyris, of the race
>   Of th'old Ægyptian kings, that whylome were;
>   With fayned colours shading a true case:
>   For that Osyris, whilest he lived here,
> The justest man alive and truest did appeare. (v, 7, 2)

Thus the gods, viewed from one angle, were real human beings, who attained divinity because of their virtue or because they were immortalized by the poets.

The euhemeristic tendency has further ramifications in Spenser. The conception of the gods as real people, thus supported by tradition, helps to explain how they become natural members of Spenser's world and are on terms of every-day familiarity with his own heroes and heroines. It lies behind the episode of Cymodoce and Marinell, which we have already noticed, and it is implicit in his treatment of such characters of mythological origin as Belphoebe, Britomart, Proteus, and Talus. It may also help to explain Spenser's practice of connecting his own characters genealogically with those of myth, as in the case of Satyrane, and of having them educated by the gods, as were Amoret and Belphoebe, Florimel, and Artegal.

The Renaissance commentators lay most emphasis on the moralistic interpretation of myth. In contrast with the medieval habit of astrologizing the gods and of referring their significance to supernatural causes, Boccaccio, and more especially Comes, are most interested in the human, moral implications of the myths. Comes' interpretations are always fullest when he is explaining 'the most useful precepts concerning the life of man', or, in the phrase which he uses repeatedly, 'quod attinet ad mores'. This shift of emphasis involves, with them, a more humanistic conception of life, a recognition that man's destiny is largely in his own hands, an interest, less in supernatural forces, planetary or other, than in men and morality. Spenser's dominant concern throughout *The Faerie Queene*, even in the Legend of Holiness, is ethical: the problem of the good life here and now. The moralistic treatment of myth in Comes and Boccaccio is, therefore, of the first importance. Among the teachers of morality to whom Spenser turned, these two should have place with Plato, Aristotle, Castiglione, and the rest.

Perhaps because of the nature of the theme, formal moral allegory is most prominent in the Book of Temperance, or Continence. The two most important allegorical passages in the book draw heavily on classic myth: the Mammon episode and the episode of the Bowre of Blis. In the Mammon episode [II, 7, 3 ff.] materials from many different sources are brought together and are held together by the bond of the allegorical meaning which they are intended to shadow forth. From moral considerations in which Comes and Boccaccio have had a share, the mood of 'the divine Vergilian pity' has gone out of the conception of Hades and it has become Hell, a place of terror, an allegory of the temptations and punishments of sinners. The interpretation of Pluto as the avaricious god of wealth, found in both Comes and Boccaccio, has influenced Spenser's conception of Mammon. The famous Golden Chain of Homer had been made by Comes into a symbol of ambition and avarice; Spenser brings it into Philotime's court and labels it 'Ambition'. The golden apples in Proserpina's garden, with the meaning attached to them by Comes, become symbols of the temptations to which Guyon is being subjected. Branded by the same commentators as a type of avarice, Tantalus finds his place there, so that Guyon can wag his finger at him and say,

> 'Nay, nay, thou greedy Tantalus, . . .
> Abide the fortune of thy present fate,
> And unto all that live in high degree
> Ensample be of mind intemperate,
> To teach them how to use their present state.' (II, 7, 60)

In the canto on the Bowre of Blis, Spenser makes use of all the moral symbolism and allegory that had grown up in commentary on the voyages of Ulysses, Jason, and Aeneas. It will not do to confine Spenser to one source, especially in an episode like this one; but it seems clear that here as elsewhere, the mythographers, especially Comes, supplied him with much of his symbolism, and with its meaning made ready to his hand. . . . As Warton noticed long ago, the description of Genius, or Agdistes, comes bodily from Comes. Quite as important as Comes' description of this figure is his statement that Genius leads men into error and lust with dreams and false spectacles. In his description of the Mermaids, or Sirens, the poet draws again on Comes, and not very far in the background is Comes' allegory: 'I believe the Sirens' song and the Sirens themselves to be nothing other than voluptuous desire'. For the poet's allegorical use of the voyage between rocks and whirl-pools, Comes' chapter on Scylla and Charybdis was an important precedent. From it Spenser has taken several descriptive details and in it he found a full statement of his own moral allegory, expressed in his own figurative idiom. By the navigator who sails between Scylla and Charybdis and finally emerges in safety,

> what else is meant but that which is written by Aristotle in his *Ethics*, that virtue is the mean between two extremes, both of which must be avoided? . . . What is life but a diligent and continuous voyage among various temptations and illegitimate desires? If a man approaches near to any of these rocks, he must keep away from them with all his strength; for there is no man who is not naturally excited by sensual pleasures. . . . Thus the ancients wished to show that life is most full of hardships and perils, like a voyage between two terrible rocks; and unless this is most wisely guided men are caught by voluptuous desire and fall into the most wretched miseries. This of Scylla and Charybdis, which the ancients clothed in the most pleasing tales and fables.

I think it is clear from such evidence that the parallelism in question is fairly close. The mythographers did more than collect the data of ancient myth and present for the poet's use treasuries of the symbol of ancient literature. By interpreting this mythology in the light of ideas which fitted Spenser's deeper purposes, they afforded him a body of poetic allegory already adapted to his own ends. The ways of Boccaccio and Comes in handling the myths were Spenser's ways in shadowing forth his own 'darke conceits'. Whether, in given cases where he is using classic myth, he took over their interpretations, or made up his own, he is following them in spirit. . . .

SOURCE: extracts from *Classical Mythology in the Poetry of Edmund Spenser* (Princeton, 1932) pp. 11–22.

NOTE

1. F. K. Rand, 'Ovid and the Spirit of Metamorphosis', *Harvard Essays on Classical Subjects*, p. 234.

H. H. Blanchard   Spenser and Boiardo (1925)

The following study does not find such closely verbal imitation of Boiardo as Spenser has of Tasso, nor such a large amount of parallel material as he has with Ariosto. It is not the contention of this paper that Boiardo's poem received the amount of attention from Spenser that either Ariosto or Tasso did. On the other hand, evidence is here given to show that Spenser had read the *Orlando Innamorato*, that it lay in his memory along with his reading of other romances of chivalry, and that parts of it asserted themselves when occasion was offered in the creation of his own poem.

Every comprehensive study of the sources of the *Faerie Queene* reveals the intricate mosaic quality of Spenser's art, the product of a poetic consciousness enriched by wide reading. Consequently, it is to be expected that, in many cases, individual incidents, situations, or longer narratives as they appear in the *Faerie Queene* represent the fusion or synthesis in Spenser's consciousness of elements taken from several sources, varying in similarity, which his past reading had left in his memory, together with the modification which his own individuality gave. . . .

1. The incident in which Red Cross and Una meet Sir Trevisan fleeing from Despair (*F.Q.*, 1, 9, 21 ff.) has several details parallel with the one in *O.I.* in which Ranaldo and his company meet a knight fleeing from the fighting Orlando (*O.I.*, 1, 17, 51 ff.).

The parallel details are the following:

1. An armed knight, with pale face and general appearance of great fear, comes galloping upon a steed.
2. He keeps looking backward as though some pursuer were close behind.
3. He does not reply upon being first questioned.
4. In speaking, his tongue shakes with his body.

> So as they traveild, lo! they gan espy
> *An armed knight towards them gallop fast,*
> That seemed from some feared foe to fly,
> Or other griesly thing that him aghast.

> *Still as he fledd his eye was backward cast,*
> *As if his feare still followed him behynd:*
> *Als flew his steed as he his bandes had brast. . . .*

> Nigh as he drew, they might perceive his head
>   To bee unarmd, and curld uncombed heares
>   Upstaring stiffe, dismaid with uncouth dread:
>   *Nor drop of blood in all his face appeares,*
>   Nor life in limbe. . . .

> *He answerd nought at all;* but adding new
>   Feare to his first amazment, staring wyde
>   With stony eyes and hartlesse hollow hew,
>   Astonisht stood. . . .
>   Him yett againe, and yett againe, bespake
>   The gentle knight; *who nought to him replyde;*
>   But, *trembling every joynt, did inly quake,*
> *And foltring tongue, at last, these words seemd forth to shake.*
>   (*F.Q.*, 1, 9, 21, 22, 24)

> Vidon venir, correndo a la pianura,
> *Sopra un cavallo un uom tutt' armato,*
> Che mostrava a la vista gran paura;
> Ed era il suo caval molt' affannato,
> Forte battendo l'uno e l'altro fianco;
> Ma l'uomo trema, ed *è nel viso bianco.*

> Ciaschedun di novelle il dimandava,
> *Ma lui non rispondeva alcuna cosa,*
> *E pur a dietro spesso risguardava.*
> Dopo, a la fine in voce paürosa,
> (*Perchè la lingua co'l cor gli tremava*)
> Disse: . . .

> Io vidi, (e ancor mi par che l'aggia in faccia). . . .
> Dugento miglia son fuggito in caccia,
> E volentier m'avria nel mar sommerso,
> *Perchè averlo a le spalle ognor mi pare.*
> Ora a Dio siate; non voglio aspettare. (*O.I.*, 1, 17, 51, 52, 55)

To be sure, as the facts are, the objects from which the knights
are fleeing are different: Spenser's knight is fleeing from the grim

and gruesome figure of Despair; Boiardo's, from the fighting
Orlando. In both cases, however, the object is terrifying, and it
seems entirely possible that the dramatic picture of Boairdo's
fleeing knight remained in Spenser's memory so that he used such
details of it as would readily fit into his own situation.

11. The battle between Red Cross and the Dragon has been found
to contain parallel details with the dragon fight in the *Seven Champions
of Christendom*, and with those in *Sir Beves of Hamtoun* and *Huon of
Bordeaux*. One detail, however, is paralleled in none of these sources,
nor have I found it elsewhere in the romances. The parallel lies in
the fact that both knights are definitely described as fighting in the
flame from the dragon's mouth so that their armor becomes heated
and they are grievously pressed.

> And from his wide devouring oven sent
> A flake of fire, that flashing in his beard
> Him all amazd, and almost made afeard:
> The scorching flame sore swinged all his face,
> *And through his armour all his body seard,*
> That he could not endure so cruell cace,
> But thought his armes to leave, and helmet to unlace. . . .
>
> *Whom fyrie steele now burnt, that erst him armd,*
> *That erst him goodly armd, now most of all him harmd.*
>
> (*F.Q.*, I, 11, 26–27)

> Gettando sempre fuoco e fiamma viva. . . .
> La bocca aperse il diverso dragone. . . .
>
> Ma come piacque a Dio, nel scudo il prese. . . .
> Era di legno, e sì forte s'accese,
> Che presto e incontinente fu bruciato;
> *E così 'l sbergo e l'elmo e ogni altro arnese,*
> *Venne quasi rovente ed affocato:*
> *Arsa è la sopravesta,* e 'l bel cimiero
> Ardea tuttora in capo al Cavaliero.
>
> Non ebbe il Conte mai cotal battaglia,
> Poichè a quel fuoco contrastar conviene;
> Forza non giova, od arte di scrimaglia,
> Perchè 'l gran fumo, che con fiamma viene,

Gli entra ne l'elmo e la vista gli abbaglia,
Nè a pena vede il brando ch' in man tiene. . . .

(*O.I.*, 1, 24, 49–51)

v. The detail in the combat between Sir Guyon and Pyrocles
in which Guyon accidentally kills the latter's horse by cutting off
its head has been compared by Kitchin to an incident in Sidney's
Arcadia. Although the *Arcadia* was published in 1590, it was probably
written in 1580–2 and circulated in manuscript. We know that the
Faerie Queene was begun and that a part of it was in the hands of
Harvey by 1580. It is difficult, therefore, to prove the direction in
which any possible influence may have operated so far as Books
I–III of Spenser's poem are concerned. There does exist, however, a
parallel incident in Boiardo, the outstanding feature of which
Spenser may well have remembered.

But lightly shunned it, and passing by,
  With his bright blade did smite at him so fell,
  That the sharpe steele, arriving forcibly
  On his broad shield, bitt not, but *glauncing fell*
  On his horse necke before the quilted sell,
  And from the head the body sundered quight.
  So him, dismounted low, he did compell
  On foot with him to matchen equall fight;
The truncked beast, fast bleeding, did him fowly dight.

(*F.Q.*, II, 5, 4)

El scudo gli spezzò quel maledetto,
Le piastre aperse, come fosser carte,
E crudelmente lo piagò nel petto,
Giunse a l'arcione e tutto lo disparte,
E 'l collo al suo ronzon tagliò via netto. (*O.I.*, III, 8, 38)

vi. Koeppel has pointed out the resemblances between the figure
of Phaedria and the *fatal donzella* of Tasso's *G.L.*, xv, 3 ff., who is
sent by an aged magician to convey in her magic bark two Christian
knights to the distant enchanted island of Armida for the purpose
of regaining Rinaldo for the Christian army. Certain details, however, which occur in Spenser and do not in Tasso, may be found in a
similar incident in Bioardo.

1. In *F.Q.* the circumstances are such that both Cymocles and

Guyon *come to a river* while on their travels (*F.Q.*, II, 6, 2 & 19).
In *G.L.* the two knights have arisen from the river bed where they
have spent the night with the aged magician (*G.L.*, xv, 1–3). 2. Both
Cymocles and Guyon in turn *desire to be ferried across* (*F.Q.*, II, 6, 4 &
19). In *G.L.* the knights are not crossing the river but planning a
long sea voyage. 3. Spenser's knights find there a damsel who is
unknown to them. In *G.L.* the knights have been previously told of
the woman by the magician (*G.L.*, xiv, 72). 4. Phaedria *betrays*
them by taking them amidst the seductions of her enchanted isle. In
G.L. the damsel is friendly to the knights and is sent to aid them by
the aged magician.

In the following parallel situation in *O.I.* it will be seen that the
knights come to a river in their travels; they find there an unknown
damsel; they desire to be ferried across; they are betrayed into the
hands of a hostile power. Ranaldo is traveling in company with
three other knights.

> E prima cercherà molte contrade,
> Strane avventure e diversi paesi. . . .
>
> Ed era già passato il quinto giorno. . . .
> Quando da lunge odîr suonare un corno
> Sopra ad un castello alto e ben murato;
> Nel monte era il castello, e poi d'intorno
> Avea gran piano, e tutto era d'un prato;
> *Intorno il prato un bel fiume circonda,*
> Mai non si vide cosa più gioconda.
>
> L'acqua era chiara a maraviglia e bella,
> *Ma non si può vadar* tanto è corrente,
> A l'altra ripa stava *una donzella*
> Vestita a bianco, e *con faccia ridente,*
> *Sopra a la poppa d'una navicella.*
> Diceva: O Cavalieri, o belle gente,
> Se vi piace passare, entrate in barca,
> Però che altrove il fiume non si varca.
>
> *I Cavalier, che avean molto desire*
> *Di passar oltre* e prender suo viaggio,
> La ringraziarno di tal proferire,
> E travargano il fiume e quel passaggio.

> Disse la dama nel lor dipartire;
> Da l'altro lato si paga il pedaggio,
> *Nè mai di quindi uscir si può, se prima*
> *A quella ròcca non salite in cima.* (*O.I.*, II, 9, 49–53)

The damsel then informs the knights that the land they are about to enter belongs to one King Monodante, and that it will be impossible for them to leave it until they have dealt with him. They meet the king, who imposes upon them a battle with Balisardo, a giant and necromancer. Here then we have the details in Spenser not found in Tasso.

It will be noted in addition that Boiardo's damsel is described *con faccia ridente*, suggesting at once the seductive mirth of Phaedria. Also, Boiardo's knights are traveling on foot, having been deprived earlier of their horses (*O.I.*, II, 9, 50), in much the same way as Guyon, whose horse had been stolen by Braggadocchio (*F.Q.*, II, 2, 11; and II, 3, 3 ff.).

VII. *Castle Joyous*, in which Britomart spends a night at the household of Lady Malecaster (*F.Q.*, III, 1, 31), seems to have been suggested in name by *Palazzo Gioioso*, which the devoted Angelica has created for Ranaldo (*O.I.*, I, 8, 1–14).

As a background to the names, the following very general similarities may also be noted:

1. The palaces are of great sensuous appeal and costly furnishing. Details:

> The roiall riches and exceeding cost
> Of *every pillour and of every post,*
> Which *all of purest bullion framed were,*
> And *with great perles* and pretious stones embost;
> That the bright glister of their beames cleare
> Did sparckle forth great light, and glorious did appeare
> (*F.Q.*, III, 1, 32)

> Di gemme e d'oro e vaga dipintura
> Son tutti i lochi nobili e gioiosi: . . . .

> Adorna molto, ricca e delicata,
> Per ogni faccia e per ogni cantone
> Di smalto in lama d'oro istorïata. . . .
> E *le colonne* di quel bel lavoro,
> Han di cristallo il fusto *e 'l capo d'oro.* . . .

Di grosse perle adorno era il suo seggio (*O.I.*, 1, 8, 5, 6, 9)

2. In each case the lady of the palace is offering her love to the guest, and in each case it is spurned: Malecaster's by Britomart, Angelica's by Ranaldo. . . .

xi. When Timias tries to rescue Amoret from the Savage Lust, the latter holds her up before his body as a shield. This incident has a parallel in Boiardo in which Orlando rescues Angelica from Santaria.

> Thereto the villaine used craft in fight;
>> For ever when the squire his javelin shooke,
>> *He held the lady forth before him right,*
>> *And with her body, as a buckler,* broke
>> The puissance of his intended stroke.
>> And if it chaunst, (as needs it must in fight)
>> Whilest he on him was greedy to be wroke,
>> That any little blow on her did light,
> Then would he laugh aloud, and gather great delight.

> Which subtill sleight did him encumber much
>> And made him oft, when he would strike, forbeare;
>> *For hardly could he come the carle to touch,*
>> *But that he her must hurt, or hazard neare*   (*F.Q.*, iv, 7, 26-7)

> Ma Santaria, che vede quella prova,
> Digran paura trema tutto quanto,
> Nè riparar si sa del colpo crudo
> Se non *si fa di quella Dama scudo.*

> Perchè Orlando già gli è giunto addosso,
> Nè difender si può, nè può fuggire;
> *Temeva il Conte di averlo percosso,*
> *Per non far seco Angelica perire.*
> Essa gridava forte a più non posso;
> Se tu m'ami, Baron, fammel sentire;
> Occidimi, io ti prego, con tue mane,
> Non mi lasciar portare a questo cane. . . .

Orlando then attacks Santaria with his fists, while the latter

> La Dama sostenea dal manco lato,
> E ne la destra mano avea la spada (*O.I.*, 1, 15, 35-8)

XII. The adventure by which Scudamore gains the Shield of Love and hence entrance to Venus' Island (*F.Q.*, IV, 10, 5 ff.) resembles the incident in Boiardo in which Mandricardo comes to the Shield of Hector (*O.I.*, III, 2, 3 ff.).

'Before that castle was *an open plaine*,
    And *in the midst thereof a piller placed;*
    On which this shield, of many sought in vaine,
    The Shield of Love, whose guerdon me hath graced,
    Was hangd on high with golden ribbands laced;
    And in the marble stone was written this,
    With golden letters goodly well enchaced:
    "Blessed the man that well can use his blis:
    Whose ever be the shield, faire Amoret be his". . . .

Ne stayed further newes thereof to learne,
But *with my speare upon the shield did rap*' (*F.Q.*, IV, 10, 8–9)

    Lo ricondusse in quella *prateria*
    Ov' eran l'opre sì maravigliose.
    L'alto edificio avanti si vedìa. . . .

    Ma, come arriva Cavaliero, o Conte,
    Sopra a la soglia de l'entrata, giura. . . .
    Toccar quel scudo, che davanti vede.

    Posto è il bel scudo, *in mezzo a la gran piaccia*. . . .

    Benchè 'l scudo d'Ettòr, ch' io v'ho contato,
    Qual era posto *in mezzo a la gran corte*,
    Non era in parte alcuna tramutato,
    Ma tal, quale il portava il Baron forte,
    Ad un pilastro d'oro era chiavato,
    Ed avea scritto sopra, in lettere scorte:
    S' un altro Ettor non sei, non mi toccare;
    Chi mi portò, non ebbe al mondo pare. . . .

    E Mandricardo fece più nè meno;
    Poi passò dentro, senza resistenza,
    E, sendo giunto in mezzo a quel bel loco,
    Trasse la spada e toccò 'l scudo un poco. (*O.I.*, III, 2, 3–9)

In both cases, the castle is approached across an open expanse:
in Spenser, *an open plaine*; in Boiardo, *quella prateria*. In Spenser, a
pillar bearing a shield stands in the middle of the plain; in Boiardo,
it is in the middle of the court within the castle – *in mezzo a la gran
piaccia, in mezzo a la gran corte*. In one case, the pillar, in the other, the
shield, bears an inscription which consists of the last two lines of the
stanza in which each occurs. To be sure, the general custom of
announcing one's challenge by rapping upon a shield exposed for
that purpose is frequently met in the romances of chivalry, but the
combination of the parallel details here quoted – the castle with
the open expanse before it, the shield hanging on a column, the
inscription consisting of the last two lines of the stanza, together
with the rapping of the shield – seems to indicate that memories of
Boiardo's specific passage asserted themselves in Spenser's mind.

Source: extracts from 'Spenser and Boiardo', *PMLA*, xl
(1925) pp. 829–32, 835–8, 845–7.

R. E. Neil Dodge Spenser's Imitations from Ariosto (1897)

If we seek for a real centre of interest in the poem, we shall find it
only in Arthegall and Britomart and their love-story. From the
beginning of the third book to the end of the fifth they are kept
pretty constantly before us, and the prophecies of Merlin (iii, 3,
26–9) and of the Priest of Isis (v, 7, 23) tell us enough of the future
to make their story complete. How much prominence Spenser
meant ultimately to give them, we have no means of telling, but, as
the poem stands, their story is the only real centre of action, and
they are in a way the real hero and heroine. Britomart, of course,
as a 'lady knight' and possessor of the magic spear, is the counterpart
of Bradamante. Arthegall may stand for Ruggiero. He is certainly
Spenser's ideal knight, strong, just, steadfast, much more real than
the magnificent Arthur, and real because he was modelled on a
real man, Arthur Lord Grey of Wilton, Spenser's chief patron. As
Ariosto, therefore, made Ruggiero and Bradamante the centre of

interest in his poem, to exalt the house of Este, so Spenser made Arthegall his virtual hero, in tribute to his former patron, to the man who more than any other had made a lasting mark on his imagination. He was presented as the lover of Britomart by analogy from Ariosto; to complete the analogy, the pair were made the ancestors of Elizabeth, through the genuinely British kings following Arthur.

When we come to trace the love-story we find that at almost every point it touches Ariosto. It is naturally brief, for Britomart and Arthegall, as the types of Chastity and Justice, are principally busied in allegorical action and have scant time for love. The passages which bear on the course of their love are few, and are scattered at rather wide intervals over the three books. As a centre of action the story is certainly rather slight. It is, nevertheless, the only plot of its kind in the poem. Its dependence on Ariosto will be worth noting in detail.

In the first place, Britomart falls in love with Arthegall by the single glimpse which she has of his image in her father's enchanted mirror (III, 2, 22 ff.). The first account which we have of Bradamante in the *Furioso* (II, 32) tells us simply that she is in love with Ruggiero, whom she has seen but once. Now, Spenser probably did not know the *Orlando Innamorato*;[1] he was, therefore, ignorant of the circumstances under which the two lovers first met (*O.I.*, III, 4, 49 to end; III, 5; III, 6, 1–33), and the passage in the *Furioso*, which was intended merely to refresh the memories of Ariosto's readers, gave him no more than a bare fact. He adopted the fact and accounted for it in his own way.

In the image which Britomart sees the knight's armor is inscribed with the legend: 'Achilles armes which Arthegall did win' (III, 2, 25). One of Ruggiero's greatest feats is the killing of Mandricardo in single combat, as a result of which he becomes possessed of the armor of Hector, which his antagonist had formerly borne (*O.F.*, xxx).

The visit of Glaucè and Britomart to Merlin in his cave and the prophecy of Britomart's future line (III, 3) is of course taken bodily from canto 3 of the *Furioso*, in which Bradamante enters the cave of Merlin by chance, and is informed of her descendants by Melissa. One may note certain differences. In the *Furioso* the spirit of Merlin speaks from the tomb, and delivers a brief welcoming address of

vaguely prophetic import; Bradamante's descendants are revealed
to her in a series of phantoms conjured up by Melissa, like the vision
of Banquo's issue in *Macbeth*. In the *Faery Queen* Merlin is sitting in
his cave, alive and visible, and reveals Britomart's future line by
word of mouth. In stanza 32, however, 'Behold the man!' etc.
would seem to indicate that Spenser had in mind the visible phantoms of the *Furioso*, and forgot himself.

Britomart wandering about Faery Land in quest of Arthegall is
like Bradamante, who at the beginning of the *Furioso* is wandering
about France in quest of Ruggiero (*O.F.*, II, 33). Britomart's long
quest after Arthegall and the brief periods during which she enjoys
his presence, periods intercalated in long months of separation,
correspond very closely to the rare meetings and the long periods of
separation which disturb the love-story of Ruggiero and Bradamante.

Arthegall's courtship of Britomart follows upon their very first
meeting (IV, 6, 40 ff.), and her consent is given before they separate.
Ruggiero and Bradamante exchange troth at their first definitive
meeting in the *Furioso* (*O.F.*, XXII, 31-6). Arthegall leaving Britomart, to pursue his quest, and promising to return at the end of
three months (IV, 6, 42, 43) is like Ruggiero pursuing his *affaire
d'honneur* with Rodomonte and promising to rejoin Bradamante
within twenty days (*O.F.*, XXX, 76-81).

Britomart waiting impatiently for the return of Arthegall, seeing
the time appointed for his return slip by, tormented by fears and
jealousies (v, 6), is the exact counterpart of the love-sick Bradamante waiting for the return of Ruggiero (*O.F.*, XXX, 84 ff.;
XXXII, 10 ff.). Talus, who brings back news of Arthegall's defeat
by Radegund and his captivity, thereby rousing Britomart's jealousy,
corresponds to the 'cavalier guascone' who brings to Bradamante
the report that Ruggiero is betrothed to the warrior maiden,
Marfisa. The conduct of Britomart when she receives the news is
exactly like that of Bradamante: she first indulges in resentful
despair, then sets out to go to her lover. The combat of Britomart
with Radegund (v, 7, 26 ff.) might be likened to the combat of
Bradamante with Marfisa (*O.F.*, XXXVI). As Bradamante discovers her jealousies to have been causeless, so Britomart.

Here the love-story of Britomart and Arthegall comes to an
end. How Spenser would have terminated it, had he carried his

poem further, we, of course, do not know. In III, 3, 28, however, we have a prophecy by Merlin of the final destiny of the pair. This destiny is almost exactly that of Bradamante and Ruggiero, as given in the *Furioso*, XII, 60 ff.

Could any imitation be more deliberate and thorough than this? Spenser has not merely taken suggestions here and there; every point of his story has its counterpart in the *Furioso*; the correspondence from beginning to end is complete. Of course, Spenser varies the details to meet the conditions of his poem, and, of course, his story has an atmosphere of its own; but he could hardly show himself more indifferent to the merits of narrative invention. He evidently had the genuine Elizabethan instinct for saving himself the trouble of inventing a plot.

SOURCE: extract from 'Spenser's Imitations from Ariosto',
PMLA, XII (1897) pp. 175–8.

NOTE

1. [But see pages 58–66 herein – Ed.]

P. J. Alpers   Spenser's Use of Ariosto (1967)

... when Spenser borrows a character from Ariosto, he is interested in a more or less conventional figure who is in a poetically interesting situation, as opposed to an individual with a unique moral nature. (The exception to this rule is his using Bradamante as the model for Britomart.) This explains a fact that has long puzzled modern critics – Spenser's basing Florimell on Angelica. The assumption is that Spenser would have to fly in the face of the poem and accept an interpretation that makes Angelica a virtuous person or the embodiment of a virtue before he could use her as the model for the virtuous Florimell. But Spenser is interested not in a character, but in the beautiful maiden who arouses erotic desire and is constantly being pursued; this dramatic situation stimulates some of his most interesting poetry about human desire. The most striking illustration

of the point we are making is Spenser's use of some situations which
involve a maiden in distress. Spenser's episodes of Sansloy's assault
on Una (I, 6, 3–7) and the old fisherman's on Florimell (III, 8,
20–31) are modeled, respectively, on Odorico's assault on Isabella
(*O.F.*, XIII, 26–9) and the old hermit's attempt to rape Angelica
(*O.F.*, VIII, 30–50). For Spenser the parts of these and other
episodes are to some extent interchangeable, and he feels no im-
pediment in the fact that some details concern Isabella, the model
of chastity, and others Angelica, the arch-flirt. Angelica is rescued
from the hermit by the sailors of Ebuda, who take her off to be
sacrificed to the Orc. This sequence of events suggests Florimell's
falling from the frying pan into the fire when Proteus rescues her.[1]
But of the three stanzas in which Ariosto laments Angelica's cruel
fate, Spenser transfers the first (*O.F.*, VIII, 66) to the Una–Sansloy
episode; he does not use the last (the wish that the lady's knights
were present, VIII, 68) in the episode with Proteus, but instead
uses it at the climax of his outcry when the fisherman assaults
Florimell (III, 8, 27–8).[2] His major rhetorical outburst in the episode
with Proteus, the praise of Florimell's chastity (III, 8, 42–3), is in its
turn taken from Ariosto's praise of Isabella's chastity (*O.F.*, XXIX,
26–7) when, rather than give herself to Rodomonte, she tricks him
into killing her.

These last examples indicate not only how well Spenser read
Ariosto's poem, but how intimately he knew it. The major sign that
Orlando Furioso was continually present in Spenser's mind is that
episodes that are important to him characteristically appear in
more than one episode of *The Faerie Queene*. Thus the Red Cross
Knight's disarming by the fountain (I, 7, 2–4) comes from Ruggiero's
refreshing himself in Alcina's grove (*O.F.*, VI, 20–5), but the
narration of Astolfo turned into a tree, which immediately follows
in *Orlando Furioso* (VI, 26–53), is used much earlier in Book I in the
story of Fradubio (I, 2, 30–44). Alcina, the enchantress who transforms men to beasts, is a characteristic Renaissance version of Circe,
and in this respect is like Spenser's Acrasia. But the unveiling of her
ugliness (*O.F.*, VII, 70–4) produces the disrobing of Duessa (I, 8,
46–9), while in a particularly skillful adaptation, Ruggiero's nervous
waiting for Alcina (*O.F.*, VII, 23–6) becomes Malecasta's agitated
creeping to Britomart's bed (III, 1, 58–61). In Astolfo's first victory
with his magic horn, his conquest of the giant Caligorante (*O.F.*,

xv, 10–62), the description of Caligorante's lair and the country around it (*O.F.*, xv, 49–50) suggests the dwelling of Despair and other Spenserian monsters; the description of Caligorante's subtly woven net (*O.F.*, xv, 56), with which he captures his victims and into which Astolfo makes him fall, is adapted by Spenser in his description of the net in which the Palmer catches Acrasia (ii, 12, 81); and the binding of Caligorante and Astolfo's leading him into Cairo to the amazement of the townspeople (*O.F.*, xv, 59–62) produce Calidore's taming the Blatant Beast (vi, 12, 36) and leading him about to the admiration of 'all the people where so he did go' (vi, 12, 37). Bradamante's defeat of Atlante not only supplies materials for the final cantos of Book iii, it also provides one of the most striking touches in Book i. The moment when Sansloy unlaces the helmet of the knight he thinks is the Red Cross Knight and uncovers the 'hoarie head of *Archimago* old' (i, 3, 38) is directly taken from Bradamante's catching sight of Atlante's face when she is about to kill him (*O.F.*, iv, 27).

Spenser's use of the episode in the Castle of Tristran (*O.F.*, xxxii, 64–110) is especially interesting. He uses the first half in Book iii and reserves the second half for Book iv, where it provides the first of a series of episodes that belong specifically to the Book of Friendship – episodes in which the conflicting desires of good knights and ladies are turned into a harmony. In the first half of her adventure, Bradamante gains the right to shelter from a storm by defeating three knights outside the castle; this is the source for the entry of Britomart, Paridell, and their companions into the castle of Malbecco and Hellenore (iii, 9, 1–18). (The special rule that makes a knight gain his entrance into the Castle of Tristran is due to the jealousy and inhospitality of its original owner – *O.F.*, xxxii, 83–94 – and this may have suggested to Spenser Malbecco's barring the gates because of his jealousy.) When it is discovered inside the castle that Bradamante is a woman, she is declared subject to the second half of the rule of the Castle of Tristran, which requires that only the woman judged to be the fairest can stay inside the castle. Ullania, who was already inside the castle, is less beautiful than Bradamante. She is about to be sent out into the storm, when Bradamante announces that she cannot be subject to the rules for both sexes, and she states that for the night she is to be considered a warrior, not a woman (*O.F.*, xxxii, 101–6).

In the opening canto of Book IV, Spenser borrows this device of
the female warrior resolving, by her paradoxical nature, a problem
created by special rules of hospitality. Britomart and Amoret come
to a castle whose rule is that no knight who does not have a lady
can stay within. A solitary knight challenges Britomart for Amoret's
hand, but after defeating him, Britomart 'that no lesse was courteous
then stout' (IV, 1, 11), devises a way to allow him to stay. After
getting Amoret secured to her as a knight, she reveals her sex and
offers herself to the stranger knight as a lady (IV, 1, 12). Britomart's
behavior is based on Bradamante's solicitude for Ullania, and her
resolution of the dilemma by letting down her hair (IV, 1, 13) turns
a striking dramatic moment in Ariosto's narration into a climactic
moment in Spenser's rhetorical mode. It is at this point in Spenser's
borrowings that the two halves of Ariosto's episode overlap. This
stanza and its analogue in the Malbecco episode (III, 9, 20) are both
imitations of the stanza in which Bradamante lets down her hair
in the Castle of Tristran (*O.F.*, XXXII, 79–80). Spenser remembered
this episode in yet another book of *The Faerie Queene*. In describing
Irena's joy when Artegall rescues her (V, 12, 13), he borrows the
simile with which Ariosto rendered Ullania's happiness at being
allowed to stay in the castle (*O.F.*, XXXII, 108).

If we start with a single episode in *The Faerie Queene* and seek out
its Ariostan sources, we will often get the impression that Spenser's
use of Ariosto is capricious and superficial. On the other hand, if we
start with an episode in *Orlando Furioso* and ask what it produces,
influences, or suggests in *The Faerie Queene*, we will get a truer sense
of Spenser's familiarity with Ariosto's poem and the ease with
which he could draw on it for his own. The best way to understand
Spenser's use of Ariosto is simply to read the first dozen or so cantos
of *Orlando Furioso* and notice how many things appear in *The Faerie
Queene*. It seems absurd to start with Archimago's meeting the Red
Cross Knight and Una (I, 1, 29–30) and point back to Angelica's
meeting with the hermit (who also turns out to be a magician,
O.F., II, 12–13), as if there were some exciting relation between the
two incidents taken in isolation. But when we are reading *Orlando
Furioso*, we see that Spenser's adaptation of the incident is precisely
not an occasion for excitement, but simply one more sign that he
had the whole poem at his fingertips. Critics have often poked fun at
Spenser for taking seriously the ironic stanza that begins 'Oh gran

bontà de' cavallieri antiqui!' (*O.F.*, i, 22; cf. *F.Q.*, iii, i, 13). Spenser appears so simple-minded here, because we assume that he solemnly sought out this individual stanza and used it as humorlessly as possible. But the opening canto of *Orlando Furioso*, in which this stanza occurs, is one Spenser must have known almost by heart and on which he draws time and again in *The Faerie Queene*. If his use of the stanza is part of a lively and immediate contact with Ariosto's poem, then it seems more likely than not that he was conscious of changing Ariosto's tone, and that his failure to reproduce it is not a sign that he mistook it.

As many Renaissance writers said, imitation is digestion and absorption, not passive copying. When a major poet is profoundly influenced by another major poet, he undoubtedly puts his own stamp on what he borrows. But we have assumed hitherto that Spenser's use of Ariosto is narrow-minded and inappropriate, like the Christian moralization of Ovid. The proper analogy is to Ben Jonson's use of Horace, Dryden's use of Virgil, Wordsworth's use of Milton, Melville's use of Shakespeare, or Eliot's use of Dante. In each case, the poet's use of his predecessor involves an unmistakable transmutation, emphasis of some qualities at the expense of others. But at the same time the borrowings of poets like these characteristically reveal a full and intelligent awareness of the poet imitated. Yet even when we have seen how well Spenser knew and understood *Orlando Furioso*, we may still wonder whether there was a temperamental affinity between him and Ariosto of the sort that we expect to find in so major a case of influence and imitation. Our accepted notions of the two poets – frivolous and ironic Ariosto, sage and serious Spenser – of course suggest that no such affinity could exist. Yet once we clear our minds of these clichés and the attendant simplistic notions of morality and irony, seriousness and play of mind, we have no trouble in seeing why Spenser felt close to *Orlando Furioso*. Are not some of his most notable and precious characteristics as a poet – his moral generosity, the poise and lucidity of his intelligence, his geniality, affectionateness, and humanity – qualities that he would have found preeminently in Ariosto?

SOURCE: extract from *The Poetry of 'The Faerie Queene'* (Princeton, 1967) pp. 195–8.

1. Spenser probably got from Ariosto the idea of having Proteus rescue Florimell. In explaining how the people of Ebuda came to scour the coasts for beautiful women, Ariosto tells of their offending Proteus, who sent the Orc in vengeance. Spenser's '*Proteus* is Shepheard of the seas of yore, / And hath the charge of *Neptunes* mightie heard' (III, 8, 30) is almost a direct translation of Ariosto's, 'Proteo marin, che pasce il fiero armento / di Nettunno che l'onda tutta regge' (*O.F.*, VIII, 54) ['Proteus of the sea, who tends the fierce herd of Neptune, who rules all the water'].

2. Robert M. Durling notices Spenser's multiple use of single passages in Ariosto and points out that *O.F.*, VIII, 66–7 is also echoed in *F.Q.*, III, 8, 1 and IV, 11, 1: see his *The Figure of the Poet in Renaissance Epic* (Cambridge, Mass., 1965) pp. 212–13.

Rosemond Tuve Spenser and Medieval Romances (1966)

The poem Spenser wrote would have been totally impossible to a mediaeval writer. This is true also of genres formally closer, of Sidney's and Lodge's pastoral romances, of Drayton's verse-tales if not of his *Nymphidia*, that delightful single success in rivaling Chaucer's doggerel mock – the minstrel-romance. Nevertheless, we see in the relation under review an especially outstanding example of a phenomenon that begins to look characteristic of the Renaissance in England as compared with other countries: that the refusal to give up mediaeval forms and habits resulted in a forced marriage between those and new forms, motifs, stuffs, imagery, which, though an unnatural union, was a fertile one. Qualities of the offspring cannot be neatly separated into distinguishable inheritances from separate parents. In qualities, inclusions and altered purposes the combination differs from either source, seeming to owe its life to them both but its typical character to neither.

Various studies that search the romances for specific influences have made the whole relationship appear trivial. The bane of studies relating Spenser to romances has been the hunt for borrowed story-motifs. These connections seem largely illusory – and all but completely unimportant; meanwhile, far too much has been argued from their absence. I shall neglect such borrowings entirely. The important connections are persistently of another kind, important to the aesthetic judgments we make, but hard to isolate and seldom securely provable; the points to be made are incorrigibly large, vague and loosely drawn, and will be falsified if not allowed to remain so. . . .

That we withdraw from precise source study and deny the importance of plot comparisons does not make the central fact any less true and important – that 'mediaeval romance' is what is responsible for the character the *Faerie Queene* has as a narrative. We ought occasionally to think of what an unimaginably different poem we should have had if Spenser had written Christian history like the Fletchers, du Bartas, Milton; if Spenser had kept to secular historical narrative like Drayton in his Legends and his two heroic poems on Mortimer, or had written of the Irish and Belgian conflicts as Daniel did of the Civil Wars; or if Spenser had written 'classical' historical epics like a Petrarch or a Ronsard, or mythicized pseudo-classical narratives like a Jean Lemaire de Belges; or if he had confined himself to (instead of merely using) Italianized, Platonized mythological poetry of the kind found in his temples of Venus or Isis or revolt of Mutability. Spenser finds use for all these kinds of narratives, but it has an extraordinary effect upon their durability and their absence of preciosity that they are set in a matrix of the most ordinary kind of storytelling in Europe for four centuries: the straightforward tale of chivalric romance.

Certain presuppositions, all now suspect, have governed criticism when it has touched upon Spenser and romance; two general observations with their sub-points may illustrate this. The relation of the *Faerie Queene* to mediaeval chivalric romances is seldom mentioned without a stated or hidden assumption that this provided 'escape'. Yet a major influence of this body of stories upon Spenser was that they taught him their flair for ordinary realism in its simplest sense: for situations drawn from daily life, natural rather than contrived or stilted conversation, unadorned reportage of a matter-of-fact presentation of what we instead isolate and call 'the marvelous', credible and unelaborated motivations, modified by a few large accepted conventions like inviolable 'customs', or the granting of quests or boons. This can be supported presently, but one might claim with justice that the romance-like portions of the *Faerie Queene* are the portions where we retire comfortably from the exotic and the thoroughly incredible into the plain affairs of serious but ordinary daily life. Feudal life was of course just as daily and just as ordinary as ours or Spenser's, and Malory's influence especially we would expect to be toward plain narrative of plain events, the romantic 'remoteness' of armor, moats, castles and jousts being still two centuries off.

Two side points are as little recognized as is the firm grasp of most mediaeval romance-writing upon actuality and the habitual use of that element as the ground of these fictions. One is that whereas it is naturally assumed that romances markedly influenced Spenser in his use of the supernatural, we notice rather that his most important large images portraying places and times beyond the natural, and actions beyond human nature, are not fundamentally romance-like. Mammon's otherworld is Dantesque and classical, the House of Pride is like a setpiece of Christian didactic literature, the Gardens of Adonis and Nature's realm in Mutability are influenced by cosmological myth of a Platonic cast, Isis' temple by Plutarchian late-classical lore, Acrasia's Bower by mediaevalized classical moral imagery.

These wonders, however, are set in a solid framework of chivalric story – real tournaments fought in visitable places (unlocated but less fanciful than the meetings and combats in Ariosto to which we are brought by a specified routing through the right countries and across the right borders). Nights are spent and wounds cured in ordinary castles; giants and monsters combatted as often as the conventional lions and bears, but as a mere variation of the inhabitants, and usually vanquished by valor not magic; the day's adventures, duties and hazards lived through without deliberate fostering of 'romantic mediaeval atmosphere'. In the prose *Lancelot* – romance par excellence, and natural source of habits and commonplaces because of its scope, frequent publication and famed hero – supernatural marvels are largely clustered around the acts and habitat of the character whose extra-human powers are meaningful: the Lady of the Lake, once no doubt a fairy mistress but now a benevolent otherworld patroness. Elsewhere large tracts of the story proceed as straightforward recounting of knightly prowess, avengings, promises, battles, mishaps, wounds, love affairs, the proving of character under stress and the relations and feelings of persons.

Spenser's use of the admittedly marvelous is roughly similar, and his significantly isolated otherworldly places or supernatural characters are set in a natural matrix which is that of the ordinary mediaeval world. Powers beyond the natural have true spiritual significance and are possessed by those meant to have such roles, while the communication or traffic between this world and the super-humanly evil or good worlds is always open but always important. These comparable narrative procedures are contrasted with, for example, Ariosto's lightheartedly fanciful and unrestrained use of the magical – of trance-inducing irresistible shields and incredibly convenient wishing-rings, of enchanted palaces that spring up and disappear as needed, psychological powers that exchange appearance and reality in the minds of 'natural' characters, conjuring-books, recognition-charms, hippogriffs guided or unguided and the like machinery. All late romances, especially other Charlemagne-romances with enlargements, like *Huon de Bordeaux*, similarly multiply machinery to advance plot, but most retain some shred of the important spiritual significance of the otherworldly elements, later so inventively developed in Spenser and integrated with Christian allegorical and symbolic meanings. There are good reasonable grounds for the effects recounted of Arthur's bright diamond shield, the unearthly landscape of the island where Venus's temple is found, Phaedria's boat that skims without power across the Idle Lake when 'only she turn'd a pin'. Since I think we may safely say Spenser learned to use the mediaeval milieu from those who lived in it, it has not the suggestions (of nostalgia, of daydream, of sentimental enthusiasm) which would threaten that serious involvement with actual life which he desires and achieves. . . .

Like the use of the supernatural, a second side point touches accepted stereotypes of what romances are. We should ask 'to *whom* are chivalric tales a nostalgic re-creation of what is lost, a harking back and wishful return to a vanished past'? Possibly only to us late-comers, prepared by *The Boys' King Arthur* for the stronger adolescent dose of *Idylls of the King*. We know considerably more than we did about the Tudor revival of Arthurian history for serious political ends, and about fifteenth- sixteenth- and seventeenth-

century English attitudes toward chivalry. From the time of Greenlaw's early suggestive inquiries, Spenser students have been aware
of the topicality and political seriousness given to Arthurian materials
by two facts: the Celtic or British origins and Arthurian connections
of the house of Tudor, combined with the legend of Arthur's prophesied return from Avalon to bring Britain again to her ancient
glory. Charles Bowie Millican's carefully circumstantial book long
ago (1932) made more obvious the inaccuracy of attaching usual
connotations of 'romantic' or 'imitation-mediaeval' to Elizabethan
use of Arthurian materials; special areas of new information were:
the number and scope of serious references relating such history to
Henry VII's Welsh lineage, the specific parallels (like Henry's
exile in Brittany, like Arthur's purging the land of false religion, i.e.
'Saracens'), the connections with interests of men like Dee and
Daniel Rogers, the Polydore-Vergil controversy, the scope and
importance of antiquarian interests and their tie to contemporary
ideals, the organization of societies, the use of Arthurian 'patrons',
support of customs, sports or manners connected with Arthurian
romances, not for their quaint remoteness but for their current
interest in a time of vigorous chivalric revival.

In the detailed study of this revival by Arthur Ferguson (*The
Indian Summer of Chivalry*, 1960), it is impossible not to observe
how completely Spenser's tone and handling fits the earlier English
developments outlined. Often in some portion of the *Faerie Queene*
where Ariosto is the undoubted immediate source, of plot motif or
character, Spenser's altered tone and different narrative impulse
show how the very changes of his source fit him into the mosaic of
this English development. We watch this development from the
time when Caxton and early printers found a motive for printing
romances in the desire to enhance England's prestige and revitalize
her institutions, down to the high tide of Arthurian interest in the
1580s. The *Faerie Queene* no longer stands so alone, as we consider
plentiful evidence that the obsolescence of chivalry as an institution
was far from obvious to a still partly feudal society, or evidence for
the aristocracy's attempt to revitalize as well as to take refuge in the
traditional ways of living and thinking, or as we observe the many
other manifestations of close relations between chivalry and developing concepts of the commonwealth, of national pride, courtiership,
or the ideals of other classes. Many of these points of view have

been obscured by our interest in satire directed against quite limited aspects of the ancient institution. . . .

Like the whole matter of Spenser's relation to 'real life' through, rather than despite, his romance genre, yet another point suggests that our commonplace stereotypes about Arthurian romances may be more mid-nineteenth century than accurate, and our conception of romance influences on sixteenth-century writers thence mistaken. The familiar assumption dies hard, that Spenser's structure, influenced by the haphazard movement of romance plots and by their Gothic wildness and multiplicity of motive, is something well passed over with charitable speed, though its oddities as evidence of changing plans have been examined of late years with a beneficial increase of both sympathy and understanding.

But modern research and criticism in fields other than Renaissance and Spenser have brought us to a quite different view of romance form. It is not only seen as an artistic design, far from haphazard, but as a form able to provide narrative excellences and subtleties which other structures cannot provide. It may be that we should be closer to the mark if we were found talking about Spenser's deliberate and wise choice of the romance structure, responsible for the *Faerie Queene*'s controlled and suitable complications of pattern, sanctioning Spenser's skilfull use of the basic romance device of entrelacement, and protecting him from the error of forcing the different logic of epic design upon materials and purposes unsuited to it. There will be time later to condemn such a galloping swing of the pendulum, as this represents, away from our current acceptance of Spenser's undisguised shifts and excusable unsuccess as a designer. At least, our discussion should consider what characteristics of *structure* would present themselves for *imitation*, to a reader who surely added numerous earlier romances to his Ariosto and his Tasso, his Homer and his Virgil. . . .

Of course Spenser read Malory. But he must have read so much else which his writing resembles more, structurally, that he surely needed to feel no discomfort about preserving the traditional role of Arthur; that is preserved (more than if he had copied Malory's incidents) in Arthur as a combined figure for the dynasty, the all-inclusive virtue, the spouse-to-be of the personified realm, the royal house through whom divine power flowed into country and people.

Whatever its origins, . . . this truly central role has been Arthur's throughout so many romances that we seldom think behind it to explanations and causes, and have ourselves accepted the irrationalities it brings (chiefly into our judgments of Arthur's character). Modern complaints get confused with those which stem rather from the ancient antipathies to the structure of romance rather than of epic, but Arthur seems inactive and minor only if we are unable to realize and allow the romance conventions which gave his role its longevity. That in the *Faerie Queene* it takes two personages to fill the functions gives no trouble, except to those who want allegory to provide us with fixed equations; it is obviously prudent, given the sex of the occupant on the throne of the returning-British-Arthur's kingdom, but also this metaphor of a marriage is the only way to state all the meanings at once, a marriage in which the Faery Queen is to be made one with all Arthur symbolizes, including establishment of the true faith, by God's grace. Arthur is given no double fidelity to correspond to Artegall's and Red Crosse's; and it is made clear in Book after Book – in this case fortunately we need not know their order of composition – that Arthur is uniquely related to the queen of the 'faeries', uniquely related to the questers or to the virtues they seek and find, and that as Magnificence he retains, divinely elected and strengthened, the kingly functions tradition gave to him. He has transcended the role of his historical kingship; but the way to the transcendent role he has in the *Faerie Queene* was pointed to by his primitive one. The mystery of Arthur's supernatural election and the question of his fitness as chief of such a fellowship is felt even in the prose romances; moderns are not the first who would prefer an epic hero with clear merits, and Malory tried to make him one. . . .

Much is said of the last-minute addition of the Letter to Ralegh, but a reader of Arthurian romance all but supplies its framework scene to the action before reading the Letter; we would invent something very like the annual feast if it were not provided by Spenser. Though once primitive, the situation had become a firmly expected part of knight-errant romances, and the donation of such trials of the realm's health to members of it, both a responsibility and a test of the sovereign, was expected too. It explains why errant knights are errant and puts a proper light upon the notion that these benefits are being secured to the realm or fellowship. That the virtues sought in the quests are secured to the commonwealth is part of the inherited design, and the Books are not separate. But an Arthur as a protagonist, parallel to and a peer with others, or as one of the questers seeking *a* virtue, would be to a habitual romance-reader a most unwelcome change in an established character whose traditional meaning is essential to the very existence, health and functioning of 'fellowship'.

Spenser's combination of this element which survived into the Arthurian romances with a theologically sophisticated and subtle presentation of Christian grace in his Arthur is one of the superlative examples of his genius for creative amalgamation. Divinely endowed Fortitude takes over as the knights approach the end of their natural powers and 'Magnificently' perseveres in a virtue, attaining a perfected and triumphant form of it. For kingship primitively understood, not personifying but *symbolic of* the realm and its health, did provide (it was thought) just such open channels to divine power. And even this late, Elizabeth the historical queen as *defensor fidei* is to be seen as one with, indissolubly united to, the instrument of God's grace for her realm, quite aside from the more particular significances of an Arthur as royal spouse, which history was *not* to see emerge. Allegorically this is a trifle; the queen of this golden England is loved by, is wooed, is married to, all the unphraseable great things Arthur symbolizes, and the multiple appearance of some of them, in shifting but perfectly real literal historical personages, reminds us that we must not suffocate an allegory with the tightly drawn noose of inflexible equations, but allow meanings to flow into and inhabit the literal so that it is symbolic also. These various ways of being real do not lend their excitement to the Arthur of earlier story, but the role which there gave continuity to his sporadic appearances seems to me retained and transmuted to give a similar continuity to his functions in the *Faerie Queene*. Such conceptions of course develop during writing, and what Arthur became in the *Faerie Queene* is to be sought in no romance. . . .

But by far the most striking element of structure which Spenser has caught from much attention to romances is the principle of *entrelacement*. . . .

Of course, I do not wish to deny the plain fact that Spenser knew and deliberately emulated epic structure and epic conventions. But the *Faerie Queene* stands like a demonstration to prove that it was possible still to avoid the misunderstanding of romance *virtues* which turns up so stubbornly in the theorists nourished on Aristotle and chained to 'his' definitions of unity, of an action, of superiority of epic, and the like. It does not seem possible that Spenser could have emphasized so neatly the 'new' merits pointed to as native to the romance form, praised them on similar principles, and relinquished contradictory 'epic' merits in their favor, if he had been quite unaware that he was taking a well-known stand on a famous question. It is sufficient for our point to recognize in the repeatedly stressed flaws for which Ariosto and romance-writers were belabored those structural flaws with which *Spenser* has been charged, from the 1700s through to the present. The 'flaws' are indeed departures from epic structure, but they are characteristic and deliberately followed principles of romance composition.

The most important complaint is that against a multiple action with multiple actors. The principle of entrelacement deliberately and inextricably attached thereto is condemned as interruption; objectors are quite oblivious to the narrative virtues of this structural device and denigrate it in phrases very reminiscent of modern comments on the structure of mediaeval romances. 'Variety' as the principle most stressed in defense is not only mentioned (as in the Letter and in treatments both by enemies and friends) but enormously developed as a chief literary pleasure, applicable to characters, supplying the place of unity, the major lesson learned by Ariosto from the romances. We seem to meet well-known friends in the condemnatory remarks about episodic structure, digression and the objection that even supposedly important characters do not stand out as 'main' or 'chief'. There is also much discussion of the suspicious importance of marvels in the action, and of their fantastic nature. . . .

One must distinguish entrelacement from the mere practice, ubiquitous in narrative, of taking one character through a series of actions, then deserting them temporarily – often with the object of introducing suspense – while another character is given primary attention, then returning to the first, and so on. This is a simple device to get around the fact that the medium of words cannot recount events happening simultaneously to different persons living through the same time; though we cannot play on several strings simultaneously, we accept the convention that we can show the polyphonic nature of what we have to tell by juxtaposing separable persons' stories. But events connected by entrelacement are not juxtaposed; they are interlaced, and when we get back to our first character he is not where we left him as we finished his episode, but in the place of psychological state or condition of meaningfulness to which he has been pulled by the events occurring in following episodes written about some one else. Moreover, though the intervening episode will look like a digression from the line previously followed, it will transpire that that line could not go on without something furnished in the seemingly unrelated second line of narrative, the 'digression'. Or, if the digression has rather the character of a flashback or an elaboration or a supplying of background, it will turn out to carry onward some second 'new' theme as well as the first one which needed the background, and from that in turn we digress, or seem to, and then come back, not to precisely what we left but to something we understand differently because of what we have since seen. . . .

This is not truly a repetitive structure, which we see exemplified, e.g. in the repeated conquests of a Tamburlaine, though the quest-organization in romances or in Spenser makes the not-truly-parallel encounters look repetitive or purely episodic – as it makes the frequent necessary transitions easy and deceptively naïve. It has always been noticed that Spenser looks at his chosen abstraction or virtue through the perspectives of several incidents, as in Book v we look at aspects of Justice and In-Justice or unrighteous tyranny through one after another token incident or fable. We therefore approach with clarified sight the real unveiling, or the climactic joining of the issue if the terms are those of a conflict, near the middle and near the end. This structure also is incorrectly termed episodic or repetitive or parallel, for the subtler effects and advantages here noted as typical of interlaced, not parallel, happenings will be seen to characterize any Book the reader cares to examine closely.

This web-structure has special possibilities of gradually discernible meaning as the woven pattern shows it *is* a pattern and *takes* shape. Hence it was a superbly invented instrument for conveying not only what we called the polyphonic nature of what is happening, but that which interested Spenser supremely, the fact that to human minds what happens 'means' something, is significant.

We may seem to digress from the pursuit of Florimell, and flash
back to the Merlin's cave episode to know why Britomart is on that
road and meets the others; we also experience, however, the way
the 'love' we condemned in Castle Joyous in III, 1, now retroacts
to complicate the love that seizes the heroine in III, 2, for we perceive likenesses as well as differences. We see that the Florimell-
pursuit is going to have meanings which the Artegall-pursuit will
clarify, that the genealogical prophecies had been given significance
(before we knew we were meeting them) by the British emphases
of Book II. No matter which was written first, the Braggadochio–
False Florimell section or the Braggadochio–Belphoebe of Book II,
the 'patchiness' with which a later-appearing character is just
lightly drawn in for an episode in a Book we read first, merely
seems patchy. For both appearances are needed, in the contexts they
are in, to fill out the presentation of the Bad Knight – as he lacks
understanding of chaste love, and as he lacks understanding of
temperance. The presentation will be properly continued in the
episode in Book V where Braggadochio is the Bad Knight since he
lacks that virtue which gives 'to each man his own', or in Book IV
where he is the Bad Knight incapable of Friendship, a knight sought
out and preferred by falsity.

The Marinell of III, 4 would not be capable of conceiving the
love he is later to give Florimell, nor have we quite distinguished
it ourselves before it occurs (or is patently missing) in incidents
involving others. Florimell must remain in the straits we leave
her in in III, 8 until those happenings occur which bring the characters and the readers through the changes that make us (and Cymoent
and Marinell) consent to the marriage in Book IV. The romance
convention of enfances furnished for Amoret and Belphoebe in
III, 6 throws light backward upon Belphoebe's actions toward
Timias and the 'love' therein portrayed (III, 5, 36), just as canto 6 also
prevents us from suspecting Spenser of oversimplification when we
confront sexual love as it is portrayed in the seemingly unrelated
episodes of Paridell and Hellenore or the tapestries of Busyrane's
house.

Meanwhile, while the real principle of unity lies in 'meanings' of
happenings, *which inform what happened* and are not separable from
the story, the events can be made to happen without pinning all
importance upon psychological motivation. In any romance, the

story can be easily advanced by such conventions as 'customs' of castles, quarrelsome knights provoking battle, stops for lodging, knights-errant who merely 'meet' adventure, enquiry into lignage and enfances, or climactic meaning concentrated in some other-worldly or symbolic *place*. It is this use of significances as the cohering factor, not the fancifulness of romance, which enables us to move in and out of symbols like the 'real' places they are.

This mode of making separate incidents cohere in a unity is even easier to see in Books where a single hero achieves some aim or learns some great definition. The series of happenings chosen by Spenser is not the sequential series natural to a biography-of-hero principle of organization; we deal with a different structural conception from that which would give us an epic action toward which every event builds, or an epic hero whom every action ultimately exalts. In a 'well-organized' single-hero Book (II), Braggadochio looks like a digression, from the Bloody Babe story or the Medina section. But we are dealing with a design wherein pattern slowly *takes* shape rather than with a design wherein a theme is stated and variants develop it. The Braggadochio episode is neither a digression from Medina nor a continuation of her theme – it is the constant problem presented in a different frame of reference. He is intemperate in every way the Knight may not be and maintain 'chivalry' by definition based on fidelity to good. He is fearful, vainglorious, advises expedient cunning not prudence or wisdom, responds to beauty with lascivious desire rather than love or wonder. In a word, his allegiance is to 'the world', and the climax is his sensuality and his vulgar advice to Belphoebe to go where she can make the most of her charms.

But for the notion that the episode ought to mean Aristotle's middle way between foolhardiness and cowardice and thus attach to canto 2, we would have noticed that foolhardiness is absent, that the character does not err by excess but by confusing vainglory with fortitude, and shows not wrong balance but wrong aims (just as prodigality is not there to answer to avarice, and as *any* traffic with Acrasia, not *too much* traffic with her, is intemperate). Having brought us to think of aspects of the problem connected with temperance defined as the mean, Spenser half-leaves this conception to illustrate temperance as defined by that element of right allegiance which Christian thought gave to it down through the centuries to

Milton's *Comus* (fidelity to 'the right loves' is the emphasis we persistently meet from Augustine onward, preventing the excesses of enslavement to Mammon or to Acrasia).

Similarly the opening up of the nature of Temperance is continued in the Guyon–Furor encounter which happens during this Braggadochio passage. So too does the Squire's Hero-and-Claudio story seem to be a digression from Guyon-and-Furor, just adventitiously attached in that Furor maltreats its teller the Squire; actually, however, it opens Temperance's nature to our view by showing how a faked 'Occasion' roused 'Furor' in the Squire. Thus the supposedly separable episode really enacts the meanings of the very characters it seems to desert capriciously.

In this interwoven structure, then, that which seems to follow (or precede) by chance is in fact discovered to be related, necessary where and when it occurs, and part of a hidden time-scheme; this is typical both of Spenser's early and later Books and of the great Arthurian romances in their best known French and English forms. . . .

But one aesthetic result is outstanding, and makes Spenser's inheritance of structural entrelacement a piece of real good fortune. He did not inherit this as an advantage, but made it one by the all but new turn he gave to the form. We change from character to character but never leave Temperance. We cannot keep straight what happened next to Artegall but we watch each canto add lines to the drawing of a just knight. We find no hero at all to embody it, but we do not misunderstand the nature of Friendship or its opposite; we are discontent with the portrayal of the Courteous Knight, but we find no objections to raise to the portrayal of Courtesy. We shift rapidly from incident to incident and place to place, but we pursue steadfastly and without agitation the question of the nature of Chastity. Especially this last unit will be seen to adhere carefully to the exposing or opening out of its subject, once we define Chastity with its traditional Christian overtones of total fidelity, love purified of idolatry, lust and self-indulgence. Incident after incident and character after character build up the inquiry into the part played by a right love in man's life – what draws him to it, its opposites, perversions, faked appearances, striking examples where it shines out, its relation to 'natural' love and generation as cosmological principles since it alone is creative and its great opposites are de-

structive principles opposed to it in their *direction* which is toward
possession and self-aggrandizement, the self-idolatrous ends of
sterile and indulgent lust. It is wanton quarrelsomeness to point
to such observations as evidence that Spenser was interested first
in the ideas, for in the piece itself there is no separating idea from
story (absurd notion); it is we late-comers who phrase these sum-
maries. For a writer with Sidneyan poetics, the mediaeval structure
which promoted ever-fresh but never repeated 'actions' and thus
allowed these meanings to re-state themselves, was a fortunate gift
of time.

The real reason for entrelacement is not necessity but choice;
it is more interesting and suits the importance of the piece. As we
pursue such analyses, we see that the plans of romances are not
visibly dictated by that principle of subordination which governs
our notions of plot, of how to outline a schema, or of how the
members of a structure are articulated. Dominance, of a character
especially, does not appear in the usual forms; the main line may
not come first, and the most meaningful character may not get most
space. . . .

Spenser's usual structure is this complex interweaving of seemingly unrelated parts that unobtrusively take shape as a pattern.
Unity is not provided by a hero's series of exploits, even when it
looks so, nor by a single mind's development (like an assumed
growth of Guyon in Book II), nor by a conflict. An opposition defined, fought out, concluded in triumph, is the structure of I, 11,
but not of Book I, of III, 12, but not of Book III. The sought virtue
is the unifying factor in *every* Book. This is usual enough in romance
(the *Lancelot* with its attempt to combine presentation of the ideal
knightly code and the ideal knightly lover is a complex example);
also, Spenser seems to have fallen into it and then realized that his
earliest portions (now embedded in Books III and IV) really do
consider what it is man seeks under the name of 'true love', and
that he had looked at aspect after aspect of a quiddity whose
Christian name was Chastity – for neither Caritas nor Agape, Eros
nor Love, will convey the meanings we are shown. When he then
chose as the design of other Books the seeking and realizing of a
virtue, his fidelity to the romance structure was wise, since it fits his
quest-organization and his narrative texture, which are conventional,
as well as his allegorical use of them, which is unusual and original.

Allegorical reading is very well served by this opportunity to realize, realize, and realize again, the full import of something we can only lamely point to by its abstract name.

I think it should be noticed as a by-point whenever chance brings it up, that through this inheritance of a structure that was neither episodic nor articulated like an epic action, Spenser could heighten the presentation of reigning themes to produce actual allegory, and yet evade the problem which teases moderns, whether and when the story is subordinate to the allegory.

I am convinced that this is a nonexistent problem which did not worry Spenser and only makes us misread when it worries us. The reason is much the same as with the point above touching 'happening and interpretation', event and meaning. The story is *read* allegorically. If I am asked to write down the notes which constitute a tune or to write down a tune, the same demand is made of me; 'the Book is Red Crosse's story' is the same statement as 'the Book is the discovery of Holiness', for there exists no man 'Red Crosse' whose story would be different if the author did not have the claims of allegorical Holiness modifying his intents. The unifying principle is not the *history* of a particular or an individual; the action is not a biography, a life, but an action. However varied the definitions of allegory, they are at one in raising to an extreme Sidney's remark about poetry, that it deals with things 'in their universal consideration' so that we view abstractions themselves interacting. It was brilliant of Spenser to realize that a structure which weaves a tapestry before us is particularly well suited to allegory, where pattern must steal upon us. He was also supremely successful at this secret conveying of unparaphrasable meaning, and we should not obscure the success by re-writing his stories into their allegories, but resolutely claim whole images with all their depicted feelings as the sole true statements of his allegorical meanings.

To observe how well these structural conventions suit Spenser's enlarged purposes gives marked pleasure. Enhancement of pleasure in a simpler form is perhaps the only result of another, and the most obvious, of the resemblances he has to romances – the *Faerie Queene*'s use throughout of the world of objects and circumstances, the adjuncts or things or furniture of mediaeval story. Spenser writes something that is not overplentiful once the great period passed – an *interesting* romance. The *Orlando Furioso* is not 'an interesting romance'; it is Ariosto that is so interesting. His twists, his turns, his ways of picking things up captivate us even when we choke upon his invention, and the sense of his presence is exhilaratingly constant. But Spenser is anonymous in the manner of the old tales. . . .

Spenser received the interestingness with the genre, when he chose it, and when he thus decided once and for all the whole wavering question of what should be the external garb of his story, the world of sights and sounds and particulars we are given to live in, the conditions and the scene-settings and the undescribed circumstances that surround his people. Spenser is the most successful of any Elizabethan in portraying his imagined characters living in a milieu. Though it appears as a consistent seamless tissue, unselfconsciously recorded as by one living in it, it was not the milieu of an Elizabethan and could not have been portrayed unlearned; he borrowed it. It is the first thing that interests us about a mediaeval romance, this quiet, constant flow past us of all the accidents, the whole superficies, of life in the chivalric world. Romance plots are not outstandingly competent, characters rise infrequently to the height of great creations, but the minutiae of a life that seems to us lived under interesting conditions quite simply engrosses the attention. . . .

A primary lesson learned from these old stories was the presentation of these sympathetic quick insights into all manner of feelings. To notice how unusually frequent they are in Spenser, as in earlier romances, we have only to allow ourselves to read him with the free and leisurely interest and pleasure which was a chief reason for writing in the romance genre. Everyone recalls the few famous examples – the delicate perceptiveness in descriptions of Britomart's jealousy, people crowding about the dragon that still seems to move, Una's rejoining of the knight she thinks to be the unjust but deceived Red Crosse, or the comic conversations when false Una or Malecasta climb into bed with startled knights. But this narrative trait is far more constantly present, and without ulterior motive, than criticism is now inclined to notice, bent rather upon detecting an unflagging awareness of significances and upon seeking equivalents in signification for each separate movement in the narrative. Yet that is not the way allegory operates, either, in such romances as use it. . . .

. . . If the whole burden of the feeling in that scene (II, 8) where the Palmer sees the protective angelic spirit at the exhausted Guyon's head is compassionate love, with stanza after stanza expressing wonder at that divine love which is unfathomable for one sole reason, that it keeps coming to man the enemy and alienated one – then the scene is not functioning as an accusation of Guyon and a warning against an insufficiency that shows him weighed in a balance and found wanting.[1] The feeling of scenes is never denied and canceled out by meanings. Where we have repeatedly been told that what we look at is that marvel of loving protectiveness which unceasingly enfolds the human creature, out of love alone and whenever he is in danger, we are not to deny the whole because some seeming verbal twist is puzzling. For that is all there is to the fact that 'good Guyon' is called God's 'wicked foe'; the whole point of introducing right loves and God's ordering love into Christian discussions of temperance lies in the fact that even a good man is God's foe and is wilfully prone to oppose rather than love God, except through the grace whose operations we are about to be shown. This is what defines the marvel, which is not turned on like extra electric power when the load is heavy; the omnipresence and gratuitousness of this love is what makes the sweetness of stanza 8 and stanza 2 so unexpectedly powerful, like an effect of music. The straightforward, free response to directly encountered emotions, indicated without elaboration but quite openly, could well be brought back into the reading of Spenser's allegory, as it had been an expected element in romances from their first development; further, it was conserved in those which are to be read allegorically, and is a guide to their allegorical points. . . .

Of course knight-errantry is a deciding factor in producing a plot of which the staples are the performance of tasks, rescue of damsels, restoring the dispossessed to their inheritances, sieges, captivities, and meetings leading to love affairs, with incidents simply 'met' rather than logically evolved, and constant movement and introduction of new characters. This factor is as decisively important to Spenser's fundamental design as the absence of certain plot motifs is unimportant (famous plot-clichés like Lancelot's swordbridge, an actual grail, tomb-incidents, court feasts, betrayal through bloodstains). More particularly, this initial *datum* brings two incident-producing elements of a romance in its train: castles with 'customs' which the errant knights must face, and the whole series of results following on the simple fact that characters are peripatetic and continually placed in new situations by each night's search for hospitality. But setting, manner, temper and texture are much more interestingly affected than plot and incident, for in those invention is far more important than influence, and Spenser borrowed them oftener from modern romances like Ariosto's. But we need tell no lies about his close dependence on Ariosto and Tasso as we notice Spenser's extreme success in reproducing the superficies of a mediaeval tale.

He learned (I think through reading) to imagine things as if they were taking place in a real and ordinary mediaeval world where chivalry, and the way of living that went with it, was a common and living institution. There are many knightly romances in the Renaissance, in England, but others do not have the flavor of ordinary though deeply idealized mediaeval life, moving with the same tempo and tone as life in the cycle romances or the lais, among the same landscapes and objects. Things take place in an England townless and untenanted, where we come upon people only resting by fountains, or on great horses charging toward us (always involved with us, never casually passing), though land is empty and spacious, with meadows and waterways interrupting the all but ubiquitous forests, or with here and there a hermitage or two or three huts of villeins, or the isolated fortified castle. Through the woods (I think more archaic than symbolic) ride the familiar characters, encountering when they should the intended person, or alternatively experiencing the chance meeting which produces so many unintended battles with unrecognized friend, brother, or boon companion. We expect characters to 'seek' desired persons simply by setting out into the forest, we know the conventions of a promised return or a sworn later meeting elsewhere or a promised delivery of oneself as trophy at court. We accept the last minute deflections from a first duty into another met en route, the dungeons where one comes upon half one's fellowship evilly deterred from their quest, and the liberations; we expect the constant single combats (bringing with them the customary easy assertions about numbers killed, blood shed, wounds and cures) which need no elaboration of motive but only a bad 'custom' bumped into on the road or a chance-met oppression that needs remedy. We take for granted

riddling inscriptions or prophecies, or tournaments universally
accepted as a way to decide matters and hence the periodical
converging of the whole action upon such a point, as well as constant
awarenesses of the code of knightly honor and occasional serious
exposition of that code – the oaths, the skills, the accoutrements
(sometimes the young knight's initiation, all usually tied to a
dominant plot motif, the enfances). . . .

This is a kind of similarity to be distinguished from parallelisms
in incident (also from the fantastic elements we call romance
machinery). It is felt even when Spenser is deliberately copying a
plot motif that would seem out of place in a mediaeval romance,
such as the Ovidian metamorphosis of Fradubio, or the Ariostan
pursuit of Florimell. It has the realism of well-known actualities
much heightened; little needed to be 'invented'. The actualities may
be archaic, but we find the same ones if we pick up next a romance of
later date which the reader will recognize: knight and lady, who
apparently are in love merely by the same chance which endowed
him with her 'quest', journey slowly toward their object, stopping to
sleep or to carry through the adventures that they evidently are
responsible for handling if they are but encountered, through woods
and past dens and caves where action takes place, past cross-
roads, hermitages, chapels, but nothing else, except the castles that
are virtually small courts, down paths which always lead to meaningful encounters. The enemy is consistently 'the Saracen', fights are
instant, combats (extremely specifically described) take place the
moment knights meet, and the accompanying damsels fall to the
victor and join his retinue. Ladies, upon desertion, wander up hill
and down dale but with the hope, always fulfilled, of meeting the
one desired lost knight; characters are benighted, trains of action
follow from the mere facts of where and with whom the travelers
take lodging (with sanctimonious deceiver or half-civilized peasant).
Decisions hang upon the outcome of single combats fought at
tournaments where we see the court under its canopy, the minstrels,
ceremonial drink and trumpet, and afterward hear of the disarming, the cured wounds, the knight who escapes by privy postern after
coming upon the inevitable dungeon with the castle's victims.
Forests are so uninhabited that they serve as places for the wild
enfances of the naïve bold youth who manages savage beasts, for
dangers met unwittingly, and tests that must be passed. Chance

wayside meetings lead to the necessary rescues from dungeons, the awakening of silent castles; religious houses serve the familiar purpose of allowing reproof and instruction of the characters, the oppressed look over their tower walls at the victorious fight that ends a captivity with the marriage of Emperor's daughter to courageous Knight, at nuptials celebrated through castle and land.

These are not the plot motifs of Book 1; they are merely the unmistakable mediaeval-romance garb in which those motifs are clothed, so unerringly that it seems folly to say, as Greenlaw did, that Spenser shows little 'use' of Malory, or as many currently writing searchers have claimed, that the influence of Arthurian romances is small. Spenser first wandered as a knight-errant through their well-wooded small lonely mediaeval counties before he knew how to describe life in his own. But though the influence of knight-errant romances, an extensive genre, is large, eminent and decisive, we shall never know just which ones 'influenced' Spenser. It does not seem sensible to rule out the most aesthetically satisfying English form, and the most common cycle – both abounding in cited traits – just because the likenesses are not shared peculiarities of plot complication.

Yet it is equally important that we not deny the vast differences. They are readily apparent from noting what has been omitted in the quick run just completed over the surface of Book 1 – from Morpheus in canto 1 to the utterly unromance-like introduction of Despair, from the thoroughly unmediaeval satyrs-canto to the Reformers'-use made of the material from Revelations. An astonishing accomplishment of Spenser's poem is that he makes one poetic whole for us without losing the intensely felt classical, or high Renaissance, or mediaeval character of materials so varied; all is not watered down into one unidentifiable drink like so many Renaissance fictions drawn from this many old tuns. Splendid large images from a very different frame of reference – Gardens of Proserpina or Adonis, marvels of Aesculapius – their classical reminiscences undisguised, do not threaten unity of tone. This was possible in part because Spenser did not create tone, milieu, conventions, from scratch. He chose a genre hospitable to varied kinds of opulence and reminds us both through our visual imaginations and the constant use of familiar narrative conventions that we are reading an especially inventive and poetic exemplar of a genre we know. It was one so firmly set in the mediaeval world that it could assimilate Renaissance uses of classical detail, just as earlier it had assimilated Chaucer's and Boccaccio's and remained 'chivalric romance'. There is no attempt to mediaevalize the great Renaissance adornments and motifs. It is not necessary.

When the plot and incidents are quite identifiably dependent upon Ariosto, as they are in Book III, it looks as if the habits Spenser learned (as I think) from mediaeval romance materials play quite as much part as plot itself in determining the quality of the *Faerie Queene*. They seem even partly responsible for the tone and characteristic temper we denote as 'Spenser's'. I think we have been too ready to find Ariosto's manner typically Renaissance; Spenser's revived idealism may have been just as Renaissance, though not so much as a change. Such effects are always a matter of the slow piling up of numerous details.

Consider the early part of Book III, where Ariostan borrowing is so consistent. We begin, as does any fresh branch or interlaced fresh unit of a cycle, with the two knights taking congé of the lady at whose castle they recovered strength, and sending the defeated and captived object of their just-finished adventure back to the court and to the sovereign who had given them the don. (Castle Joyeous is almost surely both Rinaldo's and Lancelot's Joyous Gard.) As we embark on the journey motivated only by its knight-errant aims, the meeting with a stranger-knight comes immediately to an issue in a combat, described precisely as the early models would teach one. Battle scenes are different in Ariosto, and much more ludicrously extravagant when it comes to the killings, with arms and legs chopped off and rolling, or six victims spitted on a lance like frogs. Similes are outwardly similar, but in the end, Ariosto's heads cut as if *pruning willows*, the steel cleaving flesh *like a cheese*, like *cabbage*, and the irresponsible numbers slain only serve to show up how much more Spenser's animal similes in battles resemble Malory's and all his predecessors'. Spenser exhibits the interest in exact moves of man and mount which makes Malory's combats different from later ones, and he very often includes the romance-like vigorous, rapid, even pert interchange of threat and challenge and defiance. These sets of speeches usually read like a pastiche of Malory's exchanged insults and pat rejoinders (from those with the Sans-brothers right onward, especially the comic interchanges of I, 5; or the convention-filled I, 2 or III, I, 20 ff.).

While the plot remains largely Ariostan, suggestions of romance genre-conventions, in the story's management, pile up: the 'bad custom', as usual involving the foregoing of one's own proper love to exalt the castle-Lady's beauty, a familiar irrational allegiance laid upon mortals by fées; the six fought by one; the characteristically exact portrayal of a familiar romance tête-à-tête when an unwilling knight is wooed by his Lady-hostess; the absolutely proper attempts of all knights-errant to save Florimell, and the perfectly ordinary declaration of their 'hope to win thereby Most goodly meede, the fairest Dame alive' (III, I, 18). It is not possible to mention all the examples where clustered conventions, often of manner or detail, really contribute the temper, though plot motifs have real sources outside early romance. Very occasionally the stream flows the other way, as when the Miraculous Birth motif is classicized in a way no mediaeval writer would present it (see both Marinell's chance conception, and the twins' generation by the sun). But usually, for example, we meet desmesure in the person of the well-known knight unwilling to allow passage through his domain (Marinell looks and acts like a knight, whatever his sea-deity heritage); or we move, as romances often ask us to do, into the fully 'romantic' Castle of Busyrane, though we have just accompanied our characters through the spot-scene ordinariness of the errant knight's nightly search for lodging – the storm, the pig-shed, the yelling, the waiting, the other travelers, the courtyard scenes, the drying out, the supper.

When we take our eyes from summarized plot action and rather read and imagine whole scenes at the suggestion of such details as are slipped in by the author, we observe more and more that the point to be made about the Merlin material is typical. That Spenser took his use of Merlin in III, 3 from Ariosto's *Orlando Furioso* III is completely unquestionable. He not only copies the nature of the incident and the function of the incident, but the whole intent and purpose of importing such material was suggested to him. But nothing could be more different in effect than these two visits to Merlin, and Spenser's is that of a writer to whose inner eye Merlin is the well-known character of the earlier Arthurian materials. Instead of the fanciful necromancy of Ariosto's speaking tomb, the handsome subterranean setting with no hint of a real

locale, the crowd of demons trumped up by an enchantress im-
personating the prophesied descendants, Spenser has the spirit of
the earlier tales because he has some of their details and implies
others. Suitably to the traditional Merlin, we find this one very
strictly localized in Wales (with comfortable advices to stop by
when passing through that part), his other works are noted and new
events worked in with the known tales of Vivien. The look and talk
of this living Merlin, no mere roused spirit but the important
character of the passage, show him the person we know very well
elsewhere. Ariosto's important 'character' is the enchantress who
affects plot, and he does not care about presenting a known Merlin;
Spenser does. He enters the story, and it leaves him again, but he
is that great Merlin whose story we may go elsewhere and read, a
part of England's history presented with quite a different aura and
through quite other details than Ariosto's Merlin, though the latter
is absolutely certainly responsible for his presence. It is an interesting
situation, and it is repeated, I think, time and again. Though I
would consider it a waste of time to search for the precise source in
romances of Spenser's single details, such as those on Merlin we,
should realize that we do have to add to Ariosto a further 'source'
for such characters, and for Spenser's tone and temper in romance
situations.

It would be a welcome change from the remarks about Spenser's
lack of humor or his serene gravity if we would seek some of the
reasons for his differences from Ariosto, so tirelessly noted and often
so unfairly judged, in the tone and temper of the predecessors whom
he agrees with and therefore resembles and imitates. It would be
more knowledgeable of us to look elsewhere than merely at Spenser's
personality traits. They have their place, but have been asked to
explain what is better explicable otherwise. The scene of Malecasta's
night visit, wherein dissimilar details function differently from the
Ariosto 'reversed' scene, which I have questioned as perhaps quite
unrelated, . . . is used to show Spenser 'reads his own steadfast
idealism into the most openly licentious passages of the *Furioso*'
(Dodge's phrase). . . . Did he do this? Many a such scene, with
details more like Ariosto's, used like his to show the fortitude of an
admired character, hence like his in tone, was there in earlier
materials to be struck by and followed. I would not question his
extreme dependence on Ariosto, usually a veritable 'source relation-

ship', and it seems to me to have been proven that the earliest and the most deliberately Ariostan work is found in Book III. But his steadfast idealism, an attribute we would all agree in assigning, was a stronger thing with better reasons for flourishing than the kind of sentimentality which reads idealism into licentious passages.

Of course, Spenser is far from having 'a mediaeval tone'. In fact, in this very Book III, he does what all men of his time do – elaborates old romance motifs and situations with all the sumptuousness a Renaissance imagination could command, colors images or philosophies of love with fashionable Platonism, certainly mediaeval enough but no part of love-in-the-romances. . . . Many of the differences from mediaeval writing are subsumed under one vast one, 'He wrote in the high style.' As his tone constantly shifts in accordance with decorum, a matter handled with extreme artistry, and one we are barely well enough educated to apprehend, we see the influence of something much more considered than a vague serene idealism. Spenser's attitude toward his chivalric materials, so different from that of a Cervantes or an Ariosto, antedates his definite plans to write a quest of the virtues, and he had it partly by reason of something so unavoidable as his date. Even an Ariosto would have been less ironic about knighthood and its tasks if he had written in the context of a seriously possible widespread restoration of ancient harmonies and purities with the returning house, and with the hopes for Arthur's kingdom that were agitating the 1570s and 1580s.

There were more reasons than the British blood of an Arthur to explain why Spenser read of his own country and its possible destiny when he read the great prose monuments of Arthurian romance. Even in these late French forms (late thirteenth century), one still heard a tone that was to vanish, of enthusiastic faith in the religious-political ideals of knights who were conscious of their responsibility to the chevalerie celestienne as well as of their active duties in the realm. And this is the tone which Spenser takes on as to the accent born, for use when fitting and necessary. It may have been an accident of history, but Spenser's date, the existence of Malory with his particular attitude toward Arthur and his knights, and Caxton with his, and the momentarily tenable parallel between England's destiny and the Arthurian dream as great artists had presented it, combined with lesser things to make it impossible that Spenser should write like an English Ariosto, even when he is stealing plots from him. The hands are often the hands of Esau, but the voice is the voice of Jacob.

The transposition of whole actions to a credible other time, the chief characteristic which betrays Spenser's wide reading of earlier romances and is peculiar to him, seems remarkably unselfconscious. Because it is accomplished with the unemphatic un-Romantic tone of one recording the commonplace minutiae of life as it passes, and because anachronisms do not intrude themselves, we all but accept the unselfconsciousness as if it were a deception and think of knights-errant in an England which by 1570 certainly had no visual memory of them. Spenser's additions to the romance world he pretends to keep us in are so brilliant and striking that if we avoid the one error, of forgetting that the chivalric world was not his either, we err in the other direction and tend to credit him with the total invention, matrix and poetic additions both. But chiefly his chivalry is neither nature nor invention. He got it by contagion; and his unmediaeval additions do not destroy it. They are seldom the intertwined Eliza-bethan actualities we are accustomed to find in the dramatists when they portray other periods, but the great extensions – classical or mythical fictions which his mediaeval figures enter as agents. This absence of any high threshold to cross, entering the beneficent other-world or the imagined marvelous, is of course a romance habit too. . . .

He had a further and more important reason for finding ro-mances congenial. It seems to me that Spenser recognized, from significances given to ancient romance plots in a few great well-known pieces, that romances were a sort of 'historicall fiction' naturally amenable to being read as 'continued Allegory, or darke conceit', though primarily 'historicall' and delighting. One may take quite 'au pied de la lettre' his remarks about most men delighting to read such fictions for variety of matter – this is the reason for and chief effect of romance entrelacement, and the connection is made by Ariosto when he talks of his 'web'; it is too famous as a rhetorical word and much too controversial a point for Spenser to use in-nocently. Equally serious are the claims about these stories being profitable for ensample, which was an early recommendation for urging the printing of romances from manuscripts, and modernizers and introductions did not let it die. Also, the connection with allegory is a proper part of his declared reason why he 'chose the historye of king Arthure', who was furthest from 'suspition of present time' while capable of bearing other than a single significance. The romances chiefly are what is referred to by the phrase, 'many mens former workes' that have made Arthur 'famous' and suitable because of 'the excellency of his person'.

The motif of a quest that was yet not precisely a pilgrimage lent itself, as it had before Spenser, to the combination he shows himself interested to produce from the very beginning – multiple meanings to be read in a delightful history. The physical world and furnishings of mediaeval life, within which the fiction takes place, were felt as actual parts of Britain's past, distanced from his 'present' not by fancifulness but by time. Thus the satirical point which was expected in allegory would not be made too topical through 'daunger of envy'. It was also distant enough for a treatment scarcely possible to fictions of contemporary manners; it could be combined with the fashionable newer elements from the mythographers, the Platonic temper of the decade and the richness of Renaissance artifice and decoration.

This choice, one may stress again, was a choice exalting the importance of the *fiction*. It was open to Spenser to write a didactic allegorical piece of the kind familiar in Hawes, in the *Court of Sapience*, in *Piers Plowman*, in Lydgate. He chooses instead a fully fictional kind with definite narrative characteristics. He was entirely aware that mediaeval romances, and certainly Arthurian romances, do not as a kind ask for allegorical reading. There was never a genre that held more stubbornly to the simple object of telling what people did and said, or directed such hundreds of pages simply to watching the flow of events and human participation in them. Spenser not only keeps to the idea that this is a great desideratum but has caught the knack of doing it successfully; in his success he resembles the old mediaeval models rather than their duller sixteenth-century imitators. This is great good fortune for us, since long Elizabethan poetic narratives are not outstanding for their ability to command our continuous attention without efforts of will.

In addition, however, Spenser certainly observed that these delightful historical fictions, if so written as to ask for a double reading, did not ask the persistent and detailed attention to rather tight structures of double meaning which one finds in many didactic allegories. . . . Moreover, romances demonstrate, and Spenser must have observed this, the accepted convention of being *intermittently* allegorically significant – and indeed would be unreadable otherwise. This is surely true also of the *Faerie Queene*. The word 'intermittent' does not indicate the stop and go of some mechanical inner traffic light but rather the greater or less penetration of details of an incident with metaphorical meaning, the incident as a whole lending itself to a metaphorical as well as literal reading (not a tight translation or paraphrase into equivalences, which precludes the need for metaphor). . . .

SOURCE: extracts from ch. 5, 'Romances', in *Allegorical Imagery* (Princeton, 1966) pp. 335–43, 350–3, 359, 361–72, 377–92.

NOTE

1. I am referring here to a different interpretation of Guyon's state and reasons for his faint, in H. Berger, *The Allegorical Temper* (New Haven, Conn., 1957), where Guyon's faint marks the shift from classical to Christian temperance in the 'strangely divided' two pieces of Book II, and is held to be the result of a blameworthy overdependence on his self-supported virtue. There will be disagreements on meanings of individual scenes in the *Faerie Queene* as long as it is read, and I adduce this one only to make specific enough my plea for remembering that the *Faerie Queene* is a species of romance. I do not believe the complications of the interpretation (e.g. pp. 29–44) to be in the text. But one notices in many other books as well the tendency to treat single lines, small images, or verbal tags almost as magical keys, and the imposition of dubiously applicable theorizing (here cf. the 'levels' of Berger, p. 35, absolute definitions of quite modern vintage). Current weaknesses touching what constitutes evidence have left us especially open to the dangers of overreading that accompany image-interpretation when simpler indicated meanings are left behind for possibilities suggested by similar images in other contexts. (E.g. the angel-Cupid simile of Book II, 8 must surely first relate to the iconographical identity of the winged young-man God of Love with the exactly described angel-portrait, with the direction given by the remembrance that angels ministered to Christ also after the Temptation, deliberately alluded to but of course not represented; cf. Berger's discussion of the 'world of Cupid', pp. 43–4.) Berger's and other critics' return to some consideration of Christian thought on these matters would be welcome if it were not so doctrinaire. Berger is certainly right in his perceptive distinction between 'significations' known to us, or to the character caught in action (p. 36), and in pointing out that those who think Guyon has sunk under the excessive cares of wealth have not read the story (p. 33).

2. ALLEGORY

Graham Hough   Allegory in *The Faerie Queene* (1962)

In speaking of the structure of *The Faerie Queene* we have compared its organization to that of a dream; we must now continue this argument into the allegory. If we believe that dreams have meaning at all (as by now we surely must), there is an obvious parallel between dream and allegory. The *dream-content*, as Freud calls it (the manifest content), is used to represent in a disguised form the *dream-thoughts* (latent content).[1] Thus the dream-content corresponds to what in allegory we have called image, the dream-thoughts to what we have called theme. In much allegory, however, the relation between the two elements is quite unlike that found in dreams. In naïve allegory, and even in developed religious allegory like *Everyman* or *The Pilgrim's Progress*, the image is a simple translation of the theme, by a series of one-to-one correspondences: one element in the theme corresponds to one in the image. (*The Pilgrim's Progress* escapes from naïve allegory not because of any complex relation of theme to image, but because the image-sequence has so much vitality and coherence of its own.) This is not the relation in dreams. One of the principal dream-mechanisms recorded by Freud is *condensation:* one single element in the dream-content corresponds to more than one in the dream-thoughts. To transfer this to our terms for allegory one element in the image refers to more than one element in the theme. Even from the limited observations we have made already it will be apparent that Spenser often proceeds in this way. I will now try to illustrate this in more detail.

The most obvious illustration is that in so many places there is a double reference – to the moral or psychic life in general, and to particular historical events. The attempt to read Book 1 as a transcript of Tudor history is strained and uncertain; but clearly a strong strain of allusion to the English reformation runs through it.

The Red Cross Knight is Holiness, fighting against the temptations and errors that must universally beset such a virtue. But he is also, more intermittently and imprecisely, English religion (why else should he bear St. George's cross?) struggling against the conspiracies and misdirections of the time, as Spenser saw them. But he is not always Holiness as an achieved state: he is often the universal *miles Christianus*, the militant Christian who must struggle and learn and seek to perfect himself in his journey through the world. Similarly, three themes (not unrelated but certainly distinct) stand behind the figure of Arthur – Magnificence, the historic might and glory of Britain, and the Earl of Leicester. Artegall's adventures are sometimes those of an abstract and general justice, sometimes those of Lord Grey in Ireland.

We have already spoken of the ambiguity of Britomart in another context – of her way of stepping beyond her allegorical rôle. But what is her allegorical rôle? She represents Chastity, in Spenser's special sense of the word, but not exclusively that. She represents also a quite complex Renaissance ideal of female *virtù (virtù* meaning strength and energy, not virtue) which Spenser was familiar with through the virago heroines of the Italian epic, and which has nothing to do with chastity at all.

We are of course meant to admire both equally; but there are times when this kind of dual or multiple significance can introduce a moral ambiguity as well. Duessa in Book I is the embodiment of falsehood, outwardly fair but in reality hideous and deformed. When she reappears in Book V a whole cluster of notions connected with Mary Queen of Scots has become attached to her. She is still falsehood, and still to be rejected, but she is also misguided beauty, and a decided element of sympathy for the unhappy queen as a woman has crept into the *significatio*. I do not wish to enter into the vexed question of the Bower of Bliss at this point, except to remark that it cannot represent a simple concept. The idea sometimes put forward that Spenser was secretly on Acrasia's side is obviously wrong: but it could hardly have arisen if the allegory of the bower were a totally unambiguous affair. There *is* an element of indulged and happy voluptuousness in the description of Acrasia's abode, that takes us back to Tasso's Armida, Spenser's principal source. And Armida at the end of the *Gerusalemme Liberata* is not rejected but forgiven.

Frequently, then, more than one theme lies behind the same image, and this is one of the features of *The Faerie Queene* that assimilates it most closely to the dream. 'The construction of collective and composite personages is one of the principal methods of dream-condensation', as Freud puts it. I do not believe that we should avert our eyes from this, or try to explain away any ambiguities to which it may give rise. Spenser's moral attitude as a man may have been unambiguous enough, but an element of ambiguity is an essential part of his imaginative procedure. This means in fact that there is a far greater quantity of psychic material behind Spenser's romance-figures than a simple translation of them into the obvious moral terms would suggest.

It is worth noting that Spenser's multiple significance is quite unlike the medieval four levels of meaning as applied to the interpretation of Scripture, and Spenser shows no sign of being aware of this tradition.

> Littera gesta docet,
> Quid credas allegoria,
> Moralis quid agas,
> Quo tendas anagogia.

The literal sense, that is, is concerned with historical facts, the allegorical with belief, the moral with right action, and the anagogical with man's last end. Now Spenser's literal sense is not historical; his historical allusions are always concealed. He is concerned with *quid credas* only in Book 1; and even there it is *how* we should believe, and how act on our belief, rather than *what* we should believe that is his main subject. The whole book is based on the necessity of cleaving to truth, and what happens when we depart from it; but truth is never given any doctrinal content. The moral sense, *quid agas*, is of course omnipresent; the right conduct of life in this world is Spenser's real field. But anagogia, *quo tendas*, man's last end, only appears directly in the vision of the heavenly city in 1, 10, and in the two lovely closing stanzas at the end of the Mutability cantos. The grades of reference for Spenser's allegory are not the medieval ones, they are the romantic, the historical, the moral and the psychological. And in the simpler and less developed parts, that is in the minor characters who are mere narrative or thematic conveniences – Sansfoy, Sansjoy and Sansloy, Furor,

Occasio, etc. – the underlying sense is always the moral one.

A second feature of the dream-process mentioned by Freud is the converse of condensation – it is that an individual dream-thought may be represented by several different elements in the dream-content. Or again to translate this into terms of allegory, a single theme can issue in several images. Freud is not particularly clear about this in *The Interpretation of Dreams;* but he illustrates an aspect of it more fully in the essay 'Character Types in Analytic Work in Vol. IV of the Collected Papers: and any student of recorded dreams will be familiar with the way that a single idea appears in the dream under various guises. This happens in Spenser too, and it has sometimes disquieted his commentators. Legouis remarks that Red Cross, who is Holiness, goes to the House of Holiness; that Guyon who is Temperance goes to the Castle of Temperance. Pride appears twice over in Book I, as Lucifera and Orgoglio. True we can explain this if we will; Red Cross and Guyon, besides standing for their respective virtues, are also their yet imperfect human embodiments; Lucifera and Orgoglio are two different kinds of pride. But the resemblance to the dream-mechanism can hardly be missed.

Often in the dream a single character is split up into its several components, who are exhibited in the dream-content as separate figures. There are places where Spenser seems to be working on the same lines. It is often remarked that it is not easy to give any simple allegorical interpretation of the principal woman-figures in Books III and IV. This is probably because they are dissociated parts of the total image of woman. The most obvious dissociated character of this kind is Amoret–Belphoebe. Twin sisters given totally opposite educations, one brought up by Venus, the other by Diana, they stand for two opposed aspects of womanhood – woman as the over-flowing fountain of love, and woman as the virgin, the solitary, the untouchable. Their sisterly relationship makes this particularly clear; but I should be inclined to go farther and include Florimell in this group-figure – Florimell who stands for woman as the object of desire, and who herself splits into two; the true Florimell, the right object of love; and the false Florimell, its factitious and deceiving semblance. We could include Britomart too – the active virtue of womanhood; and perhaps we should; all that forbids it is that she is a so much more developed figure in her own right.

Amoret, Belphoebe and Florimell are all aspects of the idea of woman. They do not represent virtues; they cannot be translated into clear-cut moral qualities at all. They are both more and less than that; more because they represent the unconscious, unformulated psychic background, out of which morals and virtue are yet to be developed; less because they are severally incomplete. They are a composite portrait of the anima, and they have their curious, unseizable charm not because they are romance-heroines, or not mainly for that reason, but because each is a glimpse and only a glimpse of the total image of womanhood that dominated Spenser's imagination.

Lastly (for I wish to make these dream-analogies suggestive rather than exhaustive) Freud inquires how logical relations can be represented in dreams. 'What representation', he asks, 'do "if"', "because", "as though", "although", "either–or" and all the other conjunctions without which we cannot construct either a phrase or a sentence, receive in our dreams?' And he finds that the dream has no direct means of exhibiting these. Causal relations are expressed in dreams by mere succession: alternatives by taking both members of the alternative into the same context. In fact the ample array of logical relations is reduced to a simple parataxis; apparently discrete events simply occur one after another. This is of course characteristic of romance-literature in general. Malory's typical conjunction is 'and'. But Malory's 'and' rarely means anything more; Spenser's temporal sequences often do imply more – or to put it in a fuller form, what appears as temporal sequence in the image conceals another relation, usually causality, in the theme. Immediately after the Red Cross Knight is separated from Una or Truth (I, 1) he meets with Duessa or Falsehood. This appears as mere temporal sequence in the story, but thematically it is a matter of cause and effect. It is *because* he has been separated from Truth that the knight falls into the company of Falsehood. We take the meaning without noticing the mechanism because the narrative sequence is so much the expected one; having lost one lady the romance-hero naturally meets another one. Sometimes however the sequence of images conceals a thematic meaning that is less obvious. It is on her wedding-day 'before the bride was bedded' (IV, 1, 3) that Amoret was stolen away from Scudamour by Busirane. Busirane has never cherished any designs on Amoret before; in the image-sequence this appears as an uncaused, inconsequential calamity. Thematically it means that *because* of the wedding she was stolen away; it is *because* their consummation is so much desired and is so close that the lady is tortured and her lover frustrated by the perverse cruelty of amour-passion.

Other relations similarly find expression in dream-fashion. *Although* Guyon is attracted by the loveliness of the Bower of Bliss he knows it must be destroyed and destroys it. The 'although' hardly finds expression in the narrative; there is simply an abrupt temporal transition, astonishing to most readers, from the manifest seductions of the bower (11, 12, 70–8) to its sudden hastily described overthrow (83). Alternatives likewise: woman's beauty as the object of desire can be either true beauty (the outward expression of gentleness, innocence and chastity), or its false simulacrum (the outward covering of flightiness, greed and untruth); and this is expressed by the two Florimells, absolutely indistinguishable in appearance. What appears then in *The Faerie Queene* as the simple alogical sequaciousness of naïve romance conceals a wealth of more complex thematic relations; and meaning must be sought almost as often in these relations as in the isolated signification of individual figures.

Most of these points must be taken up and illustrated more fully later on. To make an end of this general discussion we should try to sum up the special distinguishing characters of Spenser's allegory. In the first place, it *is* allegory, not symbolism in either a Blakean or a Mallarmean sense; nor fully incarnate literature like Shakespeare. It is of very varying degrees of explicitness, ranging from naïve allegory to romance with only the vaguest thematic significance. It is discontinuous – the general directing allegory announced in the Letter is only faintly developed, and the greatest allegorical intensity is reached in certain of the local stories. And as we have seen there were models of this kind near to Spenser's hand in the allegorizing of Ariosto. The allegory is in the most important places multivalent; it is on the whole only the minor characters who have a single simple allegorical significance. And last, in some ways most important, and to some readers most difficult to accept, it proceeds by loosely associative, half-unconscious methods like those of the dream, rather than by the rigorous translation of clearly formulated conceptual ideas. All the thematic content of *The*

Pilgrim's Progress could have been as easily formulated in a sermon. This is true of parts of *The Faerie Queene*, but in all the best parts the thematic content finds its only possible embodiment in the actual image-sequence that the poem presents. And the poem is both – theme and image in perpetually shifting relations, variously inter-woven, sometimes perceived separately, often talked of separately as a matter of expository convenience; but ultimately indissoluble.

SOURCE: extract from *A Preface to 'The Faerie Queene'* (London, 1962) pp. 131–7.

NOTE

1. All the features of the dream-process referred to here are described in ch. 6 of Freud's *Interpretation of Dreams*. I have used A. A. Brill's translation (London, 1913).

Maurice Evans   Spenserean Allegory (1970)

Recent Spenserean scholarship has shown a healthy reaction against earlier criticism which reduced *The Faerie Queene* either to a series of moral precepts or to a gallery of historical portraits thinly veiled by allegorical characters. The last twenty years have seen a valuable attempt to rehabilitate the image itself in place of its content, and to bring the poetry back into the poem; but there are dangers even here of interpreting it in the not wholly appropriate terms of modern critical assumptions. The insistence that form and content are one has made it almost an offence to talk about the 'meaning' of the poem or to attempt an explication in prose of an allegorical sequence.

It is doubtful whether Spenser himself would have agreed with McLeish that 'A poem "is", not "means" '; nor was he aware of the heresy of separating form from content. He was writing a didactic poem and using allegory in its accepted rhetorical sense of an extended metaphor, as Puttenham defines it in a well known passage of the *Arte:*

when we do speake in sence translative and wrested from the owne signification, neverthelesse applied to another not altogether contrary, but having
much coveniencie with it as before we said of the metaphore: as for example, if we should call the common wealth a shippe; the Prince a Pilot, the
Counsellours mariners, the stormes warres, the calme and [*haven*] peace, . . .
(III, xviii)

Such allegory allows the poet to 'translate' his concepts into a
pleasing fiction and so follow Horace's injunction to teach by
delighting. It induces the reader to read on, drawn from his chimney
corner by the attractions of the story, and at the same time it
presents experiences in a form which engraves them more deeply
in the memory and the mind. For Sidney the essential difference
between philosophy and poetry was not one of content but of
presentation: poetry activates the precepts of the philosopher by
clothing them in fictions and images which take hold of the imagination and move men to virtue.

The Faerie Queene is composed of images and they are what we
must deal with, recognizing, however, that they are not ends in
themselves but only means to an end. Spenser would not have
equated the image itself with any prose 'meaning' which we may
extract from it; but he would have recognized that the image began
with a prose concept which the rhetorical 'colours' of poetry
intensify and make universally applicable. It is the image of Phaedria's little boat which 'both from rocks and flats it selfe could
wisely save' (II, 6, 5) which lingers in the mind, not any general
precept about the capacity of mirth to melt opposition or chase
away boredom; and yet unless the image reminds us of the precept,
it fails to fulfil its purpose in the poem. Such epigrammatic images
create a moral perception which would not otherwise come into
existence: they are, in Elizabethan terms, the speaking pictures
which voice precepts in terms applicable to all manner of situations
and so provide the tools for moral discrimination.

The curiously logical structure of rhetorical extended metaphor
entails an initial distinction between the idea and the image, the
tenor and the vehicle, but an eventual convergence of the two after
a sufficient period of parallel development. The metaphysical
conceit works in this way, beginning with a simple comparison
between dissimilars, such as lovers and compasses, but ending in a
fusion as the logical development of each side reveals more and

more points of contact. The pleasure lies to a great extent in observing this process of approximation and recognizing the aptness
of tenor and vehicle for each other's purposes when the two are so
initially different. Spenser's allegory works in the same way and
delights by the endless and logical parallel which it establishes
between the metaphorical world of romance and the real world of
human moral values. At the same time, by forcing the reader to
translate the one into the terms of the other, it fulfils its primary
aim of fostering a process of continuous moral dissection.

At times, indeed, Spenser appears to be encouraging the very
thing which modern Spenserean criticism cites as the chief heresy.
We are warned against treating the poem as if it were a difficult code
to be cracked; and yet it seems to me that the poem is full of enig-
matic images whose main purpose is to tease the reader into thought.
The Enigma or riddle was by definition merely a difficult form of
allegory – 'We dissemble againe under covert and darke speaches,
when we speake by way of riddle (*Enigma*) of which the sence can
hardly be picked out, but by the parties owne assoile' (Puttenham,
III, xviii). Many of George Herbert's emblematic poems are enigmas
in this sense: his little poem, Hope, – 'I gave to Hope a watch of
mine but he/An anchor gave to me . . .' – must have set even the
seventeenth-century reader, who was well versed in the language of
symbols, an interesting exercise in interpretation not so very far
removed from that of the crossword puzzle. Herbert can do this
sort of thing in serious poetry because, as Dr Johnson recognized, it
forces the reader to think and, in discovering the logic of the image,
to define to himself more clearly than he would do otherwise the
moral point at issue. This is something which Spenser does continually. When, for example, Arthur has killed Orgoglio, he finds
Ignaro in charge of the prisoners, because it is ignorance of the
nature of the faith which has led to their downfall (I, 8, 30). He is
an old man with a bunch of rusty iron keys – the keys of knowledge,
rusty because unused, and iron because in his hands they belong
to the age of iron; and Arthur proceeds to open the prison cells with
them. When, however, he comes to Red Cross's door there is no
key in the bunch to open it, and he has to break it down. The un-
expected twist of the story, having almost the quality of a mixed
metaphor, forces us to ask why, and to recognize the point of the
riddle, namely, that although ignorance of the faith damns, know-

ledge by itself cannot save; only the Grace of God can do that. A
central tenet of theology has been condensed into a witty image, as
Herbert condenses the whole Christian system into his little parable,
'Having been tenant long to a rich Lord'. *The Faerie Queene* is full
of such dark conceits which gain their effect by demanding an
explanation. Why, for example, when he comes to the Bower of
Blisse, does Red Cross go forward with his Palmer alone and leave
behind the boatman who has done him such good service over the
Idle Lake (11, 12, 38)? Why does not Talus rescue Artegall from
Radegund, since he so easily routed her warriors earlier in the
Book (v, 5, 19)? Why is Phaedria's little boat a 'gondelay' with a
little woody bower built into it (11, 6, 2)? The answers are always
there in the context but they must be sought for, and posing the
question is the mode of instruction. On one level, and by no means
a negligible one, the poem is an enormous teaching machine pro-
grammed to its task by a technique of question and answer.

I would not for a moment claim that this is the whole or even
the main method by which *The Faerie Queene* works, but it is an
aspect of the poem which modern critical approaches tend to
leave out; and it indicates a type of sensibility in the poem which
differs from our own and makes Spenserean allegory especially
difficult for the contemporary reader. There is, however, another
reason for this difficulty, which springs not from the nature of the
allegoric method but from the choice of the allegoric vehicle. The
knights and giants and all the panoply of chivalry which charmed
the Elizabethans by their fashionable novelty, and the Romantics
by their nostalgic mediaevalism, have no such charm for the
twentieth century. They fail, therefore, on the fictional level, and
instead of leading us along by their own intrinsic interest, they tend
to make us force our way through to the 'meaning' and, having
reached it, to abandon the outward shell. Where, however, the
vehicle still retains its interest as fiction, we are less apt to object
to the method or reject the outer rind; and this is possibly why so
much contemporary criticism of *The Faerie Queene* has been concerned with the role of classical mythology within the poem, which
is agreeable to the contemporary fashionable interest in myth,
rather than with the more strictly Romance sequences. Poetry
which pursues the Spenserean method in terms of an acceptable
fiction gives no difficulty. I can see no essential difference between

many Spenserean sequences and such typical poems of Yeats as, for
example, 'Crazy Jane and Jack the Journeyman' or 'Another Song
of a Fool'. Both Spenser and Yeats offer a fiction which is capable
of standing in its own right but which carries, for those who know
the significance of the symbols from sources outside the particular
passage, an additional meaning of which it is the metaphor; and
it is this which shapes the logic of the metaphor itself. It so happens
that Spenser's chivalric metaphors interest most modern readers
less than Yeats's Fools, Irish journeymen and crazed beggar women
which have for us the sort of romantic appeal that mediaeval
fictions had for other ages. What passes in Yeats, therefore, is less
acceptable in Spenser, although the basic methods are often identical. One can see an extreme example of this in Yvor Winters's[1]
strictures on Book I of *The Faerie Queene*:

The gentle knight encounters the dragon, and after many Spenserian stanzas
he slays it. We eventually learn that the dragon represents Error. But the
dragon in general and in all its details, and merely as a dragon, is a very
dull affair; it is poorly described and poorly characterized. I do not,
frankly, know what one might do to make a dragon more interesting, but it
seems to me that unless one can do better than this one had better not use a
dragon.

Winter's criticism makes explicit what is the unspoken assumption
of many anti-Spensereans. . . .

   The Faerie Queene is not a learned poem demanding a knowledge of
esoteric literary sources but a relatively popular one using a limited
range of materials in a complex but self-defining way. In a world
which is created out of these materials, everything that happens is
necessarily allegorical: every move from plain to forest, by day or
night, by land or sea, in sunshine or storm, has by its very location a
moral significance derived from the logic of the central metaphors.
Every reference to myth or history provides a touchstone of values.
Spenser does not turn his allegory on and off; it is always inescapably
there, built into the very structure of the romance setting.

   This is not to say that Spenser's images are counters, fixed and
rigid in their significance, and that to interpret them, therefore,
is just a matter of mechanical translation. His method differs from
that of Yeats, for example, who discovers different manifestations
of a central symbol such as the gyre all around him – in the circling
flight of the falcon, or the winding stair of his tower, or the swirling

fabrics of Loie Fuller's dance – but sees them all as projections of an identical principle. Spenser's landscape, in contrast, is a mode of rhetoric which allows a single image to convey a wide range of different yet related meanings by means of distinctions in tone of voice, or choice of epithet, or by the juxtaposition of other materials; and one of his most characteristic methods is to use a 'loaded' image in such a way that it contradicts what we normally expect of it. Going into the forest, for example, can cover a wide range of human experiences, although all will in some degree be associated with entering into the presence of evil. The 'chearefull shade' of the Bower of Blisse (11, 12, 71), is a startling expression, because 'shade', although metaphorical of a variety of activities in the poem from the positive commission of sin to the relatively innocent and necessary rest after labour, is always connected with the needs and frailties of our fallen nature. In terms of its normal usage it cannot with any truth be called 'chearefull'; and the choice of adjective therefore, focuses our attention upon the context which can produce such a paradox and warns us of the sophistries of the Bower. Or consider Spenser's description of the arbour at the heart of the Garden of Adonis: it is a rich and fruitful place, belonging to Nature not Art, and yet its leafy shade is so dense

> That nether *Phoebus* beams could through them throng,
> Nor *Aeolus* sharp blast could worke them any wrong.
>
> (III, 6, 44)

At the simplest level, this is a description of the womb, secret and covered from the light of day, but the imagery implies a good deal more. The fact that it is a place of intense shade would lead us to expect it to be evil, a place of shame; yet the description of its natural wholesomeness in the previous stanzas contradicts this. Moreover Aeolus, usually hostile to all heroic endeavour, leaves it alone, which would normally be a proof of its unworthiness but is not so in this case because he cannot harm it if he would; it is beyond the reach of his power. The images pull in different ways and the whole description, if not quite a riddle, presents at least the paradox of something simultaneously virtuous and vicious.

This apparent ambiguity in Spenser's descriptive imagery is the basis of Professor Alpers's argument that Spenser passes no moral judgements in *The Faerie Queene* but presents instead a variety of possible and conflicting attitudes towards any issue, without attempting to resolve them. The aim of Spenserean rhetoric is not to persuade the reader to accept one point of view in preference to the rest, but to put him in possession of them all and so enlarge his moral consciousness. My own approach is a different one. I would interpret Spenser's paradox as his mode of asserting a fundamentally paradoxical conception of the nature of life. In his description of Adonis's Bower, for instance, he is describing the ambivalent nature of sex, at once the centre of our fallen animal nature – which is why Phoebus's light cannot reach it – yet at the same time the means of human regeneration, and so invulnerable to Aeolus. The same quality of paradox is apparent in the description of the Garden of Venus or the pageant of the rivers, as we have already seen, and it is something clearly central to Spenser's thinking.

To read *The Faerie Queene* is to be in the continuous presence of paradox and to be faced with a dilemma throughout the greater part of the poem. Good and evil are unmistakably there and the need to choose between them is inescapable; and yet the terms in which the enactment of the choice is described are often such as to blur the moral distinction for the reader, and hint that an apparently vicious choice is in reality a virtuous one, or that what is vice from one perspective is virtue from another The moral code of *The Faerie Queene* is not a simple one of black and white, nor is it laid down explicitly from the beginning. It is something which emerges gradually from the cumulative effect of apparent contradictions which are only seen in their true harmony as our experience of the poem makes the pattern plain. . . .

A world of the metaphorical kind which I have been describing would either destroy or be destroyed by a set of inhabitants who existed on the simple, naturalistic level without any dimension of allegory. The chivalric quest itself, with all its knightly trappings, is an extended metaphor of man's struggle for virtue, and the knights themselves, therefore, must share in the nature of the world they live in. The central heroes of each book are real characters of flesh and blood, conceived in the likeness of their forerunners in Homer, Virgil, or Ariosto and, in the case of Artegall, for example, possessing a necessary historical identity; but they are never merely that: each one is the generic human being, Everyman, engaged in the exploration of a particular aspect of human experience, and we should think of them in general terms as the human being discovering the nature of temperance or love or justice, rather than as the individuals, Guyon, Britomart or Artegall. The experiences which they encounter are appropriate to themselves as dramatic creations but are also shared by all mankind, including the reader and the poet himself; and Spenser moves in and out of his characters, from the particular to the general, as it suits his didactic purpose. Belphoebe, when she first appears in Book II, is not so much a person as the voice of a profound human instinct expressing itself in terms of a traditional attitude. In her dealings with Timias in Book IV, however, she is contracted into something much nearer to a historical character; and when she rescues Amoret from lust she has become, for the time being, the personification of an instinct in Britomart herself. These shifts are possible without destroying the narrative framework because Britomart and Queen Elizabeth alike are particular manifestations of the general nature of Everywoman. The action of the poem, therefore, can take place in a sort of no-man's land between the hero and the reader, common to both but limited to neither, while the poet stays outside, commenting. It is this possibility which makes the story of a Red Cross or a Guyon more than the mere biography of an individual, although based on biographical narrative.

There are very few personifications of abstract qualities in *The Faerie Queene*, and even Impotence and Impatience are the embodiments of common human experiences. As C. S. Lewis pointed out long ago, Spenser's basic method in the first three books of the poem, though not in the later ones, is that of psychological personification: the inner qualities and impulses of the human being are projected as characters who enact the inner drama in externalised form, so that a mental conflict becomes a battle between Arthur and Pyrochles, for example, representative of the warring aspects of Guyon's own nature. Alternatively, the struggle to resist impulses and temptations which spring from within may be shown as an external struggle between the character and the personification of the relevant part of himself, as Red Cross fights Sans Joy, or Florimel flees from the witch and resists the old man in the boat. This fragmentation of the human ego can be very difficult to follow, especially in Book 1, where it is extremely elaborate and where Red Cross himself often disappears behind the characters who act out his subtle and complex mental processes. In the first three books especially, the reader meets the inhabitants of the human mind as Guyon and Arthur meet them in the House of Alma:

> Some song in sweet consort, some laught for joy,
> Some plaid with straws, some idly sat at ease . . .
> This fround, that faund, the third for shame did blush,
> Another seemed envious, or coy,
> Another in her teeth did gnaw a rush; . . . (II, 9, 35)

There is this difference, however, that whereas in the catalogue of whims and moods in Alma's hall, the selection is random and the aim simply to indicate the variety of possible human impulses, the characters in the books at large follow each other with a logic which is that of human behaviour. Cymochles appears after Pyrochles because, in terms of the impulses which the two express, he is the result of his brother. Argante seizes Satyrane because the latter is no longer strong enough to hold down the spotted beast: Arthur comes to Una and to Guyon alike not by chance but because both are ready to receive him. In the allegory of *The Faerie Queene*, narrative sequence always implies cause and effect, and it is most important, therefore, to follow the details of the story. By means of the story line, Spenser anatomises the human mind and reveals with extraordinary penetration the physical and psychological springs of human action. As the hero goes on his uncertain way, surrounded by characters who act out his inner life in front of us, providing a dramatic commentary on his actions, we recognise the pattern of his behaviour, understand its sources and are forced to make a continual moral judgement.

Rosemond Tuve seems to me to pay too little attention to this aspect of the poem in her *Allegorical Imagery*. She identifies Spenser's allegorical intention and method with that of the mediaeval allegorists such as Jean de Meun, and argues that the object of 'good' allegory, whether *The Faerie Queene* or *The Romance of the Rose*, is to examine the nature of general human qualities by the gradual unfolding of their properties. In this semi-philosophical context, psychological allegory and consecutive narrative will play a less important part than more discursive methods which

allow the presentation of a central virtue in a variety of aspects
and from a variety of different points of view. Miss Tuve's analysis
of the structure of the *Romance of the Rose* is clearly true, but it is
less adequate when applied to *The Faerie Queene*. She seems to me
to ignore Spenser's more urgent didacticism: in contrast to Jean de
Meun, his prime object is moral improvement rather than intellectual enlightenment – or, at least, the sort of intellectual enlightenment which results in immediate moral action. Spenser's
allegory is essentially rhetorical; it is designed to persuade rather
than to examine, and for this reason Spenser presses more insistently
upon his reader and in a greater variety of ways than his forerunners in the Middle Ages. One of these ways is the unceasing
analysis of human motive and action which has already been described: another is by means of the 'overt moral statements' which
Miss Tuve finds incompatible with 'great' allegory. The fact that
Spenser is 'much less daring about concealing his hand than is
Jean de Meun' (p. 241), is not a sign of his failure to write good
mediaeval allegory but evidence that he is attempting a different
and more rhetorical mode.

Spenser's allegory is very much of its age: his subtle analysis
of human psychology, as well as his mode of dramatic presentation,
spring from the same national impulses which produced the drama
of Shakespeare and the Jacobeans. It is important to recognise,
however, that the allegory of *The Faerie Queene* is not all of a kind
but changes with the changes of subject. As its intention is rhetorical,
so it obeys the laws of rhetorical decorum. Psychological allegory of
the type I have been describing is only possible where the conflicts
are within the mind itself; and as the later books of the poem move
increasingly from the world of the inner man to that of man in
relation to society, other modes of allegory become necessary.
Justice, for example, is largely concerned with the conquest of other
people, and the inner personifications appropriate to the conquest
of self are denied to it. Figures such as Acrasia have a peculiar
resonance deriving from the fact that they literally find an echo in
every bosom, but it is less easy to find symbols for injustice or
communism or political treachery which move us in the same
interior way. Spenser's method in Book v, therefore, is to draw his
symbols from the great and explosive issues of public life, capable
of arousing violent sectarian and patriotic emotions. The Soldan,

or Gerioneo and his monster under the idol, are such figures, and Spenser harnesses their emotive power to the general principles of justice with which he is concerned, and of which they provide particular illustrations. It is noticeable, however, that Arthur's victory over Gerioneo or Artegall's over Grantorto are very far from being transcriptions of contemporary history: Spenser's method is that of allegory, not example; he is writing an allegory about justice, not an allegory of the history of his own times.

In Book VI we are back within the mind again, though not as in the early books of the poem. Courtesy is based on an idealistic vision which Spenser associates especially with the mind of the poet and which he projects, therefore, through the poetic genre of the pastoral idyll. Calidore's story is not designed to reveal Calidore himself so much as the poet's conception of his own craft, and Book VI is an anatomy of poetry itself, using poetic genres as allegories of its strengths and weaknesses. In contrast, the *Mutability Cantos* make the least personal, most objective statement of the whole of *The Faerie Queene*, and offer no scope for subjective allegory. They owe their peculiar richness to the fact that they draw upon the whole corpus of the poetry which has gone before: every character, incident, and myth in the cantos has already been used in a variety of forms in the six books, and here they rise out of the depths, bringing with them the wealth of association and complexity of meaning which they have acquired on their journey. It is as if all the fictions of the poem become articulate in a final fiction which speaks for them all. The cantos are literally an allegory to end allegories, as Spenser unites all the parts of the poem in this final, most literary of his allegoric statements.

SOURCE: extracts from *Spenser's Anatomy of Heroism* (Cambridge, 1970) pp. 47–51, 58–64.

NOTE

1. *The Function of Criticism* (London, 1962) p. 44.

3. RHETORIC, LANGUAGE, VERSIFICATION

P. J. Alpers The Rhetorical Mode of Spenser's Narrative (1967)

Each stanza in *The Faerie Queene* is conceived as an address to the reader, but we do not feel, as we do in *Paradise Lost*, that a decisive voice speaks to us. Spenser's manner of address is much more self-effacing than Milton's – so much so that C. S. Lewis finds it possible to claim that 'outside the proems to the books and cantos he scarcely writes a line that is not for the story's sake'.[1] Nevertheless, Spenser's style is not, as Lewis proposes, 'to be judged as the style of a story-teller'; it makes sense only as a rhetorical instrument, a means of appealing to the reader's feelings and awarenesses. Without attempting a comprehensive discussion of Spenser's style, I would like to examine a crucial phenomenon in his poetry – the pictorial effects in which his well-known verbal sensuousness seems to be in the service of fictional narration.

It has always been assumed that in his pictorial stanzas, Spenser's purpose is primarily imitative or descriptive: his language is chosen to render a 'real' object, which of course can be symbolic or emblematic. But we often find that a striking pictorial effect is not identical with visual description:

> For round about, the wals yclothed were
> > With goodly arras of great maiesty,
> > Wouen with gold and silke so close and nere,
> > That the rich metall lurked priuily,
> > As faining to be hid from enuious eye;
> > Yet here, and there, and every where vnwares
> > It shewd it selfe, and shone vnwillingly;
> > Like a discolourd Snake, whose hidden snares
> Through the greene gras his long bright burnisht backe declares.
>
> > > > > > > > (III, 11, 28)

Several words and phrases that support a pictorial effect are not at all descriptive – for example, 'vnwares', 'vnwillingly', and most notably 'faining to be hid from enuious eye', where Spenser directly suggests the kind of feeling that Busyrane's tapestries induce. Other phrases that do have a visual reference are persuasive because they are suggestive moral formulas – 'close and nere', 'lurked priuily', 'hidden snares'. A great deal of quasi-visual effect is achieved through verse rhythms, particularly in the sixth and ninth lines. Spenser is using all the verbal resources of his poetry; our sense of physical immediacy comes specifically from our experience of words and their poetic disposition, and not from any optical illusion. The last line is the most distinctly pictorial, yet we are hardly meant to see the color green. The effect of the line comes from the rhythmic crowding of words and we are to hear the alliterated formula 'greene gras'. Literally the 'long bright burnisht backe' of the snake is like a fitfully gleaming golden thread. But through alliteration, rhythm, and the concluding 'declares' with its strong rhyme, Spenser makes us feel we are dazzled, our field of vision filled – nor do we remember that the snake is 'discolourd'. The stanza has a pictorial effect because Spenser wants to achieve a certain psychological impact, not because he wants to render real visual experience. He impresses upon us, as if it were a direct sensation, the sinister moral atmosphere of Busyrane's palace.

The nondescriptive character of Spenser's 'pictures' was recognized by Coleridge, in a comment on a line about Dissemblance, in the masque of Cupid: 'And her bright browes were deckt with borrowed haire' (III, 12, 14). 'Here, as too often in this great poem, that which is and may be known, but cannot *appear* from the given point of view, is confounded with the visible. It is no longer a mask-figure, but the character, of a Dissembler'.[2] The solution to this difficulty is to recognize that Spenser's pictorial stanzas are not mimetic descriptions, but 'speaking pictures' in Sidney's sense:

Whatsoeuer the Philosopher sayth shoulde be doone, hee [the poet] giueth a perfect picture of it in some one, by whom hee presupposeth it was doone. . . . A perfect picture I say, for hee yeeldeth to the powers of the minde an image of that whereof the Philosopher bestoweth but a woordish description: which dooth neyther strike, pierce, nor possesse the sight of the soule so much as that other dooth. . . . No doubt the Philosopher with his learned definition, bee it of vertue, vices, matters of publick policie or priuat gouernment, replenisheth the memory with many infallible grounds of wisdom, which, notwithstanding, lye darke before the imaginatiue and iudging powre, if they bee not illuminated or figured foorth by the speaking picture of Poesie.[3]

We ordinarily understand 'speaking picture' to mean 'a picture that speaks'. But Sidney does not attribute to poetry any formal analogies with painting, nor does he think poetry is vivid because it renders the visual experience of external objects. He is speaking of the psychological effect of poetry. The poem enables the reader's imagination to function properly: he can, as Sidney says elsewhere in this passage, 'satisfie his inward conceits with being witnes to it selfe of a true lively knowledge'. Poetry immediately implants in the mind images that the completely sound and regenerate man would produce by his ordinary psychological activity. Observe that Sidney does not limit the resources of poetry in order to make it pictorial. All that he says assumes the full exploitation of the verbal resources that specifically belong to poetry and have nothing to do with painting. 'Speaking picture', then, means speaking that is so vivid, has so much of its own life, that it gives immediacy and clarity to its subject matter. The presentation of Time in the Garden of Adonis is a speaking picture in this sense. In using the traditional phrase as a metaphor for the psychological effect of poetry, Sidney deals with a crucial problem in any didactic theory – to show that the knowledge conveyed by poetry is necessarily dependent on the emotional force and quasi-sensory immediacy of verse.

The relation between Spenser's pictorial language and his rhetorical use of narrative materials becomes very clear in Calidore's vision of the Graces, where pictorial experience is part of the fictional action. Spenser attempts neither a real description nor a dramatization of the hero's visual experience, but rather directly conveys the vision and its significance to the reader. Hence at the climax of the passage, the observing hero and what he sees vanish into a heroic simile. The vision begins when Calidore comes to an open green on the top of Mount Acidale:

> There he did see, that pleased much his sight,
>   That euen he him selfe his eyes enuyde,
>   An hundred naked maidens lilly white,
> All raunged in a ring, and dauncing in delight. (VI, 10, 11)

Spenser does not paint a picture or portray Calidore as first seeing, then responding. Descriptive elements are absorbed into a rendering of Calidore's response, which is completely identified with our experience in reading the passage. Thus two clauses that render quality of response intervene between the verb 'see' and its object 'naked maidens'; feeling and rhythm are dammed up so that the release will imitate Calidore's surprise and delight. This rhythmic effect and the shift of tone it produces in the next to last line account for the extraordinary impression the word 'naked' makes on most readers. From the remarks of critics, we would gather that the vision of the Graces is the healthy analogue of the long erotic description of Acrasia's damsels (11, 12, 63–8).[4] Not at all – this single line is almost all we see of the dancing maidens. There are, after all, a hundred of them, and we are not meant to see a naked human body any more than Wordsworth meant to describe, or meant us to see, the leaves and petals of the ten thousand daffodils that danced in the breeze. Pictorial description renders real visual experience, while Spenser's diction uses visual suggestions to make us experience the words themselves.

The next stanza decisively shows the difference between pictorial description and the rhetorical use of pictorial diction:

> All they without were raunged in a ring,
>> And daunced round; but in the midst of them
>> Three other Ladies did both daunce and sing,
>> The whilest the rest them round about did hemme,
>> And like a girlond did in compasse stemme:
>> And in the middest of those same three, was placed
>> Another Damzell, as a precious gemme,
>> Amidst a ring most richly well enchaced,
> That with her goodly presence all the rest much graced.
>
>> (VI, 10, 12)

Clearly there is no pictorial equivalence between the two images in this stanza: if the lady is in the center of a ring of dancing maidens, she cannot be described as the jewel set into a ring for the finger. But it would be absurd to complain that Spenser is visually confusing, for he has no desire to be visually convincing. He uses sensory impressions to give a quasi-physical presence to images and words that express value.

The rationale of Spenser's verbal sensuousness is exceptionally clear in the profound and breathtaking stanza that concludes the vision. Although it is a heroic simile, it is not announced by the usual 'like' or 'as': the modification of the poet's voice does not suggest that he is turning from the narration of action (which scarcely exists at this point) in order to state an analogy. Spenser begins with 'Looke', and his simile continues and intensifies our experience of the preceding stanza:

> Looke how the Crowne, which *Ariadne* wore
>   Vpon her yuory forehead that same day,
>   That *Theseus* her vnto his bridale bore,
>   When the bold *Centaures* made that bloudy fray
>   With the fierce *Lapithes*, which did them dismay;
>   Being now placed in the firmament,
>   Through the bright heauen doth her beams display,
>   And is vnto the starres an ornament,
> Which round about her moue in order excellent. (vi, 10, 13)

What Spenser makes us 'see' is not a fixed image, an emblem in the usual sense, but a transformation of turbulence and fury into order and beauty. Our experience is specifically an experience of words and is modulated and developed in the very act of reading. The process is quite explicit in this stanza, for the crux of the simile has no iconographic or fictional reason for being there. The Centaurs and the Lapiths are not at all necessary to Ariadne's crown – they belong to another myth – nor does their bloody fray correspond to any part of the Graces' dance. Yet once there, the bloody fray is both relevant and necessary – as the syntax of the sentence makes us recognize.

There is a temporal dimension in our reading of any poem, and in a narrative poem it is conventionally identified with a sequence of fictional events. But in *The Faerie Queene*, as our last example shows, time is the dimension of verbal events – the lines and stanzas that evoke and modify the reader's responses. An episode in *The Faerie Queene*, then, is best described as a developing psychological experience within the reader, rather than as an action to be observed by him. By heeding this distinction, we can solve one of the most perplexing interpretive problems in the poem: why is Amoret tortured by Busyrane? As W. B. C. Watkins remarks, her 'captivity and torture by Busyrane seem sadism unrelated to her character or desert, since as Belphoebe's twin, she is clearly designed to represent a second kind of chastity closer to Spenser's heart – married faithfulness'.[5] The puzzle arises because the meaning of the episode is taken to be a simple translation of the story into abstract terms. Thus, 'Britomart rescues Amoret from Busyrane' means 'Chastity rescues Amoret from Lust'. We are then led to search for what Watkins calls an 'indefinable . . . fault' in Amoret that is symbolized by her torture. If we take Amoret not as a dramatic individual but as an embodied concept, we are in the same dilemma, because we must find a concept that is in need of rescue from Lust.

There seems to me no way of juggling fictional terms to produce a plausible interpretation of the episode, much less one that adequately suggests its vastness and intensity. In this episode a series of speaking pictures that creates our psychological experience as it unfolds has a clear priority over the narration of an action. Britomart disappears the moment she enters Busyrane's castle, and Spenser presents directly to the reader the series of mythological tapestries (III, II, 28–46). More important, we feel no break between this long set piece and the end of canto II, in which Britomart reappears and fictional action nominally begins. There is complete continuity from one part to the other, because the end of the canto develops and expands the poetic experience begun in the presentation of the tapestries. The image of Cupid's darts is carried over to the description of his statue (III, II, 48), and it is in the context established by the tapestries that we feel the menacing brilliance of that description. Taken by itself, Spenser's parenthetical 'Ah man beware, how thou those darts behold' is merely a pious exclamation; in the context of his continual admiration of the persuasive liveliness of the tapestries, it records the intensification of our involvement as we move further into Busyrane's palace. When we proceed into the next room, the living walls of gold and the spoils of mighty conquerors (III, II, 51–2) again intensify images of the tapestries.

The role of fictional action in this canto is to support the reader's psychological experience of images and their transformations. Spenser makes this explicit by reintroducing Britomart in the middle of the reader's exploration of the first room:

And vnderneath his feet was written thus,
   Vnto the Victor of the Gods this bee:
And all the people in that ample hous
Did to that image bow their humble knee,
And oft committed fowle Idolatree.
That wondrous sight faire *Britomart* amazed,
Ne seeing could her wonder satisfie,
But euer more and more vpon it gazed,
The whiles the passing brightnes her fraile sences dazed.

                      (III, 11, 49)

Britomart's daze is not something to be observed: it intensifies the reader's reaction to the dazzling effect of the palace. Britomart's actions in this episode never have the fictional independence that would place the reader in the role of an observer of an action. Rather they are poetic devices that develop the reader's responses and that frequently merge with a direct rendering of them. Britomart's vigil in canto 12 is absorbed into Cupid's masque, an emblematic procession of the psychological impulses that are engendered by and that characterize erotic feeling. Action in these cantos consistently turns into images that speak directly to the reader.

The nominal action at the beginning of canto 12 is Britomart's lying in wait to observe her enemy and Amoret, the object of her quest. But in fact Britomart is no more present as the masque marches by than she was when the tapestries were presented. It is the reader who first sees Amoret, and Amoret is primarily identified with her torture, the image Spenser wishes to impress upon us:

Her brest all naked, as net iuory,
   Without adorne of gold or siluer bright,
Wherewith the Craftesman wonts it beautify,
Of her dew honour was despoyled quight,
And a wide wound therein (O ruefull sight)
Entrenched deepe with knife accursed keene,
Yet freshly bleeding forth her fainting spright,
(The worke of cruell hand) was to be seene,
That dyde in sanguine red her skin all snowy cleene.

                      (III, 12, 20)

Spenser begins by developing the suggestion of artificiality in the commonplace comparison of skin to ivory. He praises Amoret's beauty in terms that recall the sinister glamor of the palace, and thus suggests the puzzling presence of a beautiful woman in Busyrane's masque. When he presents Amoret's torture, Spenser directly identifies our psychological experience with the process of reading. Subordinate clauses and exclamations intervene between the major grammatical elements, 'a wide wound' and 'was to be seene'; each is a separate unit that presents a single aspect of a multiple response to Amoret's wound. The strikingly simple last line emerges from a context of deliberate confusions with which Spenser draws us in more closely.

Once what we may call the emblematic presence of the wound is achieved, Spenser continues to involve the reader:

> At that wide orifice her trembling hart
>> Was drawne forth, and in siluer basin layd,
>> Quite through transfixed with a deadly dart,
>> And in her bloud yet steeming fresh embayd:
>> And those two villeins, which her steps vpstayd,
>> When her weake feet could scarcely her sustaine,
>> And fading vitall powers gan to fade,
>> Her forward still with torture did constraine,
> And euermore encreased her consuming paine. (III, 12, 21)

After fully presenting the emblem, Spenser does the reverse of allowing us to observe it as complete and amenable to decisive understanding. In the final lines, he makes us participate in Amoret's pain; we have a sense not only of the fact that she is tortured, but also of her endurance of torment. This stanza is the last we see of her for the moment, and we are left at a peak of tension. By thus heightening the sense of mystery that characterizes the verse throughout this episode, Spenser makes it explicit that Britomart's quest is not an action we observe, but is identified with our experience of reading. When Britomart finally enters Busyrane's inner chamber, all the figures of the masque disappear, and we see only Amoret, bound and still tortured (III, 12, 30–1). The object of our quest is the image of the pure heart transfixed by the cruel dart of desire, and Britomart's 'rescue' of Amoret is a resolution of this image:

> The cruell steele, which thrild her dying hart,
>> Fell softly forth, as of his owne accord,
>> And the wyde wound, which lately did dispart

> Her bleeding brest, and riuen bowels gor'd,
> Was closed vp, as it had not bene bor'd,
> And euery part to safety full sound,
> As she were neuer hurt, was soone restor'd. (III, 12, 38)

The meaning of these lines lies in the profoundly erotic sense of relaxation, wonder, and wholeness after the terrors of the palace have reached their height in the preceding stanzas (III, 12, 36–7). By bringing the reader into intimate contact with his verse, Spenser creates feelings and awarenesses that cannot be stated by a conceptual translation of fictional action.

Amoret's torture is a conventional image that has occurred throughout Book III. It now emerges as the culminating expression of the major issue of the book – the compatibility of sexual desire and spiritual value in human love. The meanings the image carries are most succinctly indicated by Spenser's exclamation at the sight of Busyrane tormenting Amoret: 'Ah who can loue the worker of her smart?' (III, 12, 31). 'Worker of smart' is an epithet for the object of desire, and Spenser's sententious outcry asks, 'Who can be a human lover?' Human love must involve the flesh and hence must involve desire and pain. Spenser's conception of chastity as marriage rather than virginity demands that he keep this point firmly in view, and Amoret's torture is the most drastic and comprehensive statement of it. Her torment presents something characteristic of all human love and not the unique suffering of an individual. The healing of her heart, then, expresses the resolution of problems with which the whole book is concerned, and in which Britomart – rocked by the storms of love and wounded by Malecasta and Busyrane (III. 1, 65; 12, 33; cf. 4, 6) – is fully implicated. Amoret's torture and release are a direct rendering of awarenesses that have developed in the reader throughout the book, and particularly in those passages of the final episode that have very little to do with fictional action – Busyrane's tapestries and the masque of Cupid.

In all the climactic episodes of *The Faerie Queene*, Spenser brings us into extraordinarily close, almost physical contact with his verse, in order that our psychological experience be identified as closely as possible with the direct experience of language in the activity of reading. The immediacy of the reader's psychological experience is the sign of all these episodes – the human wretchedness of the Cave of Despair, the menacing glitter of Busyrane's palace, the oppressiveness of Mammon's cave, the seductive *otium* of the Bower of Bliss. Amoret's torture is a crucial problem because it is confusing on a very simple level where Spenser's meaning is usually clear. In this episode, Spenser was able to find and express vast significance in a story that has no clear allegorical translation. In most episodes, of course, allegorical significance is plain enough in its general outlines, because symbolic encounters, emblematic figures, and the like were simply raw narrative material to Spenser. But confusion sets in the moment we try to elaborate the significance of the allegory by treating details of language as if they were fictional details.

SOURCE: extract from *The Poetry of 'The Faerie Queene'* (Princeton, 1967) pp. 9–19.

NOTES

1. C. S. Lewis, *English Literature in the Sixteenth Century* (Oxford, 1954) p. 389.
2. *Coleridge's Miscellaneous Criticism*, ed. T. M. Raysor (Cambridge, Mass., 1934) p. 39.
3. Sir Philip Sidney, *An Apologie for Poetrie*, in *Elizabethan Critical Essays* ed. G. Gregory Smith (Oxford, 1904) vol. 1, pp. 164–5.
4. See, for example, C. S. Lewis, *The Allegory of Love* (Oxford, 1936) p. 331; and Northrop Frye, *Fables of Identity* (New York, 1963) p. 86.
5. W. B. C. Watkins, *Shakespeare and Spenser* (Princeton, 1950) p. 206.

Martha Craig The Secret Wit of Spenser's Language (1967)

The language of *The Faerie Queene* to most modern readers seems alien and unaccountable. Spenser seems to have overlooked the expressive possibilities of idiomatic speech revealed so magnificently by Shakespeare and devised an artificial language which, in contrast to the artificialities of Milton's language in *Paradise Lost*, seems less significant and less forceful than the ordinary language it replaces.

Many qualities may seem unfortunate, but perhaps the most vitiating are the archaisms and an apparently purposeless distortion of words. Even after careful study, Spenser's archaism seems superficial and specious, consisting more in odd spellings and grammatical forms than in a genuine rejuvenation of obsolete words that are needed because they are particularly meaningful or expressive. And his liberties with language, the coinages and peculiar forms seem willful and meaningless; alteration of words for the sake of rhyme seems to betray not only lack of resourcefulness but irresponsibility. It is no exaggeration to say that for many readers the language of *The Faerie Queene* is at best merely curious or quaint, at worst hollow and contorted. And this is especially puzzling because the faults seem not only bad but often utterly gratuitous.

The traditional account of Spenser's language provides no reassurance but instead confirms the reader's suspicions. Spenser's diction is said to be 'decorative' and to appeal 'through spontaneity and inherent suggestiveness, independent of source or application'. If so, this has become not a defense but a condemnation. And any other defense of *The Faerie Queene*, of the structure or the allegory, for example, seems ineffectual to the modern reader, for according to his expectations, his implicit hierarchy of literary values, in ignoring the language it presupposes what is primary and most in doubt.

The most influential modern critic of Spenser, C. S. Lewis, suggests that the reader revise these values. Spenser's poetry belongs to an older narrative school in which richness or subtlety of language is not required and would even be inappropriate. It 'has in view an audience who have settled down to hear a long story and do not want to savour each line as a separate work of art. Much of *The Faerie Queene* will therefore seem thin or over-obvious if judged by modern standards. The "thickness" or "density" which I have claimed for it does not come from its language.' This account will not solve the reader's problem, however, for the language seems to call more than usual attention to itself. The peculiarities of spelling and form, the rare words, and the high degree of formal organization in the Spenserian stanza seem to encourage and even enforce close inspection of the language. If Spenser's language lacks the density of Donne or Shakespeare, it also lacks the seeming transparency of Chaucer. A language merely thin or over-obvious might be more generally acceptable, but to many the language does seem dense, not dense with meaning, but slightly muddy or opaque in a way they do not penetrate or understand and yet can not ignore.

Another account offered by W. L. Renwick explains the language in terms of the linguistic goals of the Renaissance. Spenser is said to have been influenced by the program of the Pleiade which urged the poet to revive archaic words, introduce foreign words, and construct new ones out of the existing vocabulary. The purpose was to enrich the language, ultimately the language as a whole but intermediately the language of poetry. Spenser certainly shares the spirit of the Pleiade and their belief in the creative right and creative power of the poet. But their program does not explain his style very exactly nor justify his style to the modern reader, for it does not show how the language has been truly 'enriched'. The vocabulary of *The Faerie Queene* is in general rather circumscribed compared to that of Spenser's contemporaries. Most of his archaisms consist not in the revival of obsolete words to enrich the language but simply in the substitution of archaic forms for modern ones. Though Spenser does adopt some foreign words and invent some new ones, the liberties he takes consist primarily in special modifications of current words, and even these are not consistent in the poem. Why, for example, should the text of the proem to Book I read 'scryne' instead of 'shrine' as it does in the proem to Book III?

The qualities of style that seem puzzling may be accounted for more adequately if, in place of the specific recommendations of the Pleiade, we consult a more fundamental view of language and reality which the recommendations of the Pleiade only in part represent, that is, the Platonic or 'Platonistic' view. A useful document to study in this connection is Plato's *Cratylus*, useful because as an abstract exposition of the fundamental view, it makes the view explicit.

The *Cratylus* is cited prominently by two of Spenser's mentors in their work on language, and references to the dialogue elsewhere during the Renaissance suggest that Plato's discussion had a certain vogue. Spenser must surely have been aware of it and the view of language it presents. The specific question of influence is not primary to an understanding of his poem, however. The dialogue is important to the modern reader as a rationale to account for Spenser's linguistic impulses and to disclose the attitude toward language which *The Faerie Queene* presupposes.

In the *Cratylus* Socrates sets forth the view that words must be not merely conventional and arbitrary, as many believe, but in fact 'correct' and 'true'. For if there is such a thing as reality and knowledge of it, our statements must be about reality, and they must be true to it. And if statements as a whole are to be true, the parts, that is, the words of which they are composed must be true as well. Or, on the analogy of a craft like weaving or cutting, speaking is an action performed for a certain purpose and must be done not according to our own opinion or arbitrary whim but according to nature. We must have the proper instrument correctly suited to the task. In the craft of weaving, the instrument is the shuttle used to separate the web. In the craft of speaking, the instrument is the word.

The instruments of a craft are originally made by someone; so words, too, must have been constructed by an original law-giver or name-maker. An instrument that is good must be constructed according to an ideal. The one who judges whether this has been done successfully, who superintends, is the one who uses the instrument; the carpenter judges the awl. In the case of words the one who judges is the one who knows how to ask and answer questions, who knows how to use words, that is, the dialectician.

What, then, is the principle of 'correctness' in words? Socrates says that he does not have the money for a course with the Sophists, so he suggests that the poets be consulted instead. For the modern student of Plato, this advice is tinged with irony, but the Renaissance Platonist, who took at face value the description of poetic inspiration in the *Ion*, Marsilio Ficino, for example, accepts and even approves of the appeal to the poets.

After thus carefully inquiring from whom the correctness of names, that is, the proper principle by which they are constituted, is to be learned, he mocks the Sophists, and he leads us rather to the poets, not just any of them but the divine ones, as if they had received the true names of things from the gods, among whom are the true names.

If we consult the poet Homer, we discover that correctness of words consists in revealing the nature of the things named. Words reveal reality through their etymologies. The composition of 'Agamemnon', for example, shows that he is admirable (*agastos*) for enduring (*menein*); the derivation of 'Atreus' shows that he is the destructive one (*ateros*). Words contain within them little self-explanatory statements. The subject of the statement is the word itself, the predicate is the elemental word or words from which it is made, what we would call the morphemes. Words are 'true' because they imply a true statement. . . .

The names of Spenser's characters are clearly philosophic and true, for they reveal the nature of the one named through the etymology. The heroes' names, like the names of Homer's heroes, are 'composed according to a certain allegorical rationale', as Ficino would say. Belphoebe is the 'beautiful, pure one', Artegall is the 'art of justice'. As a poet-dialectician Spenser also interprets given words truly and philosophically through etymology. 'Magnificence' is not properly conspicuous consumption but 'doing great deeds' as the etymology shows.

When a suitable etymology is not apparent in the current form of a word, Socrates looks to its archaic form or other archaic words to see if they are more suggestive, for if language has been handed down from some original name-maker, words may have been corrupted in the course of time. If so, the early form should be the right one (*Cratylus* 418–19). Through his theory of language Plato in fact acts out the etymology of 'etymology': the true explanation of words is in their origin. The original name-maker in Plato is really a metaphor for whatever principle of order and reason there may be in language. The search for older forms is a search for the true forms that are ideally expressive.

Plato's etymologizing expedient explains the sort of archaizing Spenser does in *The Faerie Queene*. Through archaism Spenser carries out the basic Platonic metaphor of the poem, the metaphor of the antique world, a time in the past when the world was more rational and comprehensible, an ideal time, 'ideal' not because there was no evil or difference, but because evil and difference could be more readily perceived and understood. The purpose of his archaisms is not primarily to enlarge his vocabulary, the concern of the Pleiade, but to make it more flexible and expressive. The archaic forms and form words, '-en' endings, 'y-' prefixes, and expressions like 'ywis' act as a sort of solvent of language, dissolving ordinary patterns and the reader's usual expectation. With archaism established as a mode of diction, Spenser is free to pick out archaic forms that are more suggestive of philosophic meaning.

The state of the language in the sixteenth century made such usage more possible and more likely than it would be now. No fixed standard of spelling and syntax had been established. There was less pattern or expectation to overcome, and the writer was free to choose among many forms available. Spenser simply exercised this freedom more widely than other writers of the time by reviving forms that were obsolete or obsolescent. Because there was no fixed standard, the sixteenth century reader always needed to be more resourceful and interpretive than we. It might not be obvious or indisputable even what word was before him. He would always examine word forms more carefully than we and so would be more apt to see their 'etymological' nature, the meaningful affinities which they suggest.

As the analysis of words in the *Cratylus* progresses, it soon becomes clear that even the aid of archaism does not yield a perfect language. The given language is clearly deficient; it is not an adequate or reliable source of truth. But for that very reason language should be improved. Words are only approximations, but as such, they can be perfected. Numbers, because they are images simply of quantities can not be; if we change II to III, we do not refer to the same number better, we refer to another number. But if we change 'demon' to 'daemon', we improve the word and make it more revealing by showing more clearly the identity of spirit and intelligence.

The poet's alterations are an effort to correct language according to his vision or insight so that it reveals reality more adequately. Forms and spellings are improved in order to disclose the etymological rationale of the word. Slight alterations in sound or spelling are admitted so that connections in meaning may be clearer. Rhyme words are spelled the same, not only implying connection in sound but encouraging comparison of meaning. Portmanteau words are devised to cover complex notions.

The lack of 'realism', the uncolloquial, unidiomatic character of the language ultimately follows from Spenser's philosophic realism, his belief that truth is not found in the everyday or in immediate surroundings, the 'world of appearances', but in a realm of ideas that are only partially and imperfectly reflected in the everyday world. Ordinary language is not adequate to this world of fuller insight. So Spenser's major heroes are not personifications of common terms, like most of the characters in medieval allegory, but of words he has invented. He writes not of 'chastity' but of 'Belphoebe', a perfected insight into chastity, not of 'courtesy' but 'Calidore', a concept something like courtesy but refined and re-defined. It is the same basic impulse at work which occasions the form 'scryne' to suggest that the shrine the poet seeks in his invocation is, according to the Latin root of the word, a *scrinium* or box of papers where the secret wisdom of the sacred muse may be found.

What the modern reader or the lexicographer sees as a distortion of language is in fact an impulse to perfect it. Like the action as a whole, individual words are allegorical; they contain hidden meaning or implied metaphors. It has frequently been said that Spenser's language suits the poem – a fancy language for a fanciful world. This should at least be supplemented: a more fully significant language for a more fully significant world. . . .

In poetry the definition is dramatized either literally or symbolically by the action. The meaning of 'Agamemnon' in the view of classical and Renaissance commentators, is implicit in the etymology, but it is fully disclosed only in the action of the *Iliad*. The reader discovers the meaning of the name by analyzing the action of the poem. Homer, with the aid of divine inspiration, originally discovered the proper name, or the true meaning of the given name, by analyzing the conduct of his character in life. Since the heroes of *The Faerie Queene* are not types but concepts and universals, their proper names must be discovered in the conduct of life as a whole. The author, if a true poet–dialectician, was inspired to direct intuition of the concept, only adumbrated in life. He then invented the proper name, a personification, and a symbolic action through which it is fully revealed.

The action of Spenser's heroes in *The Faerie Queene* continually unfolds an 'etymological' rationale, the secret wit of reality which his language is devised to disclose. Nothing, therefore, could be more misleading than the opinion that Spenser's language is negligible in our reading of the poem. In fact 'etymological' associations of language are a constant guide to the implicit meaning of the poem and form the very principle of its organization. From the beginning, the poem evolves according to such a rationale: for example, in the action of Book i, a *hero* inspired by *eros* (these terms are explicitly connected in the *Cratylus*, 398 D and make up a traditional 'etymology') rides forth as a knight *errant*. His first adventure as a knight errant is, naturally, an encounter with Errour: he defeats her but then proceeds to err through eros, the misplaced affections of his 'heroicke' heart. So misled, he goes to the house of Pride from which he emerges safely, only to err again in the *arrogance* of Orgoglio, the presumptuous spirit, the *airs* of man. He is then redeemed from Orgoglio by *Arthur*, the *ardor* and the *art* or efficacy of grace. Yet again he almost errs in *despair* before he is led to the house of Holiness by *Una* where he is restored to *wholeness* and the whole of *holiness* is symbolically revealed.

The action thus proceeds by a series of etymological puns, yet their presence is frequently unobtrusive; the wit appears to us as a secret wit. At the opening of the poem when the knight, his lady, and the dwarf enter the 'covert' to find shelter from the storm, we enter into their vision of things. The traditional catalogue of trees becomes a dramatic record of enthrallment, the process of being 'led with delight' and so beguiled. The trees, clad with summer's 'pride', conceal 'heavens light' and the guiding star: what is simply 'farre' seems 'faire'. We are warned by Una that 'This is the wandring wood, this *Errours den*', and the double meaning of 'knots' and 'boughtes' (bouts) anticipate the implication of the knight's encounter with this tortuous beast. Yet the climactic pun drawing so deeply upon the very wit of the language itself takes us by surprise: 'God helpe the man so wrapt in *Errours* endlesse *traine*.'

With the killing of Errour the knight's first encounter is complete. He proves that he is not in this sense an errant knight: he is not subject to a form of error which, as the language re-asserts again and again, can be made 'plaine'. He proves worthy of the 'Armorie' which first won his heroic heart.

The action then proceeds to show that the knight is 'errant', however, in another sense made fully clear when the word is at last used in Fradubio's speech: he is subject to Duessa or duplicity. 'The author then (said he) of all my smarts, / Is one *Duessa* a false sorceresse, / That many errant knights hath brought to wretchednesse' (I, 2, 34:7-9). '*Duessa*' is, of course, associated with *duo*, two to suggest her doubleness or deceit but also with Greek *dus-*, bad, ill and *duē*, misery to suggest the wretchedness she brings.

The Red Cross Knight is parted from Una, the one truth, by Archimago, the arch magician, and can be because '*Archimago*' in his 'Hermitage' is the architect of images, of delusive likenesses.

Archimago sends to '*Morpheus*', the former or fashioner, for a 'diverse' or, etymologically, misleading dream, subtler and more seductive than the 'diverse doubt' of Errour because the threat then made 'plaine' now becomes an ambiguous 'plaint'. The 'doubtfull words' of the dream-lady make the 'redoubted knight / Suspect her truth.' Yet 'since no untruth he knew', he is not seduced but interprets her appeal in an honorable way. Sheer ambiguity can not destroy him because if the evil is truly ambiguous, the interpreter must ascertain or supply it, and the knight as 'redoubted', reverent as well as revered, has no such evil in him to supply. Archimago must create a definite false illusion of Una as unfaithful which exploits the knight's virtue, his love of her. Una and the Red Cross are thus divided into 'double parts' or separated through duplicity and Una left 'wandring', the end of Archimago's 'drift', leaving the Red Cross to Duessa's wiles.

The nature of the Red Cross Knight's susceptibility is then further dramatized by the difference between Duessa and Sans Foy. The Red Cross defeats Sans Foy; it is not a complete loss of faith on his part which is leading him astray. But he errs, he falls prey to Duessa as Fidessa, a superficially perfect semblance of faith, through his impulse to love, the 'heroicke' character of his stout heart. His love for Duessa is certainly a crude bedazzlement revealed in the way he looks her up and down, and in respect to him she is '*Fidessa*' or little faith, but it is significant that his faith is not lost primarily but misplaced: he always believes but he may misbelieve.

The analysis of error which began in the 'wandring wood' is completed in the encounter with Fradubio, metamorphosed into a tree or an instance of error in its more refined and significant sense. In the symbolic plant the meaning of the action which began with the earlier 'plaints' is 'plast in open plaines' (1, 2, 32:9; 33:6) and made explicit. Fradubio like the Red Cross was overcome not by doubt per se but by guile, the guile to which doubt as an indeterminate state of mind makes him prey. When he tried to judge between his lady and Duessa, 'the doubtfull ballaunce' swayed equally; doubt itself determines in no way. So Duessa intervened with an act of misrepresentation, obscuring his lady in a fog. Fradubio suggests *dubius*, doubting, and reflects its dangers; more specifically, though, he is the victim of 'fraud' (1, 4, 1:3), the active evil to which the uncommitted state of doubt makes him vulnerable.

The Red Cross Knight misled by Archimago's Duessa next appears at the house of Pride, implicitly the palace of hypocrisy, as playfully derived from *Hyper chrysos*, covered over with gold.

> A stately Pallace built of squared bricke,
>   Which cunningly was without morter laid,
>   Whose wals were high, but nothing strong, nor thick,
>   And golden foile all over them displaid,
>   That purest skye with brightnesse they dismaid.   (1, 4, 4)

It is a house, as the Bible suggests, not on the strait but the broad way and built on sand, but it is 'painted cunningly'. The porter '*Malvenu*', a parody of *bienvenu* or welcome, greets them, prefiguring the evil that will come. Then '*Lucifera*' appears, the bringer of light who like Phaeton proudly burns and bedazzles with light intended 'fairely for to shyne' or *phaëthōn* (1, 4, 9:9).

In the pageant of the Seven Deadly Sins which follows Spenser's wit is comically farfetched in keeping with the gaudy cartoon quality of the parade. The first sin '*Idlenesse*', dressed like a monk in 'habit blacke, and amis thin', which may by some extravagant puns suggest the poet's condemnation, carries his 'Portesse', but unfortunately the prayer book is only a 'portesse' only carried and rarely read. Certainly the 'wayne' is poorly led with such a vacuous and inattentive fellow guiding its 'way'. Idlenesse 'esloynes' himself and challenges 'essoyne' 'from worldly cares', (*soins* in French); the legal terms suggest his Jesuitical invocation of the letter of the law to free him ironically for 'lawlesse riotise'.

Gluttony follows with the long fine neck of a crane; 'gluttony' in Latin is derived from *glutire*, to swallow. He is depicted as Silenus the satyr (*satur*, full); his drunken 'corse' reflects the course he leads. Lechery, who appears on the traditional goat, *caper*, is true to that depiction, capricious; his 'whally' eyes, white or wall eyes, are the goat's eye or *oeil de chèvre* in French.

Envy is presented primarily as a vile mouth, stressed by the rare form 'chaw' for jaw to reiterate his endless malicious and mordant backbiting. His gown of satin as 'discoloured say' seems to pun on the vicious things he says; the snake he carries in his bosom 'implyes' his mortal sting. Envy's gown 'ypainted full of eyes' reflects the root meaning of envy in Latin, *invidia*, the evil eye. He eyes all with hatred but particularly looks at his precursor 'Covetyse' or avarice with covet eyes, reflecting their close connection.

Wrath is depicted through associations in English as rash or rathe; his is a '*hasty* rage'. And when Satan tries to drive this 'laesie teme' of evils, Idleness is called '*Slowth*', spelled as if derived from 'slow'. . . .

When he leaves the house of Pride, the Red Cross Knight, wearied by the ordeal, disarms and sits down to rest by a fountain; he thus puts off the armor of faith, to which Spenser in the prefatory letter ascribes all his success, and fails to stand, according to the teaching of Ephesians (chapter 6, verses 10 ff.), having done all in the whole armor of God. Instead, like the natural man or the child of wrath in Ephesians, he indulges the desires of the flesh and the mind by bathing in the pleasure of the shade, listening to the music of the birds, and taking solace with his lady. He drinks from the fountain, the antithesis of the well of life which is later to renew him in his battle with the dragon, for this makes all who drink from it feeble and faint. It comes from a nymph who 'tyr'd with heat of scorching ayre' like the knight sat down in the midst of her race, making the goddess Diana 'wroth'. So disarmed, the knight encounters Orgoglio. The monster, boasting of his high descent and matchless might, symbolizes the knight's pride and the divine wrath such pride arouses: the pride of indulging himself in the confidence of his achievement. Duessa intercedes with Orgoglio begging him not to destroy her knight but to make him an 'eternal bondslave', the thrall of pride in works, especially works as a sign of 'high descent', of election. And he is so enthralled, erring in the arrogance of the Prince of the Power of the Air, until he is redeemed by grace.

The Red Cross is redeemed from the wrath of Orgoglio by Arthur, symbol of the ardor and art of God's grace. Arthur represents not the magnanimity of God, his potentiality or etymologically his great spirit, but his magnificence, his actuality or etymologically his doing great deeds. Arthur's image and genealogy are resplendent with the glory of such greatness. He appears with a headpiece like an almond tree on the top of 'greene *Selinis*'; '*Selinis*' in Greek resembles *selinon*, the plant from which the chaplets of victors in the ancient games were made; Virgil calls it 'palmosa Selinus' (*Aeneid* iii, 705). . . .

After his victory Arthur explains to Una and the Red Cross that he was raised by 'Timon' or in Greek honor, worth, and he is accompanied by 'Timias', his squire, 'th'admirer of his might', who is similarly derived. He was raised 'Under the foot of *Rauran* mossy hore, / From whence the river *Dee* as silver cleene / His tombling billowes rolls with gentle rore' (I, 9, 4:6 ff.). The river Dee suggests his divine origin; this is the explicit etymology of the river in the marriage catalogue of Book IV: 'Dee, which Britons long ygone / Did call divine . . .' (IV, 11, 3:4). (The Rauran seems so named because it is where the Dee gently 'rores'.) Arthur's shield is made of 'diamond', suggesting its function of representing God in the world. It was made by the great magician Merlin, the antithesis of Archimago, who created the shield to expose everything false. Merlin, too, seems related to honor and wonder through Latin *mirus* by virtue of his 'admirable deedes'. Arthur's sword was made by Merlin from metal mixed with 'Medaewart' or meadwort, so spelled suggesting that it wards off cunning and magic, *mēdea* in Greek: it is so made 'that no enchauntment from his dint might save' (II, 8, 20:6).

When Arthur appears to save the Red Cross Knight, the poet proclaims the 'goodly golden chaine' by which the virtues are linked in love, and each hero aids the other. This chain is literally 'concord', the cord that ties all things together (cf. III, 1, 12:8) through *con* and *cor*, the uniting of the heroes' hearts.

Arthur departs in search of the Faerie Queene whom he discovered in the revelation of a dream, the antithesis of the Red Cross Knight's dream delusion contrived by Archimago in Canto one. The Red Cross and Una set off and are soon accosted by a knight fleeing a ghastly sight, the sight, we soon learn, of Despair. . . .

Like most of the evils in Book I, Despair is associated with division and doubleness. The main accusation he brings is that the Red Cross was false to his faith and served 'Duessa'. The term first appears in Book I when Una is originally 'from her knight divorced in despaire' (I, 3, 2:8); she herself remains faithful, but she is 'forsaken, wofull, solitarie' through his error, his displaced faith. Spenser seems to suggest that despair is the dis-spirited state which occurs when Una or the one truth of grace and the Red Cross Knight are divided or dispaired. At any rate it is Una who now rescues the Red Cross from the rhetoric of Despair, calling him away from vain words and 'the accurst hand-writing' of God's justice to action and grace.

The knight then proceeds to the house of Holiness where the whole of holiness is symbolized. In this house he is taught repentence and the way to 'heavenly blesse', according to the argument of the canto. The spelling distinguishes 'blesse' from 'blisse', though the two were often identified in Elizabethan English and come ultimately from the same etymological source. The Bower of Bliss thus lies in contrast to the house of Holiness as the house of Unblessed Bliss, an ironic *Eden* or garden of pleasure in Hebrew. The excess of '*Acrasia*' which we see there is implicitly contrasted with the abundance of '*Charissa*'. '*Acrasia*' is presented in Book ii as a perversion of *charis* or true grace; she 'depastures' delight, a term Spenser coined, as the ironic pastor in her bower who takes life rather than nourishing it, destroying her worshippers.

In the house of Holiness Saint George at last gains his name and full identity as his sainthood is foreseen. He learns that he like Arthur is a changeling. Arthur was taken from his mother and delivered to the faery knight 'old Timon' thus, it seems, being taught by time, as Achilles was taught by Cheiron, son of Chronos. Saint George, however, was found where a faerie left him in the furrow of a field. . . . 'Georgos' is derived from the Greek term for plowman as 'Adam' was derived from the Hebrew term for earth. The etymology suggests their ultimate affinity in the moral allegory. It suggests, too, in retrospect that the earthly giant '*Orgoglio*' is George himself, inspired or blown up with the air of arrogance to which every man in his weakness may succumb.

The etymology of St. George functions also in a very different way: it presents an allusion to English literary history and the career of 'holiness' as a topic for poetry. The truth of holiness was lost but then 'fond' or found again as invention, matter for poetry in *Piers Plowman*, substantiating the traditional name of the English saint as 'ploughman' or man of the soil. Spenser eventually returns the topic to the simple, rural world through the career of 'grace' in the poem. 'Of Court it seemes, men Courtesie doe call' (vi, i, i), but Spenser eventually corrects this to show that the court is the source of false courtesy, of 'courting'; true 'courtesy' is a form of 'grace' which thrives best not at court but in the pastoral milieu, or pastoral ideal, of Book vi.

Spenser's secret wit suggests not only the moral implication of the action but political and social instances which substantiate and

exemplify. A most vivid instance occurs in Guyon's encounter with
Phaedria, Book II, Canto vi; a series of puns associates her with
Italy and the Italian way of life during the Renaissance. Phaedria's
boat is called a 'little Gondelay' and a 'little frigot'. Both terms had
been introduced into English not long before from the Italian. With
his use of them in the Phaedria passage Spenser seems to be punning
in Italian: 'gondola' suggests the Italian term *gongolare*, 'to laugh
till ones heart be sore or shoulders ake, to shuckle and be full of
joy, or excessive gladnesse'; 'frigot' suggests *frigotare*, 'to shuckle, to
shrug, or strut for overjoy'. These puns are reinforced by the epithets
of her 'shallow ship', 'painted bote' (false good), and 'flit barke',
(meaning airy, insubstantial, as well as swift). The puns become an
allusion to Italy through the meaning of 'gondola' which Florio
defines as 'a little boat or whirry used no where but a bout and
in Venice'.

Other references suggest the allusion. In repudiating war,
Phaedria refers to the kind of skirmishes she prefers as 'scarmoges'.
This spelling instead of the usual 'skirmish' (IV, 9, 20:2) associates
the term with Italian *scaramuccia*, the name of Harlequin's companion with his buffoonish battles in the Italian farce. Phaedria
locates her world 'In this wide Inland sea, that hight by name /
The Idle Lake'; 'Inland sea' is a translation of 'Mediterranean';
the *'Idle Lake'* is apparently the Adriatic, which Spenser associates
with *adraneia*, inactivity. She lives on an idyllic island suggesting
Venice, to the Renaissance Englishman the very land of Venus. The
1590 edition of *The Faerie Queene* even carried a proverbial allusion
to the pope: 'Sometimes she sung, as loud as lark in aire / Sometimes she laught, as merry as Pope Jone.' The song she sings is the
magnificent perversion of the Biblical 'Behold the lilies of the field,
they toil not neither do they spin.'

Through such puns the Phaedria incident forms an elaborate
commentary on the Italian way of life during the Renaissance and a
criticism of the young Englishman's practice of sowing his wild oats
there and affecting the Italianate style. Spenser finds reflected in
Italy the prototype of inane mirth and shallow epicureanism; in the
virtual enclosure of the Mediterranean Sea he finds a symbol of
stagnation and idleness. . . .

But the development which emerges most strongly moves in the
direction of amplifying symbolic implication rather than pursuing

social allusions in detail. Like '*Mordant*' (or '*Mortdant*' II, I, 49:9) his counterpart, '*Verdant*', the flourishing young man whose spirit Acrasia 'depastures', must receive what he gives, though in his case the outcome is happily reversed. Acrasia with her curse enacting '*Mortdant*' gives 'death to him that death does give', the Palmer, through his 'counsel sage' enacting '*Verdant*' gives truth to him that truth does give or instructs the victim in the true harm of Acrasia which he depicts and so frees him from her.

The language of the voyage projects a world of the moral imagination above the social scene to which it simply dips in specific allusion with an occasional detail of incident, image, or term. The sea-beasts encountered by Guyon and the Palmer are not the conies and quail of the Elizabethan underworld or their sea counterparts, nor even sea-lions and sea-foxes but the most fantastic monsters imaginable. The catalogue begins by literary allusion: a battle with the 'many headed hydra' is Plato's symbol in Book IV of the *Republic* (426 e) for the futility of attempting to legislate the end of fraud instead of converting the spirit of man, since without such a change of spirit new forms of fraud like the heads of a hydra will continually spring forth. The scolopendra, it was thought, 'feeling himselfe taken with a hooke, casteth out his bowels, untill he hath unloosed the hooke, and then swalloweth them up againe', which perhaps resembles certain specific devices of the sharper. But what the chosen epithets depict is images of evil monstrously general. The hazards of the course are immense and indefinable except as threat, the 'Ziffius' or swordfish, for example, and its consequence, the morse, which Spenser derives from the Latin *mors* to mean death.

This is the advantage of Spenser's secret wit. He may suggest implications at every possible level of experience without disrupting the symbolic unity and continuity of the moral world. The operation of his style was perfectly described by Spenser's first critic, Kenelm Digby, in a letter of appreciation addressed to Henry May, 1638:

Spencer in what he sayth hath a way of expression peculiar to himselfe; he bringeth downe the highest and deepest mysteries that are contained in humane learning, to an easie and gentle forme of delivery; wch. sheweth he is Master of what he treateth of; he can wield it as he pleaseth: And he hath done this so cunningly, that if one heede him not wth. great attention, rare and wonderful conceptions will unperceived slide by him that readeth his workes, and he will thinke he hath meet wth. nothing but familiar and easie discourses: But lett one dwell a while upon them, and he shall feele a strange fulness and roundness in all he sayth.

The Faerie Queene has disappointed the modern reader, for in an age that admires the difficult and complex it seems 'familiar and easy'. But, as Kenelm Digby testifies, it offers 'rare and wonderful conceptions' to the attentive reader who does not let them slide by. To discover their fullness the reader must heed the language closely, however. The language must be savored for the cunning within its gentleness and ease.

Source: extracts from 'The Secret Wit of Spenser's Language', in *Elizabethan Poetry: Modern Essays in Criticism*, ed. P. J. Alpers (New York and London, 1967) pp. 447-64, 466-7.

William Empson   Spenser's Rhythm (1930)

. . . No discussion of rhythm can ignore [Spenser]. To show the scale of his rhythm, it may be enough to list some of the ways in which he gave movement to the stanza of the *Faerie Queene*; it is by the delicacy of this movement that he shows his attitude towards his sentences, rather than by devices of implication in the sentences themselves. At the same time, once such an attitude has been fixed, it is more easily described in terms of the meaning of the words than in terms of the meaning of the rhythm; in the next example, from Sidney, I shall use this other mode of approach.

Spenser concentrates the reader's attention on to the movement of his stanza, by the use of archaic words and constructions, so that one is at a safe distance from the exercise of an immediate judgment, by the steady untroubled flow of similar lines, by making no rapid change of sense or feeling, by sustained alliteration, parallel adjectives, and full statement of the accessories of a thought, and by the dreamy repetition of the great stanza perpetually pausing at its close. *Ababbcbcc* is a unit which may be broken up into a variety of metrical forms, and the ways in which it is successively broken up are fitted into enormous patterns. The first quatrain usually gratifies the ear directly and without surprise, and the stanzas may then be classified by the grammatical connections of the crucial fifth line, which must give a soft bump to the dying fall of the first quatrain, keep it in the air, and prevent it from falling apart from the rest of the stanza.

It may complete the sense of the quatrain, for instance, with a couplet, and the stanza will then begin with a larger, more narrative unit, *ababb*, and wander garrulously down a perspective to the alexandrine. Or it may add to the quatrain as by an afterthought, as if with a childish earnestness it made sure of its point without regard to the metre, and one is relieved to find that the metre recovers itself after all. For more energetic or serious statements it will start a new quatrain at the fifth line, with a new sentence; there are then two smaller and tighter, repeatedly didactic, or logically opposed, or historically advancing, units, whose common rhyme serves to insist upon their contrast, which are summed up and reconciled in the final solemnity of the alexandrine. In times of excitement the fifth line will be connected both ways, so as to ignore the two quatrains, and, by flowing straight on down the stanza with an insistence on its unity, show the accumulated energy of some enormous climax; and again, by being connected with neither, it will make the stanza into an unstressed conversational device without overtones of rhythm, picking up stray threads of the story with almost the relief of prose. . . .

The size, the possible variety, and the fixity of this unit give something of the blankness that comes from fixing your eyes on a bright spot; you have to yield yourself to it very completely to take in the variety of its movement, and, at the same time, there is no need to concentrate the elements of the situation into a judgment as if for action. As a result of this, when there are ambiguities of idea, it is whole civilisations rather than details of the moment which are their elements; he can pour into the even dreamwork of his fairyland Christian, classical, and chivalrous materials with an air, not of ignoring their differences, but of holding all their systems of values floating as if at a distance, so as not to interfere with one another, in the prolonged and diffused energies of his mind.

SOURCE: extract from *Seven Types of Ambiguity* (London, 1930) pp. 43–5.

Northrop Frye   Verbal *Opsis* in Spenser (1957)

The relations between poetry and the visual arts are perhaps more far-fetched than those between poetry and music. Unmusical poets are often 'pictorial' in a general sense: they frequently use their more meditative rhythms to build up, detail by detail, a static picture, as in the careful description of the nude Venus in *Oenone* or in the elaborate tapestry-like pageants in *The Faerie Queene*. Where we do have something really analogous to *opsis*, however, is in the rhetorical device known as imitative harmony or onomatopoeia, as described and exemplified by Pope in the *Essay on Criticism*:

> 'Tis not enough no harshness gives offence,
> The sound must seem an echo to the sense . . .
>
> When Ajax strives some rock's vast weight to throw,
> The line too labours, and the words move slow;
> Not so, when swift Camilla scours the plain,
> Flies o'er th'unbending corn, and skims along the main.

[Frye, after general discussion, turns again to Spenser.]

The most remarkable sustained mastery of verbal *opsis* in English, perhaps, is exhibited in *The Faerie Queene*, which we have to read with a special kind of attention, an ability to catch a visualization through sound. Thus in

> The Eugh obedient to the bender's will,

the line has a number of weak syllables in the middle that makes it sag out in a bow shape. When Una goes astray the rhythm goes astray with her:

> And Una wandring farre in woods and forrests . . .

Part of the effect of this line is due to the weak rhyme of 'forrests' against 'guests'. When the subject is wreckage, the rhythm is wrecked with the same kind of disappointment-rhyme:

> For else my feeble vessell crazd, and crackt
>> Through thy strong buffets and outrageous blowes,
> Cannot endure, but needs it must be wrackt
>> On the rough rocks, or on the sandy shallowes.

When Florimell finds her way difficult to scan, so does the reader:

> Through the tops of the high trees she did descry . . .

When the subject is harmony in music, we have an identical rhyme on one of the few appropriate words in the language:

>> To th' instruments diuine respondence meet:
>> The siluer sounding instruments did meet . . .

When the subject is a 'perillous Bridge', we have:

> Streight was the passage like a ploughed ridge,
>> That if two met, the one mote needes fall ouer the lidge.

Renaissance readers had been put on the alert for such effects by their school training in rhetoric; a harmless looking line from Spenser's *January*, for instance, is promptly sandbagged by E. K. as 'a prety Epanorthosis . . . and withall a Paronomasia'. The source of Pope's passage quoted above is Vida's *Art of Poetry*, which is earlier than Spenser. . . .

The first line in the passage quoted from Pope (' 'Tis not enough no harshness gives offence') implies that a sharp discord or apparent bungle in the writing may often be interpreted as imitative decorum. Pope uses such intentional discords in the same poem when he gives horrible examples of practices he disapproves of, and Addison's discussion of the passage in *Spectator 253* shows how lively an interest such devices still aroused. Here, for example, is the way that Pope describes constipated genius:

> And strains, from hard-bound brains, eight lines a year.

Spenser, naturally, employs the same device constantly. A tasteless misuse of alliteration marks a speaker (Braggadocchio) as a liar and hypocrite:

> But minds of mortall men are muchell mard,
> And mou'd amisse with massie mucks vnmeet regard.

and when the false Duessa tempts St. George, the grammar, rhythm, and assonance could hardly be worse: the worthy knight's ear should have warned him that all was not well:

> Yet thus perforce he bids me do, or die.
> Die is my dew; yet rew my wretched state
> You . . .

Certain imitative devices become standardized in every language, and most of them in English are too familiar to need recapitulation here: beheaded lines increase speed, trochaic rhythms suggest falling movement, and so on. The native stock of English words consists largely of monosyllables, and a monosyllable always demands a separate accent, however slight. Hence long Latin words, if skilfully used, have the rhythmical function of lightening the metre, in contrast to the sodden unrhythmical roar that results 'When ten low words oft creep in one dull line'. A by-product of this latter phenomenon in English is more useful: the so-called broken-backed line with a spondee in the middle has since Old English times . . . been most effective for suggesting the ominous and foreboding:

Thy wishes then dare not be told.   (Wyatt)

Depending from on high, dreadful to sight.   (Spenser)

Which tasted works knowledge of good and evil.   (Milton)

SOURCE: extracts from *The Anatomy of Criticism* (Princeton, 1957) pp. 258–61.

Harry S. Berger Jr.   Conspicuous Irrelevance (1957)

The allegorical critics regarded the plot, or fable – to use a simile so often found in Renaissance criticism – as a mere sweet and pleasant covering for the wholesome but bitter pill of moral doctrine. The neoclassicists, limiting the sense and application of Aristotle's definition of poetry as an imitation of life, regarded the fable as the medium of this imitation, and the more perfect according as it became more truly and more minutely an image of human life.[1]

Readers of the *Faerie Queene* are confronted by two quite different levels of representation: that of the fable or image, and that of the allegory or idea.[2] When the poet states or suggests that Woman A stands for Idea B, a dilemma is forced on us. Does Woman A disappear completely into Idea B? Is this disappearance the mark of good allegorical writing? Or is such sleight of hand impossible to a poet – doesn't a fable by its very nature have some elements of concreteness (belong to the 'image of human life') that cannot be translated? Perhaps, however, the poet makes a virtue of this defect and produces pleasurable images alongside his profitable ideas.

Though theory traditionally prescribes a one-to-one relation, it also recognizes the conflicting claims of pleasure and profit, fable and allegory. From the Renaissance on, critics and theorists have encouraged the split-level response, or have at least accepted it as in the nature of things:

We may read an allegory as a pleasant piece of fiction, and we may appreciate the author's technical ingenuity; but if we fail to search beneath the surface or if the artist fails to invite our attention to a testing of the matter beneath the surface, then the allegory has lost at least one half of its function. . . . The allegory, then, if it is to be of any merit in its particular genre, must communicate both content and form, both idea and image. Great allegorists . . . have always intended . . . to present works of art which evoke a two-fold response from the pictorial imagination and the rational intellect.[3]

Modern students of literature question this strategy for a number of reasons. They have been schooled to look for poetic excellence much more intensively in the resources of the language, and they feel that the image–idea relationship projects a meaning unaffected by the manner in which it is expressed. This relationship, they are told, is to be seen in terms of the author's avowed intention. Readers must attend to the images and ideas as conceived in his mind, conveyed by his transparent words, and understood by the audience for which he wrote. A reader alert for complexity will spurn the one-to-one aspect. A reader concerned for unity may well balk at the divided response occasioned by two 'planes' of representation (image and idea) so utterly different in character.

The *Faerie Queene* in fact raises in a special and pressing manner the general problem of poetic unity. Precisely how is it a poem? How is it *one*? How do its diverse parts and elements contribute to an impression at once intricate and simple, complex and unified? We may approach this problem by glancing at a familiar pair of terms which critics have in some form or other frequently applied to the poem, either to justify it or to damn it: argument and ornament. Superficially it appears that the argument–ornament split corresponds to the profit–pleasure criterion, and that with the shift to modern sensibility and theory a poem will be found wanting insofar as it illustrates the Horatian precept. For the argument–ornament split is an either/or situation, and modern interest centers on the both/and which guarantees complexity. Argument refers to what the poem is about; ornament indicates any local delight that is irrelevant to the argument and digresses from what the poem is about.

In order to speak of ornament one must have already made the poem's argument coincide with a particular level to which all other aspects of the poem are subordinate. Allegory-minded critics identify argument with the didactic or ideological scheme; fable-minded critics identify argument with the narrative of events. The former presuppose that the poem must be read by going from one level to the other; the latter try to suppress the allegory or disregard it as an unfortunate mistake. Some critics try to justify both levels, each on its own merit. To do this they must establish two arguments not intrinsically connected, one subject to esthetic and the other to didactic judgments. Both-minded critics differ from the fable- and allegory-minded only in their divided emphasis. All of them assume that the levels are actually separable, that each level is centrifugal to the others, an alternative and self-sufficient translation which

yields a simple 'meaning'. All assume that in respect to the argu-
ment-level the meanderings of other levels produce irrelevancies
which can at best be called ornament.

. . . Is it not possible that the poem's argument and ornament are
in fact reconciled? Can we not admit hypothetically distinct levels –
fable and allegory – yet see the poem as a unified experience shaped
by the interaction of these different perspectives? Could the poem's
argument be produced by this interaction rather than identified
with one or another of the interacting levels? In short, can emphasis
be placed on the dramatic rather than didactic function of Spenserian
allegory?

In considering these questions I shall concentrate on the factor of
irrelevance, or digression. It seems inevitable that Spenser's allegorical method should create diversions from the poem's argument,
from its fable and from its allegory. Though Image A is introduced
into the fable to illustrate Idea B, the image has its own concrete
character. The relationship between A and B is therefore one of
similarity rather than identity, and it must include unlike elements;
these differences between A and B constitute the body of irrelevance
in the poem, the ornament which critics praise or damn. Now
clearly the irrelevance is in the poem and cannot be wished away.
But what can be questioned is the equation of irrelevance with
ornament. Before assuming that a digression from the argument is
purely decorative it seems only fair to test its functional value.

What is odd about Spenser's strategy is a perverse insistence on
the digressive elements. One might borrow Veblen's resounding
formula and label this the Technique of Conspicuous Irrelevance.
The irrelevance is so very conspicuous that it ought to make us
suspect the poet is more than merely clumsy or naïve. His technique
manifests itself with extraordinary consistency in the poem's smallest
details as in its larger movements. In any analogical relation such as
that between Image A and Idea B, Spenser is likely to exploit the
differences between the two. A reader desirous of clear translation
finds this disturbing, and a reader seeking meaningful complexity
may find it capricious, a vestige of the archaic Renaissance pleasure-
principle.[4]

The technique of conspicuous irrelevance is the basic strategy of
Spenser's allegorical method. In order to see how it operates, it will
be best to begin with a paradigm which presents in clear, condensed,

and concrete form the larger problems to be explored: the epic simile. The analogical character of simile notably raises the problem of justifying ornamental digressions that do not contribute to the likeness of the terms compared. . . .

> Such as Diana by the sandie shore
>   Of swift Eurotas, or on Cynthus greene,
>   Where all the Nymphes have her unwares forlore,
>   Wandreth alone with bow and arrowes keene,
>   To seeke her game: Or as that famous Queene
>   Of Amazons, whom Pyrrhus did destroy,
>   The day that first of Priame she was seene,
>   Did shew her selfe in great triumphant joy,
> To succour the weake state of sad afflicted Troy. (II, 3, 31)

A comparison is expected to enhance its subject by means of resemblance, embellishment, and elucidation. The Diana image occupying the first half of this comparison fulfills these functions. The subject of our simile may begin at stanza 30 of Belphoebe's description . . . or it may begin at stanza 22. The Diana comparison could conceivably be seen as growing out of the local situation (Belphoebe as huntress flying through the woods) and then referring back to the entire description. It may begin by providing a descriptive archetype for the flying huntress-virgin, and then describe in the sharp, summary focus of a few lines the quality, the mythic Ovidian atmosphere of Belphoebe's world, and her relation to it. Both of these functions are resemblances between the subject and comparison of the simile. The local comparison is what might be called an 'ennobling detail': though she flies 'rash' through the woods, though her 'rude haires' are full of leaves, still she is like Diana and her intense concentration on the chase has an exalted precedent. The general comparison elucidates further: Belphoebe's carelessness of others, her intensity of play, though perhaps a little odd in the human world, is perfectly in keeping with Diana's mythic wood. These are the special precincts of divinity in nature, where chastity is an inherited condition and human cries mellow into birdcalls, where a vaguely icy nimbus is at once emphasized and justified by the radiant image of Diana self-concerned.

But how are we to account for the second image of the comparison? Except for the most general resemblances the image of

Penthesilea before the gates of Troy has nothing to do with stanza 30. After we have read smoothly from the flying Belphoebe to Diana, we come face to face with a most conspicuous example of irrelevance: How is one to justify the introduction of Penthesilea's death and the mention of 'the weake state of sad afflicted Troy', neither of which adds in any way to our image of Belphoebe? If the simile begins by presenting a real likeness in Diana, the second statement of likeness is purely formal. It uses the rhetorical formula 'Belphoebe is like Penthesilea' to show that Penthesilea is unlike Belphoebe. Can one make sense of this inconsistency, or ascribe it to anything more than an indiscriminate knack for ornamental elaboration?

A clue to the problem may be found in the relation between the simile and its sources. Spenser closely copies his Diana from a familiar image in Book i of the *Aeneid* – so closely, in fact, that the source becomes an allusion. The prior work is to be viewed by the reader not merely as a historical source, material available to the needs of the historical author, but as a work which the poet points to for functional purposes affecting and revealed by his poem. Virgil's image is itself a comparison applied to Dido joyfully leading the Tyrian youth toward the temple, *instans operi regnisque futuris:*

> qualis in Eurotae ripis aut per iuga Cynthi
> exercet Diana choros, quam mille secutae
> hinc atque hinc glomerantur Oreades; illa pharetram
> fert umero gradiensque deas supereminet omnis . . . (i, 498)

Spenser's changes provide a good index of the specific effect he was seeking: *exercet* and *supereminet* are abandoned, and with them the nymphs. But the nymphs are not neglected by the poet; they are inserted as if to remind the reader that Belphoebe's Diana, quite unlike Dido's, has forgotten her nymphs. There was in Virgil's Diana a certain sense of her own majesty comparable to Spenser's Penthesilea: *supereminet* supplied this, and *gradiens*, which suggests a measured pace. But this choric quality has entirely disappeared along with the self-consciousness. By virtually pointing to Dido's Diana, Spenser reminds us of a quality temporarily withheld from his Diana, and thus from Belphoebe: a certain social feeling, a responsibility for the group she leads, and even something else which hovers vaguely over the comparison – unlike Dido, Belphoebe has no need to be concerned about justice, about the building of a future state, about anything but the fine sylvan present. It was just this kind of joy which Virgil illustrated by his comparison; it is just this kind of joy which Spenser shows as missing by his comparison. But if this seems to overburden the text before us, let us move on to Penthesilea.

Immediately before the Dido–Diana simile, Virgil had described Penthesilea, one of the *picturae inanes* seen by Aeneas on the walls of Dido's unfinished temple to Juno:

> ducit Amazonidum lunatis agmina peltis
> Penthesilea furens mediisque in milibus ardet,
> aurea subnectens exsertae cingula mammae,
> bellatrix, audetque viris concurrere virgo. [I, 490]

The proximity of the passages in the *Aeneid* would lead one to suspect that Spenser merely went from one to the other, using the Amazon figure more freely. But the details of his Penthesilea not only differ from Virgil's, they resemble another source. 'Did shew her selfe in great triumphant joy' might be taken as a transformation of 'bellatrix, audetque viris concurrere virgo': the uplift in morale provided by the warrior queen and her splendid ranks and the fact that she, a woman, defies men both contribute to the idea of self-display and 'triumphant joy'. Let us note, however, that if Spenser is trying to suggest a likeness to Belphoebe in terms of self-display and triumphant joy, he does so by a totally inapplicable example: Penthesilea, like Dido, is concerned over a particular human situation, over future as well as present glory. Belphoebe is intent on hunting.

The odd details about Penthesilea seem to come from Caxton's translation, the *Recuyell of the Historyes of Troye*. The main correspondences are to be found in three passages, the first of which is a chapter heading:

How the quene panthasile cam from Amazonne with a thousand maydens *to the socoure of troye*/ And how she bare her vayllyantly/ And slewe many grekis/ And after was she slayn by pyrrus the sone of Achilles.

she wente theder . . . for the loue of hector / And whan she was comen & knewe that he was ded he made grete sorowe/ and praid to the kyng pryant that he wold late her yssue out to the bataill ayenst the grekes/ and þat *she myght shewe to hem* how her maydens coude bere armes.

And the quene panthasilee retorned in to the cyte *wyth grete glorye*/ where

the kyng pryant resceyuyd her *with grete Ioye/* and gaf her many fayr Iewellis
& ryche/ And hym semed well that she shold avenge hym of his sorowes/[5]

[Italics mine.]

Let us note here some of the salient differences: Penthesilea came
'for the loue of hector', and this motive is not transferable to
Belphoebe or Diana. Where Spenser has overtly separated Belphoebe
and Diana from the conventional retinues, he merely says of
Penthesilea that she 'did shew her selfe'; one need not exclude her
army, and in fact a reader familiar either with the source or more
obviously the legend will assume an army. If in terms of the Diana
comparison Penthesilea seems much more self-conscious, in terms of
the source that greater self-consciousness is synecdochal: the queen's
self includes the army of maidens, the power and responsibility,
which are part of her queenly substance.

We may well ask why, when he had Virgil's Penthesilea to hand,
Spenser inserts details from another source which are irrelevant to
the resemblance under consideration. The problem of the poet's
states of mind and intentions is not of interest here; whether this
was a deliberate insertion or merely some accidental fusion of the
two sources in his mind is a question of no importance. We are
trying to find out something else: Is there a reason in the poem for
the echoes – and close echoes, too – of Caxton? If at this point we
recall the structure of Canto 10, the contrast between Arthur's
realistic and Guyon's romantic chronicles, between history and
myth; if we further recall the meaning of Spenser's Britain as related
to its ruler Elizabeth; and if we remember that Spenser links
Elizabeth to Belphoebe in his Letter to Raleigh; then the details
from Caxton may take on at least some remote relevance to the
general problems of Book II. The simile likens Belphoebe not only
to her fabulous counterpart, the chaste and withdrawn Diana, but
also to a mortal queen committed to history, impelled by passion,
and killed in war. If the Penthesilean image is inconsistent, it works
to suggest a direct contrast whose meaning is sustained by the
general structure of the poem.

Whereas the Diana image focuses on a distinctly nonhistorical
quality which characterizes Belphoebe and her world, the Penthesilea image evokes the context of history (or quasi-history which,
from the stand-point of meaning and effect, amounts to the same
thing). If both Diana and Penthesilea are mythological, only Diana

points to a certain 'mythicness': to Ovidian nature, to the recurrent act of hunting with its natural associations, to the personification of cosmic forces which mark the seasonal order of physis. The Penthesilea details point to a specific incident of a historical type, they invoke human war – a particular human war – and the vicissitudes of mortal men, the precarious character of history whose every act is new, a voyaging out from the secure circle of seasons. In this sense, Belphoebe and Penthesilea are significantly different. Though both show themselves with joy, the former is not fighting for others, not risking her life, not venturing out – not even capable of venturing out – to an embattled humanity. The reference in the simile to what she does not do serves to reinforce our impression of what she is. We are more impressed by the fact that she belongs to the woods and is by nature withdrawn from the cares of history and politics. The full meaning of her chastity is suggested to us in all the metaphysical radiance which no human exhortation can disturb.

The details from Caxton point to the mortality which the bright image of Belphoebe makes us momentarily forget: 'whom Pyrrhus did destroy' and 'To succour the weake state of sad afflicted Troy'. The picture of Penthesilea's ironic joy (an exemplum of the Fall of Princes) is in fact a close parallel to the situation of Dido excluded from Spenser's Diana. Both Dido and Penthesilea came to succour Troy. Both appeared full of the joy of a fair morning. Yet the one was overcome by desire and the other by 'pride of life'. Something of Fortune's fickleness is revealed here, and something of the need to withstand Fortune which is the chief note of Seneca's epistles. Belphoebe, by contrast, is immune. She will not be changed by life. She need only sport in the woods and Fortune cannot be her foe.

The apparently irrelevant reference to death and war throws into high relief the mythical nature of Belphoebe (Ovidian goddess, queenly virgin, sonneteer's ideal) and eases us back to reality. Like the British chronicle in Canto 10 it insinuates the perspective of mortal existence into the dramatic tissues of the poem. The 'weake state of sad afflicted Troy' recalls a more general theme which the hero and his Palmer articulate in discussing the miserable condition of those they encounter: what amounts to 'the weake state of sad afflicted man'. We move from Penthesilea's death to 'sad afflicted Troy' to 'hartlesse Trompart' (tied to 'Troy' by alliteration) in the next stanza, 'dismayed in his coward mind'. These are the faces of mortality. Without detracting from her positive virtues – without at all changing his explicitly worshipful stance as poetic speaker – the poet has placed the image of Belphoebe in perspective.

If the above account is valid, it may be seen that the digressive details serve to complicate the comparison, projecting a rich awareness, a comprehensive attitude toward life that refracts the poem's central issues onto the image of Belphoebe. The subject and comparison of a simile are seldom completely homologous; digressive elements are therefore part of its standard equipment. In a simile badly used the digression becomes meaningless, an example of 'relief', 'pleasing incongruity', or some other mode of ornament. But when the possibilities of the figure are realized it seems willful to read through the comparison as if it were transparent, an easy one-way path to the subject. The comparison has a certain opacity, a specific character, which holds it apart from the subject so that we must consider both at once:

in understanding imaginative metaphor we are often required to consider not how B (vehicle) explains A (tenor) but what meanings are generated when A and B are confronted or seen each in the light of the other. The emphasis may be on likeness or on the opposite, a kind of antithesis or repugnance . . . but in any case a co-presence of likeness and difference is necessary for the indefinite radiations of meaning, the solidity and concreteness, for which metaphor is prized.[6]

The subject is of course predominant – our simile is about Belphoebe, not Penthesilea. But the meaning of Belphoebe is quite different if we consider only the fable image and such details of the comparison as fall under the category of likeness (details that sharpen or visualize or 'ennoble' some aspect of the fable – Penthesilea's self-consciousness, for example, which will be considered in the next chapter).

The structure of the epic simile is in many ways a miniature of that which characterizes Spenserian allegory. In both cases it is possible but not desirable to collapse vehicle into tenor, ignoring the differences and completely identifying the tenor – the argument – with the simile's subject or the allegorical idea. In both cases it seems better to assume that two different perspectives on the poetic subject confront each other, momentarily demand equal consideration, and by remaining thus distinct focus a new light on the subject. The principle of analogy underlying this relationship in its various permutations (whether in simile, description, canto, allegory, or poem) is quite familiar:

in all imitation two elements must coexist, and not only coexist, but must be perceived as coexisting. These two constituent elements are likeness and unlikeness, or sameness and difference, and in all genuine creations of art there must be a union of these disparates. The artist may take his point of view where he pleases, provided that . . . there be likeness in the difference, difference in the likeness, and a reconcilement of both in one.[7] . . .

. . . The very form of a simile grammatically reflects the logic in terms of which those concrete objects are related: the categories of likeness and difference have been invoked, we are reminded that the fable image is the subject of the simile, we know that the comparison discursively embodies the poet's intention to modify the subject. Furthermore, the selection of words, their echoes in sound and meaning affect our response to the related images of the simile. The sound pattern of the Diana passage, for example, reinforces the idea of speed which the image conveys. The irony in the Amazon image is pointed by the Pyrrhus–Priam alliteration, the destroy–joy rhyme. The suggestions, placement, and reference of the word 'unwares' (Diana by Eurotas 'Where all the nymphs have her unwares forlore') imply a great deal about the Diana in the image. The sheer amount of 'space' or 'time' devoted to the comparison – one stanza – and the fact that each image occupies exactly half a stanza may also affect our response to the simile. The subjects of simile and poem are, in the final analysis, not merely the things to which the words refer, but the things altered and illuminated by verbal functions other than reference:

Poetic symbols . . . call attention to themselves as symbols and in themselves invite evaluation. What may seem stranger is that the verbal symbol in calling attention to itself must also call attention to the difference between itself and the reality which it resembles and symbolizes. . . . In most discourse we look right through this disparity. There is one-way transparent intellectual reference. But poetry by thickening the medium increases the disparity between itself and its referents. Iconicity enforces disparity.[8]

The image of Penthesilea at the gates of Troy does not make vivid the image of Belphoebe running through the woods. It is conspicuously digressive but it is irrelevant only if we take the subject, the narrative of physical persons and events, to be the poem's sole focus of dramatic attention. In the novel, and in the dramatic medium, this is indeed the predominant factor, and meaning is more directly a function of the denoted world and its inhabitants. But the epic poem is closer to the lyric (in which the poetic experience is centered in the speaker's own soul) because its subject is more explicitly transformed by the narrative speaker. Stephen Dedalus' pronouncement, though characteristically florid, is not unjust:

The simplest epical form is seen emerging out of lyrical literature when the artist prolongs and broods upon himself as the centre of an epical event and this form progresses till the centre of emotional gravity is equidistant from the artist himself and from others. The narrative is no longer purely personal. The personality of the artist passes into the narration itself, flowing round and round the persons and the action like a vital sea. . . .[9]

Stephen's quasi-genetic terms are confusing, but we may easily turn his self-absorbed statement to our uses by converting his 'artist' to the fictitious speaker, the poet-personality 'created' by the poem's style and structure. In the phrase 'the centre of emotional gravity is equidistant from the artist himself and from others', we may assume 'others' to mean the characters and events of the poem's world.

The term 'epic simile' is symptomatic of this relationship. It suggests a greater weight on the figurative side, an increase of details that belong, not to the world of the fable, but to the speaker's interpretation of that world. This analogical relationship between fable and commentary involves aspects of allegory other than those illustrated by simile. If we recall the terms used by Spingarn in the opening statement – fable and allegory – we may now feel them inadequate to comprehend the character of Spenser's poem. Image and idea are mutually exclusive concepts. They refer to sensory and mental objects with fairly determinate meanings which words only reflect. A critical attitude that limits itself to puzzling out the connections between them seems certain to respond in a divisive way. The structure of epic simile suggests that a third, more inclusive concept is required to incorporate and so unify fable and allegory.

We have seen, in the third and fourth chapters for example, how fable is altered by allegory: Alma's castle and the chronicles have allegorical functions as parts and operations of the hero's soul. It is our understanding of these functions which makes us see more deeply into Guyon's being and meaning. In like manner, the com-

parison of a simile throws light on the subject in the fable. Allegory
and comparison are both poetic techniques whereby the subject of
the poem – the adventure of Sir Guyon – is illuminated; there are
of course other techniques. But the point to be emphasized here is
that all these techniques work by exploiting the resources of the
linguistic medium.

SOURCE: extracts from *The Allegorical Temper: Vision and
Reality in Book II of Spenser's 'Faerie Queene'* (New Haven, Conn.,
1957; reprinted by Archon Books, 1967) pp. 120–32.

NOTES

1. J. E. Spingarn, *Literary Criticism in the Renaissance* (New York, 1899) pp.
277–8.
2. For convenience I shall consider the various allegorical levels – ethical,
political, historical, theological – to be one, qualitatively distinct from the
level of concrete representation.
3. E. A. Bloom, 'The Allegorical Principle', *English Literary History*, XVIII
(1951) 164. This is an excellent historical survey of the pronouncements on
allegory, concise, informative and comprehensive.
4. Some critics have emphasised the fable as revealing, others as concealing
the allegory. Some, that is, have stressed the elements of similarity, others
the obscuring elements of dissimilarity. This double relation (likeness and
difference) of terms analogically joined has always been implicitly recognised
by allegorical critics. See Bloom, 174 ff.
5. *The Recuyell of the Historyes of Troye,* ed., H. Osker Sommer, written in
French by Raoul Lefevre, translated and printed by William Caxton, *c.*
1474 (London, 1894) 2, pp. 644 ff.
6. W. K. Wimsatt Jr, *The Verbal Icon* (Lexington, Kentucky, 1954) p. 127.
7. Samuel T. Coleridge, 'On Poesy or Art', *Biographica Literaria*, ed. J.
Shawcross (London, 1907) 2, p. 256.
8. Wimsatt, p. 217.
9. James Joyce, *Portrait of the Artist as a Young Man* (New York edn cited,
1928) p. 252.

PART THREE

General Twentieth-century Studies

C. S. Lewis

'TO READ HIM IS TO GROW IN MENTAL HEALTH' (1936)

What lies immediately below the surface of the Italian epic is simply the actual – the daily life of travel, war, or gallantry in the Mediterranean world. I am not referring to those stories of the *novello* type in which the actual appears without disguise, but to the *Innamorato* and *Furioso* as a whole. Thus Agramant's war with the Franks is, on the surface, purely fantastic, and the prowess of its combatants impossible; but beneath all this we detect the familiar lineaments of a real war. There are problems of transport and lines of communication. Defeat for the invader means falling back on cities already taken. The divergent interests of allies show themselves in the councils of war. The real defeat of Agramant is plainly due not to the knightly deeds before Paris but to Astulph's blow in a different, and remote, theatre. The whole story could be plausibly re-written in headlines or generals' memoirs. When we leave the war for subordinate adventures we find the same thing. Knights may be sailing to fabulous cities of the Amazons or to the dens of ogres, but the squalls and the seamanship are those of the real Mediterranean, and so are the pirates, the brigands, the inn-keepers, the 'lousy' coloured troops (*pidocchiosi*) and all that mass of rascality which unites the romantic epic, so closely in places, to the picaresque novel. Even the loves of Roger and Bradamant have a solid background of family life and parental matchmaking: it is part of the beauty of Bradamant's character that besides being the sternest knight that ever struck with sword she is the dutifullest daughter that ever cried for an ineligible lover. Thus, in the Italians the fantastic is attached at a hundred points to the real and even to the commonplace; nothing is in the air. Even Astulph's cruises on the hippogryph are controlled by continual reference to the most recent and reliable geographers. All this lies, so to speak, an inch below the surface. But if we scratch deeper

we shall find a third layer and another sort of actuality; we shall find
below this realism, and far below the surface fantasy, the faint yet
quite decipherable traces of the original legend – the theme of the
chansons de geste, the old 'world's debate' of cross and crescent. The
presence of this theme, which the poets can suppress and revive at
will, is used to supply gravity when gravity is desired. We can always
be reminded that Roland is a senator and Charlemain the champion
of Christendom. This theme dictates that the 'machines' of the poems
should be God and His Angels instead of classical deities; it lends a
force which would otherwise be lacking to the death of Isabella or the
assault on Paris.

Such is the Italian epic: in the foreground we have fantastic
adventure, in the middle distance daily life, in the background a
venerable legend with a core of momentous historical truth. There
is no reason why the English poem should not have been much more
like this than it actually is, if Spenser had chosen. Arthur's wars
with the Saxons could have been worked up just as Boiardo and
Ariosto had worked up Charlemain's wars with the Saracens. The
scene of the poem could have been laid in Britain and a real topo-
graphy (as in the Italians) could have been used at every turn. But
Spenser keeps his Arthurian lore for occasional digressions and
detaches his Prince Arthur from Saxons, from Guinevere, Gawain,
and Launcelot, even from Sir Ector. There is no *situation* in *The
Faerie Queene*, no when nor where. Ariosto begins with a situation –
Roland's return from the East and Agramant's invasion of France.
The Faerie Queene begins quite differently. A knight and a lady ride
across our field of vision. We do not know where they are, nor in
what period; the poet's whole energy is devoted to telling us what
they look like. Ariosto begins like a man telling us, very well and
clearly, a series of events which he has heard: Spenser begins like a
man in a trance, or a man looking through a window, telling us what
he sees. And however deep we dig in Spenser we shall never get to
a situation, and never find a context in the objective world for the
shapes he is going to show us.

But this does not mean that he is all surface. He, too, has his lower
levels, though they are much harder to describe than those of the
Italians. In one sense, of course, we know already what they are
going to be: Spenser has allegorized the romantic epic (that is the
only formal novelty of his work) and what lies below the surface of

his poem will therefore be something subjective and immaterial. But, for the moment, it will be better to proceed inductively – to notice what lies beneath his poetry from moment to moment without yet inquiring into his 'continued' allegory.

Let us return to the Knight and the Lady in the opening stanzas. The knight has a red cross on a silver shield; the lady is leading a lamb. The lamb has puzzled many readers; but we now know that it had a real function in earlier versions of the legend of St. George, and (what is much more important) we know that the lady was commonly represented leading her lamb in the pageants of St. George and the dragon. In other words, the two figures which meet us at the beginning of *The Faerie Queene* were instantly recognized by Spenser's first readers, and were clothed for them not in literary or courtly associations, but in popular, homely, patriotic associations. They spoke immediately to what was most universal and childlike in gentle and simple alike. This at once suggests an aspect of Spenser's poetry which it will be fatal for us to neglect, and which is abundantly illustrated in the First Book. The angels who sing at Una's wedding probably come from the same pageant source as the lamb. The well in which St. George is refreshed during his fight with the dragon comes from *Bevis of Southampton*. The whole similarity between his allegory and that of Bunyan, which has exercised many scholars, is best explained by the fact that they have a common source – the old-fashioned sermon in the village church still continuing the allegorical tradition of the medieval pulpit. Innumerable details come from the Bible, and specially from those books of the Bible which have meant much to Protestantism – the Pauline epistles and the Revelation. His anti-papal allegories strike the very note of popular, even of rustic, Protestant aversion; they can be understood and enjoyed by the modern reader (whatever his religion) only if he remembers that Roman Catholicism was in Spenser's day simply the most potent contemporary symbol for something much more primitive – the sheer Bogey, who often changes his name but never wholly retires from the popular mind. Foxe's *Book of Martyrs* was in every one's hands; horrible stories of the Inquisition and the galleys came from overseas; and every nervous child must have heard tales of a panel slid back at twilight in a seeming innocent manor house to reveal the pale face and thin, black body of a Jesuit. The ghosts crying from beneath the altar in Orgoglio's chapel and the mystery of

iniquity beneath that other altar of Gerioneo are accurate embodiments of popular contemporary horror at these things. Gerioneo
himself, who

> Laught so loud that all his teeth wide bare
> One might have seene enraunged disorderly
> Like to a rancke of piles that pitched are awry
>
> (v, 11, 9)

is the genuine raw-head and bloody-bones of our remembered night
nurseries. A dragon's mouth is the 'griesly mouth of hell' as in medieval drama (1, 11, 12). Mammon is the gold-hoarding earthman of
immemorial tradition, the gnome. The witcheries of Duessa, when
she rides in Night's chariot and 'hungry wolves continually did
howle' (1, 5, 30), or of the hag with whom Florimel guested, are
almost incomparably closer to the world of real superstition than any
of the Italian enchantments. We have long looked for the origins
of *The Faerie Queene* in Renaissance palaces and Platonic academies,
and forgotten that it has humbler origins of at least equal importance
in the Lord Mayor's show, the chap-book, the bedtime story, the
family Bible, and the village church. What lies next beneath the
surface in Spenser's poem is the world of popular imagination:
almost, a popular mythology.

And this world is not called up, as Ariosto may call up a fragment
of folk lore, in order to amuse us. On the contrary, it is used for the
sake of something yet deeper which it brings up with it and which is
Spenser's real concern; the primitive or instinctive mind, with all its
terrors and ecstasies – that part in the mind of each of us which we
should never dream of showing to a man of the world like Ariosto.
Archimago and Una, in their opposite ways, are true creations of
that mind. When we first meet them we seem to have known them
long before; and so in a sense we have, but only the poet could have
clothed them for us in form and colour. The same may be said of
Despair and Malengin, of Busirane's appalling house, and of the
garden of Adonis. For all of these are translations into the visible of
feelings else blind and inarticulate; and they are translations made
with singular accuracy, with singularly little loss. The secret of this
accuracy in which, to my mind, Spenser excels nearly all poets, is
partly to be sought in his humble fidelity to the popular symbols
which he found ready made to his hand; but much more in his pro-

found sympathy with that which makes the symbols, with the fundamental tendencies of human imagination as such. Like the writers of the New Testament (to whom, in the character of his symbolism, he is the closest of all English poets) he is endlessly preoccupied with such ultimate antitheses as Light and Darkness or Life and Death. It has not often been noticed – and, indeed, save for a special purpose it ought not to be noticed – that Night is hardly even mentioned by Spenser without aversion. His story leads him to describe innumerable nightfalls, and his feeling about them is always the same:

> So soone as Night had with her pallid hew
> Defaste the beautie of the shyning skye,
> And refte from men the worldes desired vew – (III, 2, 28)

or,

> whenas chearelesse Night ycovered had
> Fayre heaven with an universall cloud,
> That every wight dismayed with darkenes sad –
>
> (III, 12, 1)

or, again,

> when as daies faire shinie-beame, yclowded
> With fearefull shadowes of deformed night,
> Warnd man and beast in quiet rest be shrowded –
>
> (V, 4, 45)

And, answering to this, in his descriptions of morning we have a never failing rapture: mere light is as sweet to Spenser as if it were a new creation. Such passages are too numerous and too widely scattered (often at unimportant places in the story) to be the result of any conscious plan: they are spontaneous and the better proof of the flawless health, the paradisal naïveté, of his imagination. They form a background, hardly noticed at a first reading, to those great passages where the conflict of light and dark becomes explicit. Such is the sleepless night of Prince Arthur in the third book, where the old description of lover's insomnia is heightened and spiritualized into a 'statement' (as the musicians say) of one of Spenser's main themes;

> Dayes dearest children be the blessed seed
> Which darknesse shall subdue and heaven win:
> Truth is his daughter; he her first did breed
> Most sacred virgin without spot of sinne.   (III, 4, 59)

It is no accident that Truth, or Una, should be mentioned here, for she is indeed the daughter of Light, and through the whole First Book runs the antithesis between her father as emperor of the East and Duessa as queen of the West – a conception possibly borrowed from *Reason and Sensuality* – and in the Fifth canto of that book we meet Night face to face. The contrast between her 'visage deadly sad' as she comes forth from her 'darksome mew' and Duessa

> sunny bright
> Adornd with gold and jewels shining cleare,   (I, 5, 21)

(though Duessa is but pretended, reflected light!) is, of course, a familiar example of that pictorial quality which critics have often praised in Spenser – but praised without a full understanding of those very unpictorial, unpicturable, depths from which it rises. Spenser is no dilettante, and has a low opinion of the painter's art as compared with his own (III, Pr., 2). He is not playing mere tricks with light and shade; and few speeches in our poetry are more serious than Night's sad sentence (the very accent of a creature *dréame bedǽled*)

> The sonnes of Day he favoureth, I see   (I, 5, 25)

And yet it is characteristic of him that the constant pressure of this day and night antithesis on his imagination never tempts him into dualism. He is impressed, more perhaps than any other poet, with the conflict of two mighty opposites – aware that our world is dualistic for all practical purposes, dualistic in all but the very last resort: but from the final heresy he abstains, drawing back from the verge of dualism to remind us by delicate allegories that though the conflict seems ultimate yet one of the opposites really contains, and is not contained by, the other. Truth and falsehood are opposed; but truth is the norm not of truth only but of falsehood also. That is why we find that Una's father, King of the East and enemy of the West, is yet *de jure* King of the West as well as of the East. That is why Love and Hatred, whom the poet borrows no doubt from Empedocles, are opposites but not, as in Empedocles, mere opposites: they are both the sons of Concord. And that, again, in the passage we were discussing, is why Aesculapius, a creature of Night's party, asks Night the formidable question,

> Can Night defray
> The wrath of thundring Jove that rules both night and day?
>
> (I, 5, 42)

The other antithesis – that of Life and Death, or, in its inferior degrees, of Health and Sickness – enables Spenser to avoid the insipidity of representing good as arbitrary law and evil as spontaneity. His evils are all dead or dying things. Each of his deadly sins has a mortal disease. Aesculapius sits in the bowels of the earth endlessly seeking remedies for an incurable fever (I, 5, 40). Archimago makes Guyon 'the object of his spight, and *deadly food*' (II, 1, 3). Despair is an immortal suicide I, 9, 54), Malbecco lives transfixed with 'deathes eternall dart' III, 10, 59). The porter of the garden of intemperance, the evil genius, is the *foe of life* (II, 12, 48), and so are the violent passions, red-headed and adust, who attack Guyon in the earlier stages of his pilgrimage (II, 6, 1). Over against these mortal shapes are set forces of life and health and fecundity. St. George, in combat with the beast who

> was deadly made
> And al that life preserved did detest (I, 11, 49)

is refreshed with water from the well of life and saved by the shadow of the tree of life. Babies cluster at Charissa's breasts (I, 10, 30): Belphoebe's *lilly handës twaine* crush virtuous herbs for the healing of wounds (III, 5, 33): in the garden of Adonis,

> Ne needs there Gardiner to sett or sow,
> To plant or prune: for of their owne accord
> All things, as they created were, doe grow,
> And yet remember well the mighty word
> Which first was spoken by th' Almighty Lord,
> That bad them to increase and multiply. (III, 6, 34)

– and throughout the whole garden 'franckly each paramor his leman knowes' (III, 6, 41). The love of Britomart is enobled by prophecies of famous offspring. The poem is full of marriages. Una's

face unveiled shines 'as the great eye of heaven' (I, 3, 4), and
Cambina carries a cup of Nepenthe (IV, 3, 43). The whole shining
company of Spenser's vital shapes make up such a picture of 'life's
golden tree' that it is difficult not to fancy that our bodily, no less
than our mental, health is refreshed by reading him. . . .

My claim for Spenser may take the form of the old eulogy – *totam
vitae imaginem expressit*; but perhaps my meaning will be clearer if
we omit the word *totam*, if we say simply *vitae imaginem*. Certainly
this will help to clear up a common misunderstanding. People find
a 'likeness' or 'truth' to life in Shakespeare because the persons,
passions and events which we meet in his plays are like those which
we meet in our own lives: he excels, in fact, in what the old critics
called 'nature', or the probable. When they find nothing of the sort
in Spenser, they are apt to conclude that he has nothing to do with
'life' – that he writes that poetry of escape or recreation which (for
some reason or other) is so intensely hated at present. But they do not
notice that *The Faerie Queene* is 'like life' in a different sense, in a
much more literal sense. When I say that it is like life, I do not mean
that the places and people in it are like those which life produces. I
mean precisely what I say – that it is like life itself, not like the
products of life. It is an image of the *natura naturans*, not of the *natura
naturata*. The things we read about in it are not like life, but the
experience of reading it is like living. The clashing antitheses which
meet and resolve themselves into higher unities, the lights streaming
out from the great allegorical *foci* to turn into a hundred different
colours as they reach the lower levels of complex adventure, the
adventures gathering themselves together and revealing their true
nature as we draw near the *foci*, the constant re-appearance of
certain basic ideas, which transform themselves without end and
yet ever remain the same (eterne in mutability), the unwearied
variety and seamless continuity of the whole – all this is Spenser's
true likeness to life. It is this which gives us, while we read him, a
sensation akin to that which Hegelians are said to get from Hegel –
a feeling that we have before us not so much an image as a sublime
instance of the universal process – that this is not so much a poet
writing about the fundamental forms of life as those forms themselves
spontaneously displaying their activities to us through the imagination of a poet. The invocation of the Muse hardly seems to be a
convention in Spenser. We feel that his poetry has really tapped

sources not easily accessible to discursive thought. He makes imaginable inner realities so vast and simple that they ordinarily escape us as the largely printed names of continents escape us on the map – too big for our notice, too visible for sight. Milton has well selected wisdom as his peculiar excellence – wisdom of that kind which rarely penetrates into literature because it exists most often in inarticulate people. It is this that has kept children and poets true to him for three centuries, while the intellectuals (on whom the office of criticism naturally devolves) have been baffled even to irritation by a spell which they could not explain. To our own troubled and inquiring age this wisdom will perhaps show its most welcome aspect in the complete integration, the harmony, of Spenser's mind. His work is one, like a growing thing, a tree; like the world-ash-tree itself, with branches reaching to heaven and roots to hell. It reaches up to the songs of angels or the vision of the New Jerusalem and admits among its shining ones the veiled image of God Himself: it reaches down to the horror of fertile chaos beneath the Garden of Adonis and to the grotesque satyrs who protect Una or debauch Hellenore with equal truth to their nature. And between these two extremes comes all the multiplicity of human life, transmuted but not falsified by the conventions of chivalrous romance. The 'great golden chain of Concord' has united the whole of his world. What he feels on one level, he feels on all. When the good and fair appear to him, the whole man responds; the satyrs gambol, the lances splinter, the shining ones rise up. There is a place for everything and everything is in its place. Nothing is repressed; nothing is insubordinate. To read him is to grow in mental health. . . .

SOURCE: extracts from *The Allegory of Love* (Oxford, 1936) pp. 308–16, 357–9.

A. C. Hamilton

THE *ARCHITECTONIKE* OF THE POEM (1961)

The relation of Books I and II to the theme of man's fall becomes more explicit when each knight falls into the power of his enemies. Guyon's fall which heralds the coming of Arthur parallels the same mid-point of the narrative in Book I where the Red Cross Knight whose powers are similarly weakened also falls to the ground and is imprisoned until he is rescued by Arthur. As Una is the means by which Arthur intercedes for the Red Cross Knight, the Palmer is the means by which Arthur pledges to aid Guyon. Afterwards the knight praises Una as one 'whose wondrous faith, exceeding earthly race, / Was firmest fixt in mine extremest case', even as Guyon joys to see the Palmer: 'firme is thy faith, whom daunger neuer fro me drew' (I, 9, 17; II, 8, 53). More important, however, is the significant contrast which the parallel provides. After his fall to the ground, the Red Cross Knight, being 'disarmd, disgrast, and inwardly dismayde' (I, 7, 11), suffers a second fall into Orgoglio's dungeon where 'all his vitall powres / Decayd, and all his flesh shronk vp like withered flowres' (I, 8, 41). Since he undergoes spiritual death, Arthur faces a double task: first, to slay Orgoglio, and then to descend into the dungeon. Guyon, however, is only 'dead seeming': his death-like trance renders allegorically an event that happens literally in Book I, as far as the conventions of romance allow. Being so dominated by the affections, he too needs grace: 'for every man with his affects is born, / Not by might master'd, but by special grace.'[1] His foes are prevented by Arthur from disarming and disgracing his fallen body; accordingly, when they are slain, he 'from his traunce awakt, / Life hauing maistered her sencelesse foe.'

Arthur's roles in Book I as the instrument of divine grace, and in Book II as the symbol of magnanimity, appear so different that he has been considered two distinct persons. Yet the parallel between his two roles shows them to be compatible in one person. We have seen how his rescue of the knight in Book I imitates Christ's harrowing of hell. In Book II Spenser uses the same analogue though in terms appropriate to the argument. We see Arthur claim Guyon's fallen body from the Satanic forces represented by Pyrochles and Cymochles. Against the enemies who seek in their wrath to inflict punishment for sin, he sues for pardon. In the debate which follows he is called Guyon's 'dayes-man' (II, 8, 28): such was sought by Job to mediate between him and God's wrath. He suffers the symbolic wound in the right side, 'wyde was the wound, and a large lukewarme flood, / Red as the Rose, thence gushed grieuously' (II, 8, 39). Finally he slays his foes, and like Christ, claims man's body in the name of Mercy.

Spenser contrasts the scope of each book at certain key points. In Canto 10 of the first book where the opening stanza sums its argument, the final lines provide a formula for the whole book: 'if any strength we haue, it is to ill, / But all the good is Gods, both power and eke will.' The first line summarizes the knight's moral history during the first half of the book; the second prepares for the second half where the knight under Una is continually sustained by grace until he wields the power to slay the Dragon. 'All the good is Gods', as later in Book II he bears witness: 'his be the praise, that this atchieu'ment wrought, / Who made my hand the organ of his might; / More then goodwill to me attribute nought' (II, 1, 33). Until this final adventure, he remains the prostrate figure over whom the cosmic forces of light and darkness, represented in Una and Duessa, battle to possess him. In Book II the two opening stanzas of Canto 11 sum its argument:

> What warre so cruell, or what siege so sore,
>   As that, which strong affections do apply
>   Against the fort of reason euermore
>   To bring the soule into captiuitie:
>   Their force is fiercer through infirmitie
>   Of the fraile flesh, relenting to their rage,
>   And exercise most bitter tyranny
>   Vpon the parts, brought into their bondage:
> No wretchednesse is like to sinfull vellenage.

But in a body, which doth freely yeeld
  His partes to reasons rule obedient,
  And letteth her that ought the scepter weeld,
  All happy peace and goodly gouernment
  Is setled there in sure establishment;
  There *Alma* like a virgin Queene most bright,
  Doth florish in all beautie excellent:
  And to her guestes doth bounteous banket dight,
Attempred goodly well for health and for delight.

The first stanza repeats the argument of Book I in moral terms, that
is, the weakness of human nature; but the second declares the
strength of the temperate body. Together they assert the power and
limitations of natural virtue. Since Guyon manifests its power
throughout his journey, he 'euermore himselfe with comfort feedes,
/ Of his owne vertues, and prayse-worthy deedes' (II, 7, 2). When he
sees the damned in Proserpina's garden, he lectures them upon their
folly. But the Red Cross Knight whose only strength is to do ill
despairs at the memory of 'his deformed crimes, / That all his manly
powres it did disperse' (I, 9, 48). And when he sees the damned
suffering in hell, he sees himself as one of them. But Guyon's display
of the power of natural virtue reveals at the same time its limitations.
In meeting his enemies, he cannot slay Furor and Disdain; and
though he may subdue Pyrochles and Cymochles, he is prevented
in the name of temperance from slaying them. Moreover, though
the temperate body may resist temptation, it cannot defeat its
besiegers. The image of the besieged body given in the first stanza
above is the unifying metaphor of the book. It is expressed in Mortdant and Amavia whose 'raging passion with fierce tyrannie / Robs
reason of her due regalitie' (II, 1, 57), in Medina surrounded by her
two sisters with their warring suitors, in Phedon whose strong affections 'cruell battry bend / Gainst fort of Reason, it to ouerthrow'
(II, 4, 34), and culminates in the first half of the book with the image
of Pyrochles and Cymochles ready to despoil Guyon's senseless
body. The full limitation of natural virtue is seen when Guyon falls,
and Arthur must come to rescue him. For though the temperate
body is strong, being continually besieged, it stands only by the
power of grace.

The significant contrast that we see between the Red Cross

Knight's fall and Guyon's, together with the contrast between their rescue by Arthur, defines the scope of each book. The senseless Red Cross Knight dominated by Orgoglio is an emblem of the total depravity of human nature, the death of the spirit. Though he undergoes spiritual death, however, he may be reborn and regenerated through God's grace and finally restored to a higher state. Guyon, prostrate upon the ground under the wrathful Pyrochles and the lustful Cymochles, is an emblem of man's body dominated by the irascible and concupiscent affections. His fall is given in moral, rather than spiritual, terms; and through Arthur's intervention he recovers his natural moral state. He remains, then, upon that natural level which the Red Cross Knight transcends. The cyclical movement of Book I, the spiritual descent and ascent, contrasts with that linear movement upon the natural level described in Book II. In the terms suggested by Professor Woodhouse, we may say that Book I moves upon the level of grace while Book II remains upon the level of nature; but it is important to add that the levels are not exclusive. Though Guyon neither shares the depths of the Red Cross Knight's descent nor rises to his heights, he is not excluded from that knight's regeneration which follows Arthur's rescue: instead, he enjoys its counterpart upon the natural level. From the parallel structure of the second half of both books, it becomes clear that Book I transcends the natural level explored in Book II by including it.

After being rescued by Arthur, each knight must realize the perfection of his own nature in three stages before completing his adventure. Guided by Una, the Red Cross Knight is first purged of sin in the house of Penance; later in the holy Hospital he is taught to frame his life in holy righteousness; and finally he ascends the hill of Contemplation where through a vision of the New Jerusalem he learns his name and nature. Thus fully prepared for his final adventure, he leaves to slay the Dragon. Guyon is not purged, for he need not learn to cherish himself; instead, 'with rare delight' he enjoys immediately the perfection of the temperate body in the castle of Alma. His delight as he moves through the castle, and his feasting, contrast sharply with the Red Cross Knight's agony in a dark lowly place where he diets with fasting until he 'had past the paines of hell, and long enduring night' (I, 10, 32). The 'goodly workmanship' of the castle of Alma, its 'wondrous frame' (II, 9, 21, 44), elaborates at

some length matter contained in Book 1, that 'wondrous workeman-
ship of Gods owne mould' (1, 10, 42) which is maintained by the
seven bead-men in the holy Hospital. In the final state of his preparation within the castle, Guyon also ascends to see a vision of

> This parts great workmanship, and wondrous powre,
> That all this other worlds worke doth excell,
> And likest is vnto that heauenly towre,
> That God hath built for his owne blessed bowre. (11, 9, 47)

What is revealed to the Red Cross Knight as his spiritual nature
appears to Guyon as his natural body. The Red Cross Knight is
taught his future state as Saint George, his present duty to aid Una,
and his past history; Guyon is shown the body's power in the three
sages who teach the future, the present, and the past. Heavenly
Contemplation teaches the Red Cross Knight his 'name and nation':
Eumnestes teaches Guyon his country's ancestry. The episodes are
clearly parallel upon different levels, the religious and the secular;
but again these levels are not exclusive. Man's spiritual nature
which is revealed in Book 1 is embodied in the second book in the
perfection of man's natural body governed by temperance and up-
held by divine grace.

The spiritual regeneration of the Red Cross Knight, that continual
casting out of sin from the time he regains Una as his guide until he
slays the Dragon, provides the pattern for Arthur's fight with
Maleger and his troops in Book 11. The parallel may help us understand the nature of this fight which has become a crux in the
allegory. While Guyon voyages to the Bower of Bliss, Arthur confronts Alma's besiegers who are described earlier as that body so
'distempred through misrule and passions bace: / It growes a
Monster, and incontinent / Doth loose his dignitie and natiue grace'
(11, 9, 1). Maleger is this Monster, the parody of man's body: 'his
bodie leane and meagre as a rake, / And skin all withered like a
dryed rooke' (11, 11, 22). The pattern for his attack upon the castle
of Alma, his counterpart, is given in Book 1 by the Red Cross Knight's
spiritual regeneration, the casting-out of his fallen self. When he
first emerges from the dungeon, he looks like Maleger with 'bare
thin cheekes . . . his rawbone armes . . . were cleane consum'd, and
all his vitall powres / Decayd, and all his flesh shronk vp like

withered flowres' (I, 8, 41), for each manifests that state of sin by
which our body is totally depraved. Awareness of his sinful state
aroused by Despair so pierces the Red Cross Knight's heart that he
seeks to pierce his heart: like Maleger, he tries 'to spoyle the Castle
of his health' (I, 9, 31). He is saved by Una who leads him to the
house of Penance where he undergoes true despair: 'prickt with
anguish of his sinnes so sore, . . . he desirde to end his wretched
dayes: / So much the dart of sinfull guilt the soule dismayes' (I, 10,
21). In the end he is purged of 'inward corruption, and infected sin'
(I, 10, 25), further instructed by the cardinal virtues and Mercy,
and assoiled by Contemplation. Finally, he is regenerated by the
three-day battle with the Dragon: twice he is cast to the ground
where he is washed in the Well of Life which can cleanse 'guilt of
sinfull crimes', and anointed by the Tree of Life which 'deadly
woundes could heale' (I, 11, 30, 48). In Book II Alma the soul is
similarly besieged by the darts of Maleger so that she was 'much
dismayed with that dreadfull sight' (II, 11, 16). She too is saved by
divine grace whose instrument is Arthur. From the parallel with
Book I we understand that Maleger is the state of sin, both actual
and original; it is that state of sin from which the Red Cross Knight
must be purged before he may slay the Dragon, and which must be
slain before Guyon may overthrow the power of Acrasia. Spenser
uses the myth of Antaeus in both books to describe the overthrow of
sin. When the Red Cross Knight falls to the ground apparently slain
but rises with greater strength, the Dragon is amazed:

> No wonder if he wondred at the sight,
> And doubted, whether his late enemy
> It were, or other new supplied knight.
> He, now to proue his late renewed might,
> High brandishing his bright deaw-burning blade.
>
> (I, 11, 35)

And on the second day when the knight arises healed of his wounds,
again the Dragon is amazed:

> When now he saw himselfe so freshly reare,
> As if late fight had nought him damnifyde,
> He woxe dismayed, and gan his fate to feare.   (52)

When Maleger is cast to the ground but rises 'much stronger then before', Arthur is amazed:

> Nigh his wits end then woxe th'amazed knight,
>   And thought his labour lost and trauell vaine,
>   Against this lifelesse shadow so to fight:
>   Yet life he saw, and felt his mightie maine,
>   That whiles he marueild still, did still him paine:
>   For thy he gan some other wayes aduize,
>   How to take life from that dead-liuing swaine,
>   Whom still he marked freshly to arize
> From th'earth, and from her wombe new spirits to reprize.
>
>   (II, II, 44)

There is no paradox in this contrast between the two books. In Book I the knight is Georgos, or Earth; and the ground upon which he falls, Eden, being watered and nourished by the Well and Tree of Life, sustains him. In Book II we see Guyon fall to the ground and rise 'with so fresh hew' once Arthur slays the affections which dominate his body; but the ground belongs to that fallen nature which perverts man because it was perverted by him at the Fall, and so sustains his enemy. Like the Dragon, Maleger is that terrifying image of the enemy whom man in his own power cannot wound or slay. As the Dragon is slain by the knight's baptized hands wielding his 'deaw-burning blade', Maleger is slain by being cast into the standing lake.

The climax to the two books where the knights arrive at the entrance to Eden offers full parallel with contrast. When the Red Cross Knight marries Una, everything serves his pleasure: the posts sprinkled with wine, the great feast, the precious perfumes, the song of love, the heavenly music of the spheres through which he was 'reft of his sences meet, / And rauished with rare impression in his sprite', and above all, Una whose glorious beauty 'his heart did seeme to melt in pleasures manifold' (I, 12, 39, 40). These pleasures are parodied in the Bower of Bliss: the wine offered by its porter, the sweet smells, the song of the rose, the earthly melody of the birds, waters, and wind, enchant man in order to enchain him in Acrasia's bower. Her beauty makes her knight 'quite molten into lust and pleasure lewd' (II, 12, 73). The heavenly music which lifts man above himself contrasts with the earthly music which binds him to his senses: the pleasures which fulfil man for further duties contrast with those which put him to sleep. The Red Cross Knight 'swimming in that sea of blisfull ioy', yet who 'nought forgot . . . vnto his Farie Queene backe to returne' (i, 12, 41), contrasts with the sleeping Verdant who forgets all honour of arms, 'but in lewd loues, and wastfull luxuree, / His dayes, his goods, his bodie he did spend' (ii, 12, 80). But the Red Cross Knight's final state is parodied earlier, and it is with this earlier state that the significance of the parallel with Book ii may be realized.

Earlier at the mid-point of his adventure, the Red Cross Knight yields all to pleasure: disarming himself, he rests by a fountainside where he feeds upon the cooling shade of the leaves 'wherein the cherefull birds of sundry kind / Do chaunt sweet musick to delight his mind.' With Duessa in this bower of 'greene boughes decking a gloomy glade', he 'bathe[s] in pleasaunce of the ioyous shade' courting Duessa 'both carelesse of his health, and of his fame'. In just such state is Verdant with the enchantress Acrasia until Guyon frees him. This parallel between the climax of Book ii and the mid-point of Book i, and the contrast between the climax of Book ii and the climax of Book i, justifies fully the elaborate paralleling of structure which the poet sets up between the two books. By destroying the Bower of Bliss, Guyon overthrows all those forces by which the Red Cross Knight falls into sin. The overpowering sloth, the carnal lust by which he yields to Duessa, the great weakness which leaves him helpless before his enemy: this terrible vision of the noble knight 'forlorne, / And left to losse', now is set against the power of virtue to release man from enshrouding nature, the womb which imprisons man upon the level of nature without possibility of rebirth. In terms of their archetypes which are present at this point, the Red Cross Knight moves toward man's final state in the Heavenly City when he will be fully restored to God, while Guyon turns back to man's original state when he entered Eve's garden and through her enchantments fell from God's grace. The apocalyptic significance of the Red Cross Knight's slaying the Dragon becomes the pattern for Guyon's release of man from imprisonment in the Garden of Eden. As the Red Cross Knight is an image of that second Adam who harrows hell to redeem mankind from Satan's power, Guyon, who runs a like race, imitates him to become a new Adam. He is one who, in Milton's phrase, 'might see and know, and yet abstain'; one who binds Eve and destroys the Garden that man may pass successfully through the world towards his final restoration.

SOURCE: extract from *The Structure of Allegory in 'The Faerie Queene'* (Oxford, 1961) pp. 98–106.

NOTE

1. Shakespeare, *Love's Labour's Lost*, 1 i 150–1.

William Nelson

THAT TRUE GLORIOUS TYPE (1963)

. . . Among the many sixteenth-century editions of Vergil's poems a considerable number are substantial folio volumes in which the text is surrounded by a sea of commentary. Commonly, such editions include the annotations of various scholars, the work of the late classical grammarians Servius and Donatus and of Renaissance humanists. Of the later commentaries that of Jodocus Badius Ascensius, otherwise Josse Bade van Assche, famous Flemish scholar and publisher, is surely one of the most frequently reprinted.

After explaining the form of the title of Vergil's poem, Badius announces its purpose as 'simul et iucunda et idonea dicere vitae'. This is the second line of that distich of Horace's *Ars poetica* which Ben Jonson translates:

> Poets would either profit or delight
> Or mixing sweet and fit, teach life the right.

The Poet, Badius declares, undertook the task of teaching 'life the right' because he knew that there could be nothing more useful to a commonwealth than to be led by a prince who was clement, prudent, brave, temperate, and endowed with the other virtues. He therefore depicted such a prince in the *Aeneid*, prophesying that he would be imitated by Augustus, just as Xenophon had portrayed a Cyrus, not exactly as he was, but as he should have been ('ut Xenophon de Cyro fecisse perhibetur, non semper qualis fuit, sed qualem fuisse decuit perscribens'). By this means he suggested to Augustus both the necessity of imitating the ancestor to whom he traced his origin, a man whom he described as most pious, just, brave, temperate, etc., and the disgrace that he would incur if he degenerated from the honorable customs and virtues of his forebears. Besides this general intention which he shares with all good writers, Badius explains, Vergil had a number of particular ones ('speciales atque peculiares'). He wished to crown his poetic career with a work in the grand manner, as he had begun it in his youth with the humble pastoral and progressed in his maturity to the middle style of the *Georgics*. And since he had equaled Theocritus in his eclogues and Hesiod in his *Georgics* he desired in his great work to equal that prince of poets and fountain of ingenuity, Homer. Indeed he overwent Homer ('illi praestare demonstrat'). What the Greek poet needed the forty-eight books of his *Odyssey* and *Iliad* to express, Vergil said in twelve. For Homer had described the contemplative life in the person of Ulysses and the active life in his account of the Trojan war, while Vergil combined them both in one, treating the former (which he signified by the word *virum* in 'arma virumque cano') in his first six books and of the latter (*arma*) in the last six books. Besides considering other 'special' intentions of the *Aeneid*, Badius summarizes the events of its story in chronological or historical order, pointing out as he does so that poetical narration follows a very different sequence. . . .

It is in terms of matter and emphasis that Spenser's letter shows itself to be modeled after the kind of introductory essay that is found in sixteenth-century editions of the *Aeneid*. As Vergil's intention is said to be the portrayal of a virtuous prince, so Spenser begins by asserting his purpose 'to fashion a gentleman or noble person in vertuous and gentle discipline'. For the fabulous Aeneas Spenser offers Arthur 'before he was king'. Arthur cannot serve as a figure for Elizabeth, as Aeneas for Augustus, but Spenser explains that she is 'shadowed' in Arthur's beloved Gloriana and in Belphoebe. If Vergil's method is justified by an appeal to the precedents of Homer and Xenophon, Spenser relies for authority upon those two writers, upon Vergil himself, and upon Ariosto and Tasso. Badius' division of the subject of the nature of the hero-prince into the branches designated by *virum* and *arma* is paralleled by Spenser's partition into *ethice* and *politice*. The list of virtues ascribed to Aeneas is like the list of virtues combined in Arthur and represented separately by the twelve subsidiary heroes; the one catalogue begins with 'pius,' the other with 'Holinesse'. And Spenser's letter ends with a summary of the events of his story told, not according to 'the Methode of a Poet historical', but in the manner of a historiographer who 'discourseth of affayres orderly as they were donne, accounting as well the times as the actions'.

For his linking of Ariosto and Tasso with Homer, Vergil, and Xenophon as writers on the theme of the virtuous hero, Spenser had ample authority in contemporary comment on their poems. The editions in which he must have read the Italian poets were supplied with introductions resembling that of Badius to the *Aeneid*. Tasso himself provided explanatory prefaces to his *Rinaldo* and his *Gerusalemme Liberata*, and his essay on the latter, like the letter to Ralegh, repeated the accepted dogma concerning the division of the great subject: 'Of the life of the Contemplative Man, the Comedy of Dantes and the Odysses, are (as it were) in every part thereof a Figure: but the civil Life is seen to be shadowed throughout the Iliads, and Aeneids also, although in this there be rather set out a mixture of Action and Contemplation.'[1]

There has been much argument as to whether Tasso's moralizations of his poems reflect his original intention or a more or less grudging concession to the pressures of counter-Reformation critical theory, but the question is irrelevant to the present purpose. Like Tasso's poems, the *Orlando Furioso* came to Spenser's hands as a work in this didactic tradition. Few readers today will believe that Ariosto's purpose was to portray a prince like Aeneas or Cyrus. But there are a number of plainly moralistic episodes in the *Orlando*, fully equipped with appropriately named allegorical personages, and the problem of extracting a useful meaning from the rest of the poem was easily within the capacity of the critics of the time. Sixteenth-century editors of the *Orlando* regularly discovered in it a portrait of the heroic leader, and one of them, Orazio Toscanella, compiler of *Belleze del Furioso di M. Lodovico Ariosto* (1574), describes Ariosto's method in just the way that Spenser describes his own. Ariosto, he says, 'placed several virtues in several individuals, one virtue in one character and another in another character, in order to fashion out of all the characters a well-rounded and perfect man. A well-rounded and perfect man is one adorned with all the virtues.' Spenser calls this well-roundedness 'magnificence . . . which vertue . . . (according to Aristotle and the rest) . . . is the perfection of all the rest, and conteineth in it them all.'

By Spenser's own account, then, the intention of *The Faerie Queene* is 'to fashion a gentleman or noble person', and this he confirms by announcing in the prologue to his poem that its 'argument' is 'that true glorious type' of Queen Elizabeth, the type of gentleness and nobility. The word 'fashion' in his statement of purpose is open to misconstruction. It may be taken to mean that Spenser proposed to show how experience and training make a truly virtuous man out of one who is only potentially virtuous. But in the present case, Spenser's use of 'fashion' echoes a long-established tradition which shows that he must intend by it not 'educate' or 'train' but 'represent', 'delineate'. Cicero's *De oratore* introduces its subject with the statement 'we have to picture to ourselves in our discourse (*fingendus est nobis oratione nostra*) an orator from whom every blemish has been taken away'. Castiglione makes Sir Frederic propose that one of the company 'take it in hand to shape in wordes (*formare con parole*) a good Courtier', and the author declares his intention to 'fashion such a Courtier as the Prince that shall be worthie to have him in his service, although his state be but small, may notwithstanding be called a mighty Lord'.[2] It is in this acceptation that the *Oxford English Dictionary* understands 'fashioning' as it appears on the title page of Spenser's poem: 'The Faerie Queene. Disposed into twelve bookes, Fashioning xii. Morall vertues.' And in the sentence immediately preceding that in which 'to fashion a gentleman' occurs, Spenser explains that the purpose of his letter is 'to discover unto you the general intention and meaning, which . . . I have fashioned'. Furthermore, Spenser goes on to explain that in fulfillment of his design he has labored 'to pourtraict in Arthure, before he was king, the image of a brave knight, perfected in the twelve private morall vertues'. He does not say that he has shown Arthur in the process of achieving that perfection. Of course, since the 'fashion' of a man includes that which determines his character, training and experience enter into it to the extent that one believes them to be effective agents. But Spenser announces here, not that he has written the story of an education, but that, like Badius' Vergil and Toscanella's Ariosto, he has described a man who combines in himself the chivalric and the moral disciplines, a virtuous gentleman. And when he exclaims at the beginning of the last canto of the Legend of Temperaunce,

> Now gins this goodly frame of Temperance
>   Fairely to rise

he is saying that he has portrayed the virtue itself, not the growth of that virtue in its champion.

It is difficult for most modern readers to disabuse themselves of the idea that character development must be an essential feature of any extended narrative that pretends to be more than merely an entertainment. Stories in which the growth of the hero is a principal motif are of course not uncommon in medieval and Renaissance literature: *Parzifal* is a notable instance, and the progressive lightening and illumination of Dante's soul is obviously important to the structure of the *Commedia*. The humanist Christophoro Landino reads the *Aeneid* as an ascent of the hero from the fleshly concerns of Troy to the purity of the contemplative life symbolized by the conquest of Latium. But although the question of the role of character in an epic poem was endlessly discussed by Renaissance critics, no writer on the subject with whose work I am familiar recommends the growth or education of the hero as a subject for the narrative poet. Indeed, the Aristotelian principle of consistency ('The fourth point [with respect to character] is consistency: for though the subject of the imitation, who suggested the type, be inconsistent, still he must be consistently inconsistent'[3]) and the Horatian emphasis on decorum were read as prescribing stability of character, so that one Italian critic says flatly, 'The poet, once he has undertaken to imitate somebody, keeps him always and everywhere exactly the same as he was when first introduced.' Tasso's Godfrey is typical, I think, of the kind of heroic figure envisaged by Renaissance criticism. His victory is achieved, not through the perfecting of his nature, but through the overcoming of obstacles which prevent that nature from exercising its proper functions. These are the victories won by Spenser's gentle knights.

A gentleman or nobleman is distinguished from Everyman by the fact that he bears both a private and a public character. Spenser's use of the words *ethice* and *politice* to describe the study of these two aspects of the gentle nature suggests a reference to Aristotle's *Ethics* and *Politics*, linked treatises the first of which concerns the good man, the second the state in which men are made good. In describing the *Odyssey* and Tasso's *Rinaldo* as concerned with the former, the *Iliad* and the *Gerusalemme* with the latter, and the *Aeneid* and the *Orlando Furioso* with both, Spenser accepts the conclusions of the criticism of his time. His own work is to deal with 'ethics', as portrayed in Arthur before he became king, 'which if I finde to be well accepted, I may be perhaps encoraged, to frame the other part of polliticke vertues in his person, after that hee came to be king'.

The division between the 'ethical' and 'political' realms needs to be understood as precisely as possible, particularly because Spenser is often accused of abandoning it in the later books. What he has to say about Queen Elizabeth and the role she plays in the poem helps to clarify the matter. After identifying Gloriana as 'glory' in his general intention but 'the most excellent and glorious person of our soveraine the Queene' in his particular, Spenser continues: 'For considering she beareth two persons, the one of a most royall Queene or Empresse, the other of a most vertuous and beautifull Lady, this latter part in some places I doe express in Belphoebe.' The poet's language indicates a familiarity with the famous legal doctrine of 'the king's two bodies', a doctrine which a recent student describes as 'a distinctive feature of English political thought in the age of Elizabeth and the early Stuarts' . . .[4]

Spenser's Gloriana was evidently intended to represent this union and so the necessary connection between *The Faerie Queene* and that second 'polliticke' poem. Often it required great legal subtlety to distinguish between the king natural and the king politic. But Spenser's understanding of the difference appears most clearly, I think, where it has been most often challenged. In the Legend of Justice, Queen Mercilla sits surrounded by the emblems of her regality as presiding officer at the trial of Duessa. But when the court, the body of which she is the head, arrives at its verdict, she does not pronounce it. She does not let 'due vengeance' light upon the culprit but

> rather let in stead thereof to fall
> Few perling drops from her fair lampes of light;
> The which she covering with her purple pall
> Would have the passion hid, and up arose withall.
>
> (v, 9, 50)

The passion and tears, inevitable and praiseworthy in a virtuous queen natural, are nevertheless the sign of an 'imbecility' to which the queen politic, by definition, cannot be subject.

The theme of the noble man as 'body natural' having been determined, Spenser then chose the 'historicall fiction' of Arthur as the most suitable means by which to express it. So, at least, he describes the process. It has been argued most ingeniously that in fact he did not begin in this way at all, that the moral intention came late and was superimposed upon what was originally a romantic narrative. In the absence of unambiguous independent testimony – and it is absent – such an argument cannot be decisive. It may be that in 1589 Spenser himself would not have been able to say whether it was a dream of Britomart or a determination to benefit the commonwealth that led to the composition of his poem. But the question in any case is not directly pertinent to an attempt to understand the meaning of *The Faerie Queene*, a poem which we read, not as it evolved in the mind of its author, but as it was dedicated to Queen Elizabeth and published in 1590 and 1596.

The choice of Arthur as hero was dictated by a number of considerations, among them those which Spenser mentions: he was 'most fitte for the excellency of his person, being made famous by many mens former workes, and also furthest from the daunger of envy, and suspition of present time'. Certainly the myth so sedulously fostered by Henry VII that Arthur was of the line of British kings whom the Tudors claimed as their ancestors and a descendant of Vergil's Aeneas also played a part in his election. Spenser recalls the story by deriving the family of Elizabeth from his own fictions, Artegall and Britomart, and so eventually from Aeneas' grandson, Brutus. . . .

The Faerie Queene does not pretend to be an account of events that actually took place. We are now so accustomed to the convention of serious fiction that it requires an effort to recapture the attitude that demanded of a writer that he account to the world for his telling of a story palpably false. The argument of Sidney's *Apology for Poetry* in fact turns upon such a justification: a poem is not a lie, he says, both because the reader is not invited to accept it as history and because it is tied to 'the general reason of things' if not to 'the particuler truth of things'.[5] It is this 'general reason of things' that Spenser claims to be expressing when he describes his work as 'a continued allegory or darke conceit'.

In recent years a number of brilliant studies have thrown much light on the use of allegory in the Middle Ages, and that use was surely a powerful influence upon later allegorists. But what may be said of the method of the *Divine Comedy*, the *Romance of the Rose*, and *Piers Plowman* does not necessarily apply to *The Faerie Queene*. Spenser claims as his models not those poems but the *Aeneid*, the

Orlando, and the *Gerusalemme*. Whatever *allegory* may have meant in medieval usage, it had both a particular and a general acceptation in the Renaissance, the particular defined in terms of its nature, the general in terms of its function. The former sense, that given in textbooks of rhetoric from classical times onward, makes allegory a species of metaphor, 'a Trope of a sentence, or forme of speech which expresseth one thing in words and another in sense'. It is distinguished in its class by the fact that its literal elements and the meanings they signify are multiple rather than single: 'In a Metaphore there is a translation of one word onely, in an Allegorie of many, and for that cause an Allegorie is called a continued Metaphore.'[6] The examples of this figure of speech given by the rhetoricians are derived indifferently from prose and poetry, the Bible and secular letters. One writer offers as a typical instance the following line from Vergil's eclogues: 'Stop up your streames (my lads) the medes have drunk ther fill', explaining it thus: 'As much to say, leave of now, yee have talked of the matter inough: for the shepheards guise in many places is by opening certaine sluces to water their pastures, so as when they are wet inough they shut them againe: this application is full Allegoricke.'[7]

Spenser's familiarity with this sense of 'allegory' is obvious both from his application to the word of the standard epithet 'continued' and from his frequent use of such extended metaphors in the poem. Amoret with her heart laid open and bleeding is a figure of speech for a woman tormented in spirit; Orgoglio deflated like an empty bladder tell us that pride is merely puffed up; Arthur's dream of Gloriana is a metaphorical statement of the noble vision of glorious achievement. These are 'allegories' within the definition of the rhetoricians and there are many like them in *The Faerie Queene*. In Spenser's practice they are often presented dramatically or pictorially, a technique resembling that of medieval allegory and of the allegorical pageants, paintings, and 'emblems' of the Renaissance. But Spenser says that his poem is an allegory, not merely that there are allegories in it.

It is the functional significance of the word which is uppermost in Spenser's mind. Tasso's explanation of his *Gerusalemme Liberata* provides the gloss:

Heroical Poetry (as a living Creature, wherein two Natures are conjoyned) is compounded of Imitation and Allegory: with the one she allureth unto her the Minds and Ears of Men, and marvellously delighteth them; with the other, either in Vertue or Knowledge, she instructeth them. And as the Heroically written Imitation of an Other, is nothing else but the Pattern and Image of Humane Action: so the Allegory of an Heroical Poem is none other than the Glass and Figure of Humane Life. But Imitation regardeth the Actions of Man subjected to the outward Senses, and about them being principally employed, seeketh to represent them with effectual and expressive Phrases, such as lively set before our Corporal Eyes the things represented: It doth not consider the Customs, Affections, or Discourses of the Mind, as they be inward, but only as they come forth thence, and being manifested in Words, in Deeds, or Working, do accompany the Action. On the other side, Allegory respecteth the Passions, the Opinions and Customs, not only as they do appear, but principally in their being hidden and inward; and more obscurely doth express them with Notes (as a Man may say) mystical, such as only the Understanders of the Nature of things can fully comprehend. (trans. Edward Fairfax.)

Beyond the vague statement that it is difficult to understand and is expressed by obscure 'notes' – a 'dark conceit' in Spenser's phrase – Tasso is not concerned with the method of allegory. What is salient for him is its purpose, instruction in virtue and knowledge and investigation of the inward as well as the outward motions of man, the presentation of 'the Glass and Figure of Humane Life'. Sir John Harington's 'Briefe and Summarie Allegorie of Orlando Furioso' shows how such a definition is applied.[8] The 'two principall heads and common places' of the *Orlando* he takes to be love and arms. Under the former he expounds the meaning of Rogero's adventures with Alcina, the temptation of pleasure, and Logestilla, or virtue. These episodes are 'allegories' in method. But Harington also declares that 'the whole booke is full of examples of men and women, that in this matter of love, have been notable in one kinde or other'. His exposition of the theme of arms begins with 'the example of two mightie Emperours, one of which directeth all his counsels by wisdome, learning, and Religion; But the other being rash, and unexperienced, ruined himselfe and his countrie.' These are exemplary fictions, metaphoric only in the sense that their characters are types representative of many individuals, but they find place in the 'generall Allegorie of the whole worke' because they contribute to its didactic purpose. Renaissance allegorical explanations of the *Aeneid* similarly depend indifferently upon the elucidation of 'continued' metaphors and the lessons to be learned from the example of the characters of the story. Spenser himself makes no sharp division between allegory and fictional example: although at one point he describes his work as 'clowdily enwrapped in Allegoricall devises', at another he declares the method of the *Cyropaedia* to be doctrine 'by ensample' and adds, 'So have I laboured to doe in the person of Arthure'.

Spenser's method is in fact best disclosed by his practice. The episode of Malbecco, Hellenore, and Paridell, the principal subject of the ninth and tenth cantos of the Legend of Chastitie, serves as a convenient illustration, for while its intention is unmistakable, the rhetorical techniques employed in its telling are marvelously varied and complex. The tale begins as a fabliau of the hoariest type, a comedy involving the miserly, jealous husband, his pretty, wanton wife, and the polished seducer. Such situations are sometimes called 'realistic', yet the names of the characters at once give the story a meaning beyond the particular: 'Malbecco' is from the Italian *becco* which means both 'cuckold' and 'he-goat'; 'Hellenore' and 'Paridell' are intended to suggest the types of Helen and Paris of Troy. Malbecco's passions for his money and his wife are presented in parallel so that one becomes a figure for the other: he is not properly entitled either to the gold or to the girl, he makes no use of either, he keeps both locked up and fears constantly for their loss. His blindness in one eye serves as a metaphor for the watchful blindness of jealousy, for although he keeps up a sleepless, self-tormenting vigil he is unable to see what goes on at his side, the seduction of Hellenore by Paridell. That affair is described realistically: Paridell 'sent close messages of love to her at will'; metaphorically: 'She sent at him one firie dart, whose hed / Empoisned was with privy lust, and gealous dred'; and symbolically: '[she] in her lap did shed her idle draught, / Shewing desire her inward flame to slake'. That inward flame leads to the fire set by Hellenore to cover her escape, a fire compared with the conflagration which consumed Troy, Helen and Hellenore, wantons both, joying in wanton destruction. Now the realm of realism is left quite behind, for Hellenore, having been abandoned by the rake Paridell, finds refuge as the common mistress of a band of satyrs, half-goats who herd goats, her sexual passion satisfied at last. And when Malbecco tries to rescue her from her happy predicament, the goats butt him with their horns – give him the 'horn' for which he was named at his christening. Finally, consumed by the 'long anguish and self-murdring thought' of his jealous nature he is changed into a strange creature with crooked claws dwelling in a cave overhung by a tremendous cliff

> which ever and anon
> Threates with huge ruine him to fall upon,
> That he dare never sleepe, but that one eye
> Still ope he keepes for that occasion (III, 10, 58)

There he lives forever, so deformed 'that he has quight / Forgot he was a man, and Gealosie is hight'.

This is not a story in the ordinary sense of the word, for the movement is inward, not onward. The transformations of Malbecco and Hellenore are not really transformations at all but revelations of their essence. The poet's purpose has been to lay bare the sterile, destructive, and dehumanizing power of the passions of greed, jealousy, and lust, and to this end he has made use of every means at his command, exemplary tale, myth, metaphor extended and simple, simile, symbol, and direct statement. As narrative, the episode is self-contained, for neither Malbecco nor Hellenore appears earlier or again, but the ideas which it expresses are presented in parallel and contrast, echoed, analyzed, developed, and refined throughout the Legend of Chastitie. To distinguish among the rhetorical tools by which this is accomplished is a task which would require the sharpest of definitions and infinite subtlety in applying them, for the poetical stream flows unbroken from one into another. Fortunately, it is not a task that need be undertaken here, for it offers little help in understanding the poem. Rather, the theme of discourse suggests itself through its repeated statement in a variety of forms, and once manifested reciprocally illuminates the 'dark conceits' by which it is expressed.

The models for his method which Spenser acknowledges in the letter to Ralegh include only classical and Renaissance works. He is also indebted, though I think not as profoundly, to specifically medieval traditions. The influence of the morality drama is particularly evident in the Legend of Holinesse. Since the subject of many of these plays is human salvation, their protagonists meet obstacles similar to those which hinder the Red Cross Knight, and like that Knight they must be saved by God's mercy. The central characters of the later moralities – for their popularity persisted well into the sixteenth century – tend to be one or another kind of human rather than Mankind in general, and John Skelton's *Magnificence* presents a prince, or magnificent man, as its hero. The trials of Magnificence parallel those of St. George. The vicious influences playing upon him are disguised as virtuous ones, just as Duessa poses as Fidessa and Archimago as the Red Cross Knight. As a result of his delusion he falls into the clutches of Despair and is about to commit suicide when Good Hope snatches away his dagger and he is regenerated by Redress, Sad Circumspection, and Perseverance. The influence of the long tradition of medieval allegorical poetry on *The Faerie Queene* is also clear. Spenser owes to it such devices as the gardens of love, the pageant of the sins, the arms of the Red Cross Knight, the masque of Cupid, and the Blatant Beast. An analogue to the Beast occurs in a late example of such poetry, Stephen Hawes's *Pastime of Pleasure,* a poem which is strikingly similar to *The Faerie Queene* in general conception, for Graunde Amour, like the Red Cross Knight, is clad in the armor described by St. Paul, and his passion for La Belle Pucelle is as much a metaphor for the noble man's hunger for glory as Arthur's love for Gloriana. Indeed, the idea of a quest for a high goal as the central motive is common to medieval story of many kinds, from saints' lives to chivalric adventures. And since a heroic quest is central to the *Aeneid* also, Spenser found it appropriate to his Vergilian treatment of the matter of Arthur.

But the goal is not Prince Arthur's guide, as the hope of a new Troy is for Aeneas and the conquest of Jerusalem for Tasso's Godfrey. The narrative structure of *The Faerie Queene* is, in fact, almost frivolously weak. Having fallen in love with the Faerie Queene in a dream, like Sir Thopas in Chaucer's burlesque tale, Arthur thereafter wanders in and out of the poem, rescuing the unfortunate, contending with villains, and chasing the beautiful Florimell. Only a parenthetical observation that he wished his beloved were as fair as Florimell reminds the reader that his romantic attachment persists. The chivalric quests of the titular heroes of the successive books can be taken no more seriously. St. George sets out to kill the dragon besieging the castle of Una's parents and that is all we hear of his interest in the matter until the very end of his legend. In the second book, Guyon's task is to destroy Acrasia's Bower, but he is otherwise occupied for most of his career. Britomart is absent from much of her Legend of Chastitie and she learns of Amoret's imprisonment and undertakes to rescue her only in the eleventh canto. The story of Cambel and Triamond is merely an episode in the Legend of Friendship. Neither the rescue of Irena nor the hunt for the Blatant Beast dominates the action of the last two books, and there is no sign of a champion or of a quest in the fragmentary seventh. There are, to be sure, hundreds of stories in Spenser's poem, many of them brilliantly told, but *The Faerie Queene* is not, in any significant sense, a story. If plot is soul, the poem cannot escape damnation.

Nor does *The Faerie Queene* become coherent if the reader seeks for a continuing moral tale of which the literal one is a metaphor. In the first episode of the first book, the Red Cross Knight enters the Wandering Wood and conquers monstrous Error. When he leaves the Wood does he leave Error behind him and thereafter walk in the way of Truth? In fact, he, like all men, spends his mortal life in the Wood battling with the monster. Has he done with despair when he escapes from Despair? Even in his final struggle with the Old Dragon he wishes he were dead. Seduced by Will and Grief, he abandons Una, his true faith. If he is therefore faith-less he is nevertheless able to conquer Sans Foy, or faithlessness. Then he enters Lucifera's House of Pride in company with the figure of Falsehood, Duessa. In this state he fights with Sans Joy and is at the point of defeat when his 'quickning faith' rescues him and turns the tide. This happens in Canto 5, yet St. George is not reunited with his Faith until the end of Canto 8. By the dwarf's help he escapes from that House of Pride only to be caught in the arms of Duessa by the giant of pride, Orgoglio. Those commentators who read the Legend of Holinesse as a Christian's progress make a difference between Lucifera and the giant; I cannot find it in the text. To be sure, the carcasses behind Lucifera's palace are those guilty ones who have been destroyed by the sin of pride while the bodies on the floor of Orgoglio's castle are the innocents and martyrs who have been destroyed by the sinfulness of the proud. Lucifera, usurping queen of man's soul, is attended by the mortal sins of which she is chief and source; Orgoglio, usurping tyrant of the world, by a seven-headed monster whose tail reaches to the house of the heavenly gods. These are inward and outward aspects of the same sin, that sin of pretended glory which is false at its foundation, as the House of Pride is built on a hill of sand and the great Orgoglio is brought down by a blow at the leg. A recent student of *The Faerie Queene* analyzes the Legend of Holinesse into ten 'acts',[9] but if the episodes are properly so described the whole is scarcely a neatly constructed play.

Confusion also besets the reader who follows the characters of *The Faerie Queene* in the hope of extracting from their adventures an orderly lesson in morality. In the course of Florimell's desperate flight from her various pursuers she escapes from a horrid spotted beast by leaping into the boat of a poor old fisherman. As she does so she loses her golden girdle. Since in later books we learn that this girdle will not stay bound about ladies who are unchaste we may be led to conclude that Florimell has now lost her maidenhead. One commentator[10] accepts this logic and finds confirmation for it in 'the apparently innocent line that she was driven to great distress "and taught the carefull Mariner to play" (III, 8, 20)' although the grammar of the passage in question makes it quite clear that Fortune, who drove Florimell to distress, taught her to play the troubled mariner, not that Florimell taught the fisherman erotic games. Surely, the unhappy girl is here made to lose her girdle only in order that Satyrane may have it to bind the spotted beast, for when the fisherman attacks her she cries to heaven, and not in vain:

> See how the heavens, of voluntary grace
> And soveraine favour towards chastity,
> Doe succour send to her distressed cace:
> So much high God doth innocence embrace (III, 8, 29)

Even if God is deluded about Florimell's chastity, it seems unlikely that the poet is also. Yet later in the same canto he exclaims in her praise, 'Most vertuous virgin!' The fallacy of reading Spenser's allegory rigidly becomes patent when it is observed that the Snowy Florimell, who is not enough of a virgin to wear the girdle in the fourth book (5, 19–20), has somehow become able to bind it about her waist by the time of her trial in the fifth (3, 24).

Reading the Florimell story as a continued narrative leads to the suggestion that she is a kind of Proserpina, that her imprisonment beneath the sea by Proteus and her eventual betrothal to Marinell constitute a retelling of the vegetation myth.[11] Indeed, her flowery name, the icicles on Proteus' beard, and the effect of the warmth of her presence on the moribund Marinell seem to support such a reading. But if this is what Spenser intended by the story taken as a whole, he was perverse enough to addle his readers unmercifully by making the duration of Florimell's bondage not six months but seven. . . .

One kind of inconsistency in Spenser's narrative which is sometimes ascribed to changes in his plans and to shifting literary influences upon him is, I think, an essential part of his grand design, although it has not previously been recognized as such. It is apparent and it has often been remarked that the style of *The Faerie Queene* is not uniform throughout: the Legend of Chastitie is notably in Ariosto's manner; the Legend of Courtesie has the character of pastoral romance. If this is inconsistency, it is of the kind the reader should be led to expect from a consideration of Spenser's practice in his other poems. . . .

The varying styles of the successive books of *The Faerie Queene* serve a purpose of greater weight than the avoidance of monotony. The 'patrons' of those books are indeed different from each other and engage in different kinds of action. This is so, I believe, because Spenser intended his readers to recognize in them reflections of particular literary models in just the same way as they recognized in the first half of the *Aeneid* an imitation of the *Odyssey* and in the latter half an imitation of the *Iliad*. The Legend of St. George echoes the saint's life in *The Golden Legend*. Sir Guyon is a hero of classical epic, like Aeneas and Odysseus. Britomart and Florimell inevitably recall Ariosto's Bradamante and Angelica. The titular story of Cambel and Triamond in the Legend of Friendship is based on Chaucer's unfinished *Squire's Tale*, and reminiscences of that story and the one told by the Knight recur frequently throughout the book. Artegall is compared directly with Hercules, Bacchus, and Osiris, the mythical founders of civilization. The adventures of Sir Calidore are of the type found in the Greek romances and imitated by Sidney in the *Arcadia*. The fragmentary Cantos of Mutabilitie clearly imitate Ovid's *Metamorphoses*. . . .

This hunger for complexity, for binding into one the multiple and for revealing the multiple in the one, shows itself in almost every aspect of Spenser's technique. The stanza which he invented for the poem is itself such a various unit. Its closest relatives are the Italian ottava rima (*abababcc*), rhyme royal (*ababbcc*), and the stanza used by Chaucer in the *Monk's Tale* (*ababbcbc*). In the first two forms the final couplet rhymes independently of the rest; the *Monk's Tale* stanza lacks a clear-cut conclusion. By adding an alexandrine rhyming with *c* to this last verse pattern, Spenser introduces metrical variety and at the same time supplies an ending which is linked to rather than separated from the remainder. Stanza is joined to stanza by frequent echoes in the first line of one of the sound or thought of the last line preceding it, and analogous links tie together canto with canto and book with book. To the amalgamation in his stanza of Italian and English forms Spenser adds a Vergilian touch by occasionally leaving a verse unfinished in the manner of the *Aeneid*.

The invention of the names of the characters of *The Faerie Queene* betrays a similar habit of mind. They are designedly derived from different languages: Pyrochles is Greek, Munera Latin, Alma Italian (and also both Latin and Hebrew), Sans Foy French, the first half of Ruddymane English. Many of the names are portmanteaus into which Spenser has stuffed a multiplicity of meanings. 'Britomart', for example, reminded his Elizabethan readers of Ariosto's heroine Bradamante as well as of Britomartis, the chaste daughter of Carme whom ancient myth identified with Diana, while at the same time the etymology 'martial Briton' must have been inescapable, for Boccaccio calls Britomartis 'Britona, Martis filia'.

The key ideas of his moral teaching are expressed by as many different symbols as the poet can imagine: the power which binds the disparate or antagonistic is represented by the figure of Concord flanked by Love and Hate; by the hermaphrodite Venus and the snake about her legs whose head and tail are joined together; by the lady Cambina, her team of angry lions, her Aesculapian rod, and her cup of nepenthe. These reciprocal processes of unification and multiplication reflect a conception of the universe which makes it all one, yet unimaginably rich.

There is a plenitude of story in *The Faerie Queene*, martial, amatory, and domestic; myth, fairy tale, chivalric adventure, and anecdote. Some of these tales Spenser invents himself; others he borrows from biblical, classical, medieval, and contemporary sources. He has no sense of impropriety in setting together the true and the fabulous, the familiar and the heroic, the Christian and the pagan. Rather, he seems to seek occasion to do so, either 'for the more variety of the history' or to demonstrate the universality of the theme he is expounding. What he borrows he makes his own, without the slightest respect for the integrity or the intention of the original. His ruthless use of Vergil's story of Dido and Aeneas serves as an example.

The words spoken by Aeneas when he meets his mother on the Carthaginian shore are put into the mouth of the buffoon Trompart, while the portrait of Venus is made over into a portrait of the Diana-like Belphoebe. Aeneas' account of his past experiences at dinner with Dido inspires Guyon's table conversation with Medina. Dido's alternate name, Elissa, is given to Medina's morose sister. Dido's dying speech is echoed by the suicide Amavia, and as Iris shears a lock of hair from the one so Guyon does from the other. Again, elements of the legendary story of St. George are used in several ways in Book I, but the incident of George's binding the dragon with a girdle and leading it about as a tame thing is transferred to Sir Satyrane in Book III. Chaucer's *Squire's Tale* provides the basis for the story of Cambel and Triamond; the episode in which a lovesick bird is restored to its fickle mate 'By mediacion of Cambalus' suggests the reconciling of Timias and Belphoebe by mediation of a lovesick bird. . . .

This reshaping and reworking of borrowed material is neither random nor perverse. Behind it lies the constant determination to make story the servant of intention. . . .

Within *The Faerie Queene*, the unit is the book or legend. It is made up of episodes and 'allegories' invented to illuminate its theme. Typically, a book begins with an encounter between new characters and those of its predecessor, there is a climax or shift of emphasis approximately at midpoint, and the end is marked by some great action. Apart from these loose formal characteristics, however, the constituent elements are not sequential in their arrangement; they are truly episodic, obeying no law of progress or development. Rather, they are so placed as to produce effects of variety and contrast. They are tied not to each other but to the principal subject of discourse, and to this they contribute analytically or comprehensively, directly or by analogy, by affirmation or denial.

In Spenser's poem, intention is the soul, while the stories, characters, symbols, figures of speech, the ring of the verse itself constitute the body:

> of the soule the bodie forme doth take:
> For soule is forme, and doth the bodie make.
> ('An Hymne in Honour of Beautie', 132–3)

Only from the made body can the form be inferred, however, and this is the kind of inference that Spenser expects of his readers. One may take hold of the meaning of a book almost anywhere in it, for it is everywhere there. I have entitled the chapter dealing with the Legend of Holinesse 'The Cup and the Serpent', the symbol which Fidelia holds, but it might as well have been called 'Mount Sinai and the Mount of Olives,' 'Sans Joy and the Promise,' 'Hope in Anguish', 'The Burning Armor', 'Una and the Veil', or 'The Tree and the Living Well'. Each of these in its own way and with its own inflection is a figure for the paradox of life and death which I take to be central to the book. What that paradox means and how it may be resolved Spenser never says directly. I think it was the nature of his mind rather than the fear of losing his audience that kept him from delivering his discipline 'plainly in way of precepts'. He could no more state his abstract theme apart from its expression in this world than a painter could draw the idea of a chair. The result is the richness of *The Faerie Queene*.

SOURCE: extracts from *The Poetry of Edmund Spenser* (New York, 1963) pp. 118–36, 139–43, 145–6.

NOTES

1. *Godfrey of Bulloigne*, trans. Edward Fairfax (London, 1600).

2. Sir Thomas Hoby's translation of Castiglione's *Il Cortegiano* (1561); Everyman Library edition (1928) pp. 16, 29.

3. Aristotle, *Poetics*, xv, 4, trans. S. H. Butcher (1895).

4. E. H. Kantorowicz, *The King's Two Bodies: A Study in Medieval Political Theology* (Princeton, 1957).

5. Sir Philip Sidney, *Apologie for Poetrie*, in *Elizabethan Critical Essays,* ed. G. Gregory Smith (Oxford, 1904) I, p. 164.

6. Henry Peacham, *The Garden of Eloquence* (1593).

7. George Puttenham, *The Arte of English Poesie* (1589).

8. Sir John Harington, *Orlando Furioso in English Heroicall Verse* (London, 1591).

9. A. C. Hamilton, *The Structure of Allegory in 'The Faerie Queene'* (Oxford, 1961).

10. Ibid.

11. Northrop Frye, 'The Structure of Imagery in *The Faerie Queene*', *University of Toronto Quarterly*, xxx (1961).

Frank Kermode

'THE ELEMENT OF HISTORICAL ALLEGORY' (1964)

What I have now to say takes issue with some learned and acute modern guides to Spenser; but I say it not in a spirit of contention, but with proper gratitude for the help I have accepted from them. Spenser is very diverse, and lends support to many generalizations which seem flatly counter to one another. Thus, as everybody knows, *The Faerie Queene* fluctuates from a philosophical extreme – as in The Garden of Adonis, and the Mutability Cantos – to relatively naïve allegory such as the House of Alma. It contains passages – such as Guyon's stay in the Cave of Mammon, or Britomart's in the Church of Isis – which seem to deal with high matters, but deliberately conceal their full meaning; yet it also contains transparent historical allusions to the trial of Mary Queen of Scots and the campaigns in the Netherlands. Its mood varies from the apocalyptic in Book I to the pastoral in Book VI. Sometimes, as with Florimel, one senses the need to complete Spenser's allegory for him, and sometimes one feels that he has for the time being almost forgotten about it; yet there are other times when one wonders at the density of meanings the fiction is made to bear. Readers of Spenser's own epoch seem to have enjoyed the allusions to great men of the age as well as the moral allegories, but later there was some danger of his sinking under the explanations of scholars, and in recent years there has been a noticeable trend towards simplicity of interpretation.

Obviously, we should not cumber his world with our own planetary ingenuities; but I think this process has gone too far. I shall now briefly characterize some of these simplifications, and then examine some aspects of the poem which seem to me to remain stubbornly what the simplifiers do not wish them to be.

At the beginning of this century it was assumed by all who considered Spenser's more philosophical passages that he knew Plato's

dialogues, and that he may have interested himself in Renaissance
Neo-Platonism. Later there came a different understanding; philo-
sophical sources were found in Lucretius, in Empedocles, in 'old
religious cults'. And it became a commonplace of scholarship that
Spenser could be illuminated by reference to the learning of Ficino,
Benivieni, or Bruno.

The picture of Spenser as a very learned man is not in itself
absurd, since he understood that the heroic poet should be a 'curious
and universal scholar'. But perhaps only an unfamiliarity with the
conditions of Renaissance scholarship could have permitted anyone
to imagine him to be systematically acquisitive of learning. Also
there was prevalent an oversimple view of the Renaissance as a clean
new start, which implied a failure to understand the extent to which
medieval syntheses – including much Aristotle and Plato which
scholars have misguidedly traced back to the original – persisted in
the learning of Spenser's time. Thus the Garden of Adonis, which has
attracted much speculation, possibly contains little philosophy that
would have surprised an educated reader in any age between that
of Spenser and that of Boethius. Not surprisingly there has been a
reaction, and such influential books as those of W. L. Renwick (1925)
and C. S. Lewis (1936) presented a more credible philosopher-poet,
Lewis even labelling him, in a famous passage, 'homely' and
'churchwardenly'. Whether or no we accept this provocative
formula, it remains true that Spenser used compendia, handbooks
of iconography and so on; that he learnt from popular festivals; and
that it would have been harder than used to be supposed to catch
him working with an ancient classic open before him.

Yet we should not make the mistake of thinking that what seems
exotic or far-fetched to us necessarily seemed so to Spenser. It is
enough, perhaps, to remind ourselves of the great differences between his map of knowledge and ours – to remember, for instance,
the continuing importance of astrology; the over-riding authority of
theology; and a view of classical antiquity which seems to us simply
fantastic. Spenser's mind was trained in forms of knowledge alien to
us, and habituated to large symbolic systems of a kind which, when
we read of them in Huizinga's *The Waning of the Middle Ages*, are
likely to strike us as almost absurdly frivolous. Yet he was very
serious in his wish to 'make it new' – 'it' being the sum of knowledge
as it appeared to an Englishman at what seemed to be a great crisis

of world history. It is hard for us to remember that Spenser served a queen whom he regarded as technically an empress, and whose accession was regularly thought of as the sounding of the seventh trumpet in the Book of Revelation. Spenser saw this world as a vast infolded, mutually relevant structure, as inclusive as the Freudian dream; but he also saw it as disconnected, decaying, mutable, disorderly. We should expect to find his mind, especially when he deals with systematic ideas of order, very strange to us; and we should not easily allow this strangeness to be lost in learned simplifications.

I turn now to a second device for reducing the proportion of relatively inaccessible meaning in *The Faerie Queene*. This is to minimize the importance of a characteristic which had certainly appealed to Spenser's contemporaries, namely the element of historical allegory. Dryden thought that each of Spenser's knights represented an Elizabethan courtier; even Upton, who in his way knew so much more about *The Faerie Queene* than we do, stressed the historical allegory and elaborately explained allusions to Elizabethan history. This way of reading Spenser persisted and, perhaps, reached its climax in the work of Lilian Winstanley half a century ago. But it was dealt a blow from which it has not recovered at the hands of the great American Spenserian, Edwin Greenlaw, in his book *Studies in Spenser's Historical Allegory* (1932).

Greenlaw's object is, broadly, to subordinate historical to ethical allegory. Historical allegory, he says, has reference principally to general topics; it refers to specific persons only momentarily and with no high degree of organization. This is now, I think the received opinion, and it certainly makes sense to relieve Spenser of barrenly ingenious commentary relating his poem to obscure, forgotten, political intrigues. But if we apply Greenlaw's criteria indiscriminately we are likely to be left with a Spenser drained of that historical urgency which seems to be one of his most remarkable characteristics; it is the adhesive which binds the dream image to immediate reality. And certainly one consequence of the modern simplification of Spenser has been to loosen the bond between his great First Book and an actual world by denying the complexity of his historical allegory.

Finally, there is a third and very sophisticated mode of simplification, and this we can represent by reference to two critics, Mr. A. C.

Hamilton in his *The Structure of Allegory in the Faerie Queene* (1961) and
Mr. Graham Hough in his *Preface to the Faerie Queene* (1962). Mr.
Hamilton is an enemy of 'hidden allegorical significance', at any
rate in Spenser, though of course he knows how much Renaissance
critical theory has to say about 'dark conceits'. He suggests that we
have now established 'a fatal dichotomy' between poet and thinker,
and that the despised old romantic habit of reading the poem for
the beauties of its surface was no more harmful than the modern way
of looking straight through to the emblematical puzzles beneath.
We have, he argues, made the poem a kind of Duessa 'whose borrowed beauty disguises her reality'. Or, ignoring the fiction, we seek
historical allusion, treating Book 1, for example, as a concealed
history of the English Reformation; or we devise some 'moral reading yielding platitudes which the poet need never have laboured to
conceal'. Offering some instances of this, he asks, 'Is this the morality
which More found divine? . . . The "conceit as passing all conceit?"'
And he proposes his 'radical reorientation': by concentrating upon
the fiction – the image – he will show that the poem is not like
Duessa but like Una, who 'did seem such, as she was'. He finds support for his policy of subordinating all allegorical meanings to the
literal in some remarks of Sidney, and asks us to see the moral
senses not as kernels of which the fiction is the shell, but as the
expanding petals of a multifoliate rose – the meaning 'expanding
from a clear centre'.

Mr. Hamilton shows much skill and sensibility in developing a
reading along these lines. But the method, attractive as it sounds,
will not serve. We lose too much. Not that I deny the pre-eminence
of the literal meaning, which Aquinas himself would have accepted;
only it does not mean quite what Mr. Hamilton thinks. The praise
of Henry More, for example, which was not in the least extravagant,
depended upon a well established view that images could combine
old truths to make a new one; the whole was greater than its parts,
and if you broke down the 'icon' into its original constituents the
parts together would have less meaning than the whole icon. The
pleasure and instruction, you may say, is double: it is the intellectual
delight of breaking down the icon and the intuitive benefit of per-
ceiving its global meaning. In short, although we may welcome the
figure of the multifoliate rose, we still need the idea of the kernel and
the shell, or of the fiction as a means of concealment: it will not, in

Spenser, be as perversely opaque as it is in Chapman, but it may well be as elaborate as the sixth book of Aeneid, as read by Renaissance mythographers.

What you find under the surface depends upon your learning and penetration. Behind the Garden of Adonis are philosophic constituents; behind the First Book constituents of world history; behind the Fifth Book and especially the elaborate dream of Britomart, high matters of imperial and national legal theory. I want, so far as it is possible to have the best of both worlds, to enjoy the fiction much as Mr. Hamilton does, but also to deny his contention that the 'universal reference prevents our translating events into historical terms'. Thus I am sure that Book v is impoverished if the Church of Isis passage is treated simply as a figurative rendering of the love-relationship of Artegall and Britomart; and this is how Mr. Hamilton, following a note in A. S. P. Woodhouse's famous essay, would have us read it.

Mr. Hough tries, in his very agreeable book to satisfy the contestants in his kind of quarrel by arguing that there are intermediate stages in literature between complete 'realism' and naïve allegory; Shakespeare is equidistant between these extremes, his magic fully absorbing his theme so that one might speak of an 'incarnation'. Nobody, I suppose, using Mr. Hough's chart, would care to put Spenser – so far as the epic poem is concerned – anywhere save where he puts him, between Shakespeare and 'naïve' allegory, as a maker of 'poetic structures with various degrees of allegorical explicitness'. And Mr. Hough's insistence that the allegory is 'relaxed and intermittent' ought to remind us of the constantly varying 'thickness' of Spenser's thematic meanings. But I do not think he serves us so well in asking us to depend in our reading upon our 'general sense' of how 'mythical poetry' works. *The Faerie Queene* is an epic and so historical; we simply do not have an instinct which enables us to participate in historical myths relating to the religious, political and dynastic situations of Spenser's day. And our feeling for 'mythical poetry' tells us nothing relevant to the juristic imperialism of his Church of Isis.

I have respect for both of these books; each in its way says that Spenser is a great poet who can mean much to modern readers; and I have given only a very partial account of them. But I quarrel with them, as with the others, because they habitually ignore what I think may be the peculiar strength of Spenser. Probably no other English poet has ever achieved so remarkable a *summa* as his. And it seems to me that we must not modernize him at the cost of forgetting this. 'Poetry is the scholar's art.' We should be glad to find in *The Faerie Queene* not only the significances of dream, but that fantastic cobweb of conscious correspondences, running over all the interlinked systems of knowledge, which a scholar-poet and a courtier might be expected to produce. Leaving out of account the philosophical simplification I began with, I intend now to speak of two parts of the poem: the historical allegory of Book i, and the allegory of justice in two parts of Book v. In each case, I myself find that the hidden meanings contribute to the delight of the fiction, because some of this delight arises from recognition of the writer's complex intent. And I do not think it does the dreamlike narrative any harm to include in it elements recognizable by conscious analysis.

The First Book of *The Faerie Queene* is well known to be apocalyptic, in the sense that it presents a version of world history founded rather closely upon the English Protestant interpretation of the Book of Revelation. I have elsewhere tried to explain how the force of the book – as I see it – stems from a peculiarly subtle and active interplay of actual history with apocalyptic-sibylline prophecy. In its more political aspect, Book i is a celebration of the part of Elizabeth Tudor, the Protestant Empress, in the workings of providence. This a writer sufficiently sympathetic to Spenser – Milton, for example – would take in at a glance; and nothing in Milton is more Spenserian than the apocalyptic exhortations to England in the pamphlets *On Reformation* and *Areopagitica*, with their emphasis on God's manner of dealing with the nations, and the special role chosen for his Englishmen in the overthrow of antichrist. The Puritan commentators on Revelation, especially Bullinger and Bale, had long insisted upon the degree to which the text foretold the history of the Church, now reaching a climax; and for the better part of a century English opinion accepted Foxe's reading of ecclesiastical history as prefigured in the flight of the woman clothed with the sun – the true catholic church – into a wilderness from which, after forty-two months, she returns to her own as the Church of England. Discussing elsewhere the profusion of references to Revelation in Spenser's text, I expressed some surprise that the very scholars, who, by the citation of patristic and Reformist commentaries, have made these identifications so sure, should, under the inhibition of Greenlaw, have forborne to study them in their obvious historical dimension. The text of *The Faerie Queene*, Book 1 is admittedly studded with the prophetic emblems of Revelation; it admittedly suggests that the Elizabethan settlement – the *renovatio mundi* brought by the Phoenix, the Astraean Elizabeth – fulfils the plan of history laid down in the Bible. Would it not seem likely that the narrative should allude to the history of the Church in the wilderness – that the story of Una and Duessa should, like Foxe's history of the Church, demonstrate the culmination of the divine plan in Elizabeth's accession?

It is clear that the limited series of allusions admitted by most editors to the course of English Reform under Henry VIII and Edward VI would not be enough for the apocalyptic-historical purpose Spenser announces with his imagery from Revelation. If you once identify the English with the primitive Catholic Church, you begin its history, as Jewel said, 'after the first creation of the world'. After that, Joseph of Arimathaea brought Eastern Christianity to England; later there was a Christian king, Lucius; hence the early splendours and purity of the English Church, and the historic English independence of Rome and the 'ten-horned beast' or Latin Empire, impaired only by the treachery of Hildebrand and his successors. The imperial claims of Elizabeth, however, defined the papal power and were traced back to Constantine.

Now the celebration in image and allegory of the Foxian version of history is not a remote and learned fancy; just as *The Faerie Queene* had her 'yearly solemne feaste', so had Elizabeth. Her Accession day (17 November) was celebrated with increasing fervour, especially after the Armada, so that the Papists called it blasphemous and a parody of the adoration of the Virgin. Mr. Roy C. Strong has well surveyed the main themes of sermon, tract, ballad and entertainment relating to this feast. Elizabeth is *rarissima Phoenix, ultima Astraea*, the renewer of the Church and faithful true opponent of antichrist. She has undone the work of the wicked popes who usurped the emperor's power and rights; she inherits both Lucius' recognized position as God's vicar, and the imperial power of Constantine and Justinian. Antichrist, the murderous sorcerers of the see of Rome, stands finally exposed. The queen is the defender of the true Church in an evil world. In a sense she *is* that Church. When Mr. Strong's preacher speaks of her as the sun shedding beams of religion, he is remembering 'the woman clothed with the sun', who turns into the Una of whose sunshiny face Spenser speaks, 'glistening euery way about the light of the euerlasting Gospel'. As Mr. Strong observes, 'the complexities of eschatological and imperial theory are never far away from the Accession Day themes'. Foxe's book, available with the Bible in every church, had become part of the body of patriotic thought, a textbook of English imperialism.

Now 'homely Spenser' made, in the First Book of his poem, an epic of these very Accession Day themes, and he too chains up Foxe beside the Bible. An appeal to history was a prerequisite not only of the claims of the Catholic Church of England to antiquity and purity, but also of the queen's claim to possess imperial power over the bishops. *The Faerie Queene* may be mythical poetry; but its myths are the myths of English polity in the fifteen-eighties and nineties. Greenlaw himself observed that the use of Arthurian legend was for the Elizabethans not a Tennysonian archaism, but an argument from antiquity. The Elizabethans in fact saw Arthur's not as Malory's world, but as a unified Britain, and Arthur himself as king of the whole island, which, under the diadem of Constantine, was an empire according to *Leges Anglorum*. Greenlaw observed also that it was commonplace in popular pageants to present the queen as True Religion; and that Spenser's poem reflects the view that her greatest service was the establishment of true religion in England. We are speaking of an age that venerated Foxe – the age of Archbishop Parker, of Sandys, of a queen who herself insisted upon her role as head of a church founded by Joseph of Arimathaea and a State that inherited the powers of the Constantinian Empire. Indeed she had, the claim ran, reunited the two. Spenser could not avoid allusion to the whole of church history according to Foxe in describing the struggle between Una and antichrist.

Earlier interpretations of this kind – such as those of Scott and Keightley – have been ignored or coldly dismissed by Spenser's modern editors. I think Scott and Keightley were wrong in detail, since they did not look at the history of the church through the medium of Elizabethan propaganda; but they had the right instinct. Any apologist of the Elizabethan settlement was obliged to produce historical arguments, and Spenser, as an allegorical poet, did so by means of hidden meanings in his fiction.

No one is in much doubt about the relationship of Una and

Duessa. Una is pure religion, which came to England direct from the East: she is descended from 'ancient Kings and Queenes, that had of yore / Their scepters stretcht from East to Westerne shore' (I, I, 5). Duessa, on the other hand, claims descent only from an Emperor 'that the wide West under his rule has / And high hath set his throne, where *Tiberis* doth pas' (I, 2, 22). Her false description of her father as emperor alludes to papal usurpations on the imperial power, a constant source of Protestant complaint. As Miss Frances Yates rightly says, Duessa and Una 'symbolize the story of impure papal religion and pure imperial religion'. The success of the Tudors against the papacy is a restoration of Una, of imperial rights over the *sacerdotium*. The emperor, or empress, is, as Jewel says, the Pope's lord and master; Rome is not directly descended, he adds, from the primitive Eastern church, whereas the reformed Church of England can make exactly this claim. Duessa is in fact a representative of a religion not only antichristian but also anti-imperialist, anti-universalist. Duessa's very name accuses her of schism.

The Red Cross Knight has dealings with both ladies, appearing first with Una in his capacity of defender of the true faith. It is part of the dreamshift technique of the poem that he begins thus, and as *miles Christi*, to end as the knight *fidelis et verax* or Christ himself (whose bride Una is the Church) – after a career of error typical of the human pilgrimage and also of the history of England. In confronting him with Error in the opening Canto, Spenser fulfils a multiple purpose, having in mind not only Christ's victory over sin in the wilderness, but Una's great enemy, heresy, against which the early English Church protected her. Scott thought Error stood for Arianism; it probably corresponds more generally to that series of heresies which Bale associates with the opening of the second and third apocalyptic seals: Sabellianism, Nestorianism, Manichaeism, as well as Arianism. Modern heresy, for which Jewel firmly places the responsibility on Rome, is the brood of these earlier errors. The locusts of stanza 14 derive, as Upton pointed out, from Revelation 9:7, and were traditionally associated with heretical teaching – a point made by that herald of reform, Matthew of Paris, whom Foxe quotes approvingly. The association is also remembered by Bale. The enemies of Una had existed as long as there had been a Roman antichrist; Red Cross is her champion, since God had entrusted her, as Milton thought it natural, to 'his Englishmen'. The victory of

Constantine, which made possible the Christian Empire, was achieved, according to Foxe, with the aid of British troops; he thought it represented the end of 294 years since the Passion, and the binding of Satan for a thousand years. Constantine was himself of course British, born of St. Helena at York.

Archimago, as is generally agreed, corresponds to the false prophet and the beast from the land, and so to antichrist. But it is worth observing that Spenser gives him a name which suggests that he is a magician; and this is a charge incessantly made against popes by Foxe and many others. Marlorat's compendious commentary on Revelation, published in 1574, says, on Rev. 13:15 (where the dragon seeks by supernatural means to destroy the woman clothed with the sun), that popes were often 'nigromancers'. . . . Gregory VII himself, 'erst called Hildebrand', was a 'notable nigromancer' . . . who was specially detested because, having gained authority in England through the Conqueror, he began that interference with English government which disfigures so many subsequent reigns, notably those of Henry II (who claimed judicial authority over the clergy) and John. Foxe singles him out as the Pope who started the encroachment on the rights of the temporal governor 'whereby the Pope was brought to his full pride and perfection of power in the fourteenth century'. I have little doubt that Spenser was thinking chiefly of Hildebrand when he made Archimago a master of magic arts and described his plots against Red Cross.

We hear of Archimago's arts in 36, and in 38 he produces a succubus, a false church 'most like that virgin true' until her real nature is revealed. She deceives Red Cross with her claim to be *una sancta ecclesia*, and makes outrageous demands on his body. Spenser may not have been thinking only of the troubles of the eleventh to the fourteenth century; the Synod of Whitby, where, according to Foxe, Wilfrid first led England into the power of Rome, may also have been in his mind. But Gregory VII, who first claimed control of both the swords, ecclesiastical and temporal, and so usurped the power of the emperor . . . was the greatest papal villain. . . . Spenser allows Archimago to conjure up the demonic church which tried to rule the world, and which the British Tudors were to exorcise. But the disgrace of Red Cross, which begins here, represents the long misery of the English Church from the time of Gregory VII until the first stirrings of reformation with Wyclif.

Other crucial events in the Anglican version of church history are reflected in Spenser's narrative. . . . Red Cross first meets Duessa in the company of the infidel Sansfoy (2, 13). She is adorned with a Persian mitre which, together with the bells and flounces of her 'wanton palfry', signify the union of popish flummery and oriental presumption. Sansfoy is the pagan antichrist, defeated by Red Cross as Arthur defeated the pagan Saxons and the crusades the Saracens. I do not say he does not, with his brothers, make a triad opposed to that of the Theological Virtues; the readings are perfectly consistent with one another. Sansloy and Sansjoy are also aspects of antichrist and paganism. . . .

There is surely reason to suppose that Spenser would think along these lines. Let me, to avoid tedium, spare analysis of the Fraelissa and Fradubio episode, clearly another allegory of the wrong choice of faith, and pass on to the story of Kirkrapine, Abessa and Corceca. Corceca is obviously blind devotion. Abessa, as Sr. Mary R. Falls established, is not an abbess but absenteeism, from *abesse*. The main difficulty is with Kirkrapine. I agree with Sr. Mary Falls that he cannot refer to the evils of monasticism; she argues, with some force, that the reference to church-robbing is more likely to apply to the behaviour of English bishops and courtiers after the Reformation. She cites much evidence, and more could be adduced. Sandys, for example (though himself not innocent of the charges he brings against others), asked the queen to end the abuses of the 'surveyors' 'that trot from one diocese to another, prying into churches. The pretence is reformation; but the practice is deformation. They re-form not offences, but for money grant licences to offend.' And he asks the queen – 'our most mild Moses' – to stay the hand of these 'church-robbers'. But he also calls this a perpetuation of a characteristic antichristian practice; and this is really our clue. Spenser is not thinking exclusively of a topical issue; what he has in mind is the duty of the newly restored church to abolish a practice typical of popery, that of using the goods of the church for personal and temporal purposes. Luther gloomily foresaw that churchrobbers would not be checked till Armageddon. Long afterwards Milton echoed him in *Of Reformation* speaking fiercely of prelates:

How can these men not be corrupt, whose very cause is the bribe of their own pleading, whose mouths cannot open without the strong breath and loud stench of avarice, simony and sacrilege, embezzling the treasury of the church on painted and gilded walls of temples, wherein God hath testified to have no delight, warming their palace kitchens, and from thence their unctuous and epicurean paunches, with the alms of the blind, the lame, the impotent, the aged, the orphan, the widow?

Milton accuses the prelates of theft in several kinds; Jewel specifically calls the Roman hierarchy *sacrilegos*, which is in the contemporary translation 'church-robbers', for refusing the laity the wine at communion. Clearly any act which impoverished the church could be called church-robbing; there were contemporary instances, but Spenser has in mind the long record of antichrist and his misdeeds. In *The Shepheardes Calender* 'September' he is more specifically attacking contemporary misappropriations; but when he speaks of the foxes replacing the wolves in England he is thinking of the clergy as having taken over the role of thieves from the pagans. To compare the antichristian clergy to foxes is an old device stemming from Christ's description of Herod as a fox, and from a gloss on Canto 2, 14; Sandys uses it and so does Spenser when he gives Duessa, revealed in all her ugliness, a fox's tail (1, 7, 48). What is scandalous is that this ancient wrong should have survived in the reformed church. Kirkrapine, incidentally, lives in concubinage with Abessa. This certainly suggests the unholy relation between simony and absenteeism in Spenser's time, but also suggests that it is a leftover from an earlier period; for Abessa reproaches Una with unchastity, which hints at the Romanist distaste for the married priesthood of the reformed church, and again associated Kirkrapine with the bad religion before reform.

Archimago, disguised as Red Cross and having Una in his charge, represents a bogus English church betraying true religion. That Sansloy should bring Archimago near to death suggests the self-destructive follies of Urban VI (1318–89, Pope from 1378), who seems in fact to have been more or less insane; Wyclif said that he destroyed the authority of the papacy; after him 'there is none to be received for the pope, but every man is to live after the manner of the Greeks, under his own law'. This lawless folly, and the contemporary inroads of the Turks, probably account for the episode. The rescue of Una from Sansloy by satyrs, as Upton noticed, means the succour of Christianity by primitivist movements such as the Waldensian and Albigensian; some primitives fall into idolatry (hence the follies

of some puritan heretics) but the true Reformation line is represented by the well-born primitive Satyrane, who instantly knows the
truth and opposes Sansloy

The subjection of Red Cross to Orgoglio is the popish captivity
of England from Gregory VII to Wyclif (about 300 years, the three
months of 8, 38). The *miles Christi*, disarmed, drinks of the enervat-
ing fountain of corrupt gospel and submits to Rome. He is rescued
by Arthur, doing duty for Elizabeth as Emperor of the Last Days,
saviour of the English Church. The viciously acquired wealth of
Duessa is confiscated. In 9, 17 Red Cross places Una under the
charge of Gloriana, head of the Church. In this warp of allegory the
capitulation to Despair must mean the Marian lapse; after that
Red Cross is assured of his Englishness, and shown the New Jerusalem, of which Cleopolis or London, capital of the Earthly Paradise,
seat of the empress, is the earthly counterpart. Only then does he
assume the role of the warrior *fidelis et verax* and, with the aid of the
two sacraments of the true church, enact the slaying of the beast, the
harrowing of hell, the restoration of Eden and the binding of
Archimago. The English settlement – to which, as Revelation proved,
all history tended – is a type of that final pacification at the end of
time. Spenser makes it clear that it is *only* typical; but the boldness
with which he conflates history and the archetype in Revelation
proves how fully he accepts Foxe's bold formula, 'the whole church
of Christ, namely . . . the church of England'.

I have tried, in making this sketch of the allegory of ecclesiastical
history in Book I, not to forget that Spenser's historical view was that
of Anglican church historians. This, after all, is rather to be expected
than not, in view of the apocalyptic and protestant-imperialist
nature of Spenser's poem. What I suggest, in short, is that given the
apocalyptic character of Book I – which cannot be denied – allegories
of the kind I propose *must* be present in the poem; consequently the
historical allegory is not the flickering, limited affair it is sometimes
said to be; nor can we pick it up in all its depth by a learnedly
ignorant contemplation of the surface of the fiction. . . .

SOURCE: extracts from 'The Faerie Queene, I and V', originally
published in the *Bulletin of the John Rylands Library* (1964);

subsequently republished in his *Shakespeare, Spenser, Donne* (London, 1971) and in the paperback edition entitled *Renaissance Essays* (London, 1973). Material reproduced here is from the paperback edition, ch. 2, pp. 34–49.

Peter Bayley

THE POETIC ACHIEVEMENT (1971)

. . . In every book, except, significantly, the pastoral Book vi, the hero or heroes visit or sojourn at a great house or castle. Such visits are common in medieval Romance, in medieval love allegory, in Elizabethan pageantry and spectacles, where they usually have a moral significance; even Ariosto provides obvious moral lessons in Atlante's magic castle of deceit and in Logistilla's house, representing reason and virtue. (Tasso's action, being confined to an actual place, Jerusalem, and its environs, except for Rinaldo's truancy to Armida's isle, affords no scope for similar significant buildings.) Spenser re-inforces the point of his argument in each book by temporarily arresting the quick-moving narrative while the Red Cross Knight encounters Pride and the other deadly sins at the House of Pride, falls victim to the pride of the flesh in Orgoglio's castle, and is then instructed in the ways of Holiness at the House of Temperance; while Sir Guyon encounters the personification of the golden mean at Medina's House and sojourns at the House of Temperance; while Britomart – not that she is tempted, in danger or needs to be instructed – is confronted with the shallow pleasures, latent sorrows and ultimate enslavement of sexual indulgence at Malecasta's and Busirane's houses. Further, the Castle of Venus with her temple in its island-gardens enshrines an ideal virtue and beauty; Rade-gund's 'unnatural' regimen presents a disordered world of female rule and male subjugation, and Mercilla's Court clarifies the mes-sage – of love and mercy in judgement – of Britomart's earlier dream at the Temple of Isis. Spenser does not organise too precisely; there is no rigid scheme, the houses or castles are not regularly spaced in the sequence of books, and it is not possible to say that there is any 'type' of house or castle automatically endowed with good or bad properties. Yet there is enough of a scheme . . . for the reader to

perceive a definite pattern which tells him of repeating emphases
in the poem and of its essentially cyclic repeating unity.

In four of the books a similar repeating significance may be found
in the lavish descriptions of gardens. In Book II the Bower of Bliss
provides the only example (with the exception of the brief if vivid
description of the hellish Garden of Proserpine in the same book)
of a garden which is not a place of virtue, however beautiful it may
appear. (C. S. Lewis long ago made clear beyond dispute the careful
detail with which Spenser presented the Bower as a place superficially charming to all the senses but meretricious, artificial and
bad. . . .) In contrast Spenser emphasises the natural in his depictions
of the Garden of Adonis in Book III, and, as the place where stands
the Temple of Venus, in Book IV. Book VI, which has no symbolic or
allegorical house or castle, has instead, in the depiction of the
pastoral world and of the grassy Acidalian mount where the Graces
dance, two splendid natural 'gardens' which symbolise the ordered
virtuous perfection which God intended for his world.

Bowers, arbours and pavilions exist in all these gardens. In Book II
Cymochles is first seen in the arbour 'framed of wanton Ivie' and –
'art striving to compaire With Nature' – garnished all within by
flowers which 'bring out bounteous smels, and painted colours shew'
(II, 5, 29). Phaedria's gondola is

> . . . bedecked trim
> With boughes and arbours woven cunningly,
> That like a little forest seemed outwardly,   (II, 6, 2)

a very artificial boat. Proserpine's 'thicke Arber' is set next to the
tree of golden fruit but in a garden in which the herbs and fruits are
all 'direfull deadly blacke with leafe and bloom' (II, 7, 51). The
climax of these artificial and wanton bowers – bowers of wantonness
– is the arbour-like gate to Acrasia's bower.

> With boughes and braunches, which did broad dilate
> Their clasping armes, in wanton wreathings intricate.
>
> (II, 12, 53)

Very different are the woods on Mount Acidale

> In which all trees of honour stately stood
> And did all winter as in sommer bud,
> Spredding pavilions for the birds to bowre,   (VI, 10, 6)

and the natural arbour of Nature herself, not fashioned by craftsmen.

> But th' Earth herself, of her owne motion,
> Out of her fruitfull bosome made to growe
> Most dainty trees . . .   (VII, 7, 8)

The correspondences, which are close enough for similarities to be recognised and at the same time to emphasise the differences between places of good and of bad resort, extend to the nearby streams. 'Fast beside' Cymochles's bower, a stream trickles softly down with 'murmuring wave', making a sound

> To lull him soft sleepe, that by it lay,   (II, 5, 30)

fit place for the idle wanton Cymochles. Near the Bower of Bliss is a lavishly decorated fountain 'overwrought' . . . with 'shapes of naked boyes', and its 'silver flood' grows into a little lake paved with jasper. At the Bower itself the water musically falls with 'base murmure'; the pun – a common Spenserian device – is emphatically pejorative. But below the woods of Mount Acidale

> . . . a gentle flud
> His silver waves did softly tumble downe,
> Unmard with ragged mosse or filthy mud;
> Ne mote wylde beastes, ne mote the ruder clowne
> Thereto approch, ne filth mote therein drowne;
> But Nymphes and Faeries by the bancks did sit,
> In the woods shade, which did the waters crowne,
> Keeping all noysome things away from it,
> And to the waters fall tuning their accents fit. (VI, 10, 7)

The happy reminiscence of one of the 'Epigrams' from his earliest work, the translation of Marot's version of Petrarch's *canzone*, must have pleased him to make. It confirms one's view of Spenser as the most consistent and homogeneous of poets, constant always to his preoccupations, subject-matter and images. In the original 'epigram' (No. 4) the vision of Muses and Nymphs sweetly in accord tuning

> . . . their voice
> Unto the gentle sounding of the waters fall

is suddenly wiped out:

> I sawe (alas!) the gaping earth devoure
> The Spring, the place, and all cleane out of sight.
> Which yet agreves my heart even to this houre.

The disappearance of the Graces and their dancing attendants more powerfully and more poignantly makes the same point about the vulnerability of virtue. The history of Spenser's development from simple allegories to complex and potent symbolism is summed up in this connexion between the fourth epigram of *A Theatre* and Book VI of *The Faerie Queene*.

At the houses, castles and sometimes in the gardens there are often masques, dances or processions: in Book I the procession of the seven deadly sins at the House of Pride; in Book III the procession and the masque at the House of Busirane; in Book IV the procession of the rivers, seas, water gods and sea-nymphs at the marriage of the Thames and the Medway; in Book VI the dance of the Graces, that great symbol of ordered virtue, and in the Mutabilitie Cantos the procession of the seasons, months, days and hours. (Book V, the book of Disorder, has no place for any dance or procession; nor has Book II, in which the knight-hero has to resist the unruly and disordered passions to which man is subject; but in the other books the ordered power of virtue or the dreadful power of vice is often symbolised in terms of dance or procession.)

All of these recurring *motifs* help to clarify the poet's moral concerns, give abstract power to his exploration of them, and enable him to provide much pleasing imaginative detail. At the same time they are mostly conventional elements in epic and Romance literature: *locus amoenus* or pleasance, *hortus conclustus*, or secluded garden, castle, court and palace. Yet in many cases they give also an effect of real contemporary life; real houses, real courts and courtly ritual, real gardens. They also emphasise again the recurring cyclic structure and purpose of *The Faerie Queene*, and of course they strengthen the sense of the poem's unity: they are like the 'bonders' used in dry-stone walls, great stones placed at irregular intervals and running through the entire thickness of the wall.

Another recurring factor in the poem is reference to Ireland or reminiscence of it. This extends from the slightest allusion or comparison, either generalised, like the cloud of gnats molesting a shepherd (I, I, 23) or, specifically placed, the swarm of gnats at the 'fennes of Allan' (II, 9, 16), to descriptions, for example, of the Red Cross Knight's wasted appearance (I, 8, 41) or of the 'vile caytive wretches' encountered outside Alma's castle (II, 9, 13–17) which seem to echo passages from Spenser's own prose *View of the Present State of Ireland*. There are also many topographical references to and extended treatment of Irish matters and places in Book v and in the Mutabilitie Cantos. . . . Irena's land is Ireland and its disorder, violence and cruelty Irish; many an Irish skirmish, siege, battle and ambush in Book v, together with the hatred, treachery and guile so often presented derives from Spenser's real-life experiences in that 'salvage Island'. And in the Mutabilitie Cantos he charmingly makes a new myth – a second, for there is one in 'Colin Clouts Come Home Againe' – out of two Irish rivers near his estate of Kilcolman, and places the assembly of the gods and the great debate between Nature and the goddess Mutability on the neighbouring Arlo Hill.

There are also a number of ideas, beliefs or preoccupations which constantly recur throughout the poem, and add their contribution to the unmistakable sense of its unity in diversity. Chief among these are the Aristotelian notion of the golden mean, most prominently deployed in Book II 'Of Temperaunce'; the conflict of Reason and Passion, and the dissonance between appearance and reality, which dominate Books II and I respectively, concerned as they are with self-discipline and with man's need of truth; the contrast between courtliness which often means falsehood, corruption and insincerity and the simple virtuous ways of pastoral, shown in the lavish depictions of evil courts such as Pride's or Malecasta's and in the virtues of simple folk, unsophisticated knights like Sir Satyrane and Timias, and the Fauns and the Lion which gently tend Una, and chiefly of course in the self-contained pastoral world in Book VI.

An even stronger bond is the patriotic impulse which permeates the whole poem. Every time Arthur appears (once in each book), in the three books in which Britomart, that virtuous British lady-knight, is the dominant figure; whenever Belphebe – type of 'the most excellent and glorious person of our soveraine the Queene'– appears; and in many sidelong references to Gloriana (Elizabeth) or her court or 'her kingdome in Faery land' and to England's fame; we are reminded of it. From time to time there are more extended references, especially when – surprisingly enough in view of his character – Paridell at dinner in Malbecco's house (III, 9, 33 ff.) tells of his descent from Paris and prompts Britomart to amplify the Trojan connexion with Britain and to prophesy the greater future glory of Troynovant (new Troy). Britomart's lineage and future progeny are also recounted by Merlin in Book III, Canto 3. A greater, and to modern readers somewhat tedious, account of lineage and royal descent is given in Book II, Canto 10, which is devoted to the '*chronicle of Briton Kings*' and the '*rolls of Elfin emperours till time of Gloriane*' which Arthur and Guyon respectively read in the chamber of Memory in Alma's castle. But the whole Arthurian background of the poem, its continuous allusions to English contemporary historical events and personages, and especially Book I with its constant reference to the Church of England in its unending war with Catholicism, and Book V with its continual pointing at the political and military menace of the Catholic powers in Europe, emphasise Spenser's desire – and his powerfully successful achievement of it – to make his great poem not only an enchanting romantic narrative, a work of moral instruction, and an exploration of human motive, character and behaviour, but also a profoundly national epic.

Most pervasive of all, in the end, is Spenser's preoccupation with mutability. Nearly all of his writing contains this, a commonplace of Christian thinkers and writers, but *The Faerie Queene* shows increasingly powerful expression of it. It is this element which is chiefly responsible for the grandeur of *The Faerie Queene* as a philosophical and religious poem, as well as a romantic epic and an allegory. While the early books show the achieving of their quests by the Red Cross Knight and Sir Guyon, the Dragon slain and Acrasia's Bower of Bliss destroyed, increasingly Spenser depicts Faerie land as the world since the Fall, a world governed by imperfection, sin and death. If he had written other books he could not have shown, as he did in the early books, the achievement of ideals in the Faerie world. The flux of the world, its imperfectability, its corruption and decay, the transitoriness of human life and the ultimate inadequacy of human endeavours are aspects of life of which Spenser was deeply conscious. They presented him with the great dilemma of faith, which always confronts the Christian writer who enjoys and loves life: how to reconcile the alluring variousness of the mortal world with its imperfection and instability. Chaucer made several attempts to untease the dilemma: in *The Parlement of Foules* in which he dodged the issue by inventing or incorporating the parliament; and in the *contemptus mundi* of the palinode to *Troilus and Criseyde*. Spenser triumphantly made use of Chaucer's Nature and Chaucer's *débat* in the Mutabilitie Cantos, with which the poem concludes. All the paradoxes and antitheses which the poem rehearses, the perfect and the imperfect, the real and the illusory, the ideal and the actual, good and evil, fertility and sterility, sophistication and innocence, happiness and misery, are resolved in Nature's brief reply to Mutabilitie. But any element of *contemptus mundi* is largely overborne by Spenser's understanding, which is the theme of the Mutabilitie Cantos, that change is not only the sad human consequence of the Fall but that some change is an essential part of God's purpose for that fallen world. Nature herself, God's vicar in Chaucer's 'Foules' Parley', with her changing seasons and the pattern of birth, growth, death and renewal of her creatures whether animal or vegetable, stands for the very principle.

This links the Mutabilitie Cantos closely with the ideas of perpetual renewal and divinely ordained change presented in the account of the Garden of Adonis, especially in Book III, Canto 6. . . . At the beginning of the next Canto (Canto 7, stanza 3) Sir Guyon comes to a gloomy glade which like the Wandering Wood of Book I is so thickly overgrown as to be cut off 'from heavens light'. That is no euphemism; it is indeed cut off from the light of heaven. Here he finds sitting

> . . . in secret shade
> An uncouth, salvage, and uncivile wight,
> Of griesly hew, and fowle ill favour'd sight;
> His face with smoke was tand, and eyes were bleard,
> His head and beard with sout were ill bedight,
> His cole-blacke hands did seeme to have beene seard
> In smithes fire-spitting forge, and nayles like clawes appeard.

> His yron coate all overgrowne with rust,
> Was underneath enveloped with gold,
> Whose glistring glosse darkned with filthy dust,
> Well yet appeard, to have beene of old
> A work of rich entayle, and curious mould,
> Woven with antickes and wyld Imagery:
> And in his lap a masse of coyne he told,
> And turned upsidowne, to feede his eye
> And covetous desire with his huge threasury.

This is a subtle and temperate description, more varied and detailed than the earlier one of Error, but it is composed in exactly the same way, and with similar hyperbole, alliteration and onomatopoeia. Mammon is cleverly compounded of elements of Plutus, God of Wealth, Pluto, God of the Underworld, and Vulcan. A powerful suggestion of the symbolic is combined with a great sense of actuality: his face 'tand' with smoke; 'bleared' eyes; his sooty head and beard; the 'nayles like clawes'; and the rusted 'yron coate' its 'glistring glosse darkned with filthy dust'. Mammon comes before our eyes first as a dirty, bent all-too human smith; gradually we learn of the rusty but rich iron coat with fine chasing in gold, and the telling of his coins, and he appears as the quintessential miser: *miser* despite his riches, wretched hoarder of gold, furtive and fearful of its theft, a mean human wretch, before he reveals himself to Guyon as 'God of the World and worldlings . . . Great *Mammon*, greatest god below the skye'.

There are echoes throughout the episode of Guyon's three-day sojourn in the underworld of Christ's three days and nights in the heart of the earth (Matthew 12:40), and of the temptation of Christ by Satan (Matthew 6:24 and Luke 4), which deepen the gravity and significance of Guyon's sojourn. We can see why – and how successfully – Spenser introduced the infernal subject with those premonitory chords at the end of the preceding canto: he rightly prepared the reader for a transition from an Ariostan romantic epic to deeply significant moral epic narrative.

I have shown how Spenser developed his portrait of the god Mammon slowly, not identifying him as a god until he had told us of his abjectness, foulness, meanness, fearfulness and misery. We are forced into dislike or hatred before we can be impressed. (Milton's Satan we are allowed to admire before we are required to hate.) This is Spenser's common practice. An earlier example was the presentation of Despair:

> That cursed man, low sitting on the ground,
> Musing full sadly in his sullein mind;
> His griesie lockes, long growen, and unbound,
> Disordered hong about his shoulders round,
> And hid his face; through which his hollow eyne
> Lookt deadly dull, and stared as astound.

> His raw-bone cheekes through penurie and pine,
> Were shronke into his jawes, as he did never dine.
>
> (I, 9, 35)

Here a character first introduced to us as a 'cursed man' gradually evolved into a personification. In the course of the process, he attempted to lure the hero into suicide. Failing, he attempted the deed himself. And, as we leave him, this is what we see him doing, as he has done many times before, attempting to kill himself in despair, but in vain; he cannot die, and has become an animated emblem of Despair. A later example is to be found at the end of Book III, Canto 10. Malbecco, the jealous old husband of the faithless and immoral Hellenore, turns into an emblem of Jealousy, and is left for ever wakeful, for ever in pain, hating and hateful, deformed and ill yet unable to die, living on for ever miserably in a cave.

How characteristic it is of Spenser, to leave us with not so much a character as a personification, a picture, an allegorical presentation as in a Tudor pageant, show or morality-play. He employs this method because it is an exemplary teaching method. The identity of the vice or evil is not just presented to us. We meet the figure as an intriguing character in the narrative, and get to know and recognise him and his activity. Often we understand him as an abstraction or emblem before Spenser proclaims his identity, and so he is all the more persuasive because identifying him has been a mental process performed by ourselves. *We* have done a lot of the work. It is a superb justification, if justification were needed, of the use of the allegorical method in a romantic epic with a vital moral purpose. The allegory does not obtrude (as Ariosto's rare use of it does) for in the extra dimension in which Spenser works, a romance figure can easily 'zoom' into character close-up and 'fade' into moral emblem, a vivid episode end by 'freezing' into exemplary tableau. Such sequences refute the perennial complaint of critics about the incompatibility of Romance and allegory, fairyland and moralising, and also about Spenser's being 'remote from life'.

The emblematic – the encapsulating of a moralising idea or a moral lesson in a simplified image – contributes valuably to Spenser's didactic purpose. It is a peculiarly appropriate device, with its ancient lineage, long history and Christian sanction. Its recent recrudescence in the emblem-books of the sixteenth century, together

with the Elizabethan passion for the emblematic shown in so many
pageants, shows and moralities, encouraged the poet to use it in his
moral, patriotic, Elizabethan romantic epic, itself a 'continued
Allegory, or darke conceit'. A number of emblems from the emblem-
books are released from the woodcut and set to move in his narrative.
His chief quarry was Alciati, numerous editions of whose *Emblemata*
appeared from the first edition in 1532; there were nearly one hundred in several European languages before the end of the century.
Spenser's detail of the elongated crane's neck of *Gula* (gluttony) in
the procession of the deadly sins in the House of Pride (1, 4, 21)
probably comes from Alciati's emblem of *Gula*, which itself was inspired by Aristotle's story of a glutton who wished his neck was long
as a crane's that he might the longer enjoy the taste of his food.
Similarly, while his depiction of Duessa when she becomes Orgoglio's
leman (1, 7, 16–17) has its obvious source in the words describing
the Scarlet Whore of the Apocalypse in Revelation 12:17, in his
mind's eye as he wrote was Alciati's emblem, illustrating it, called
Ficta religio (false religion). His *Occasion,* whose locks

> Grew all afore, and loosely hong unrold,
> But all behind was bald, and worne away,
> That none thereof could ever taken hold.   (11, 4, 4)

embodies a detail from Alciati's wood-cut, itself illustrating the
proverbial saying about seizing opportunity 'by the forelock'. He is
also in debt to Alciati for his Tantalus (11, 7, 58), his *Envie* (v, 12,
29 ff.) whose 'dull eyes did seeme to looke askew', whose bones you
might see through her cheeks, whose 'lips were like raw lether, pale
and blew' and who feeds on 'her owne maw' and gnaws hungrily a
venomous snake, and many others. There is nothing elementary or
superficial about Spenser's use of others' emblems: he wants to
simplify and clarify big issues as much as he can, and this purpose
the emblem – and allegory generally of course – notably serves. But
his own 'emblems' are superb: Despair; Mammon; Ignaro (Ignorance) blind and slow, his head turned backwards on his neck (1, 8,
3 ff.), who impedes Arthur in his search for the Red Cross Knight
in Orgoglio's castle; Maleger the evil, sick leader of the besiegers of
Alma's castle (in 11, 11, 22); and many more. They function admir-
ably on the moral plane, but they are also excellent characters in
the narrative. Spenser is careful to humanise them as much as he

can as he sets them moving. When Arthur urgently searches Orgoglio's castle and receives no answer to his calls,

> At last with creeping crooked pace forth came
> An old old man, with beard as white as snow,
> That on a staffe his feeble steps did frame,
> And guide his wearie gate both too and fro;

but Ignaro is 'senceless' and 'doted' as well as blind, and answers to every question 'he could not tell'. Our impatience grows with Arthur's. And Maleger – surely the most un-picturable of all abstractions, this 'badly-diseased evil-doer', leader of the passions attacking the soul – is vividly evoked in the simplest of similes drawn from ordinary life: his 'looke' is 'pale and wan as ashes', his 'bodie leane and meagre as a rake', his skin 'all withered like a dryed rooke'. They are combined with skilful suggestions of the unearthly: his 'helmet light' is 'made of a dead man's skull'; he is large-limbed and broad-shouldered, and yet

> . . . of such subtile substance and unsound,
> That like a ghost he seem'd, whose grave-clothes were unbound.

It is a good example of Spenser's ability to conjure up an abstraction, make clear its moral function and at the same time promote in us a moral and emotional response to it, while successfully keeping our interest in the romantic narrative.

This astonishing power of making the reader see and feel different things at the same time in a character or episode is best shown in his presentation of the Bower of Bliss. A brief comparison of Spenser's depiction of Acrasia with Ariosto's of Alcina and Tasso's of Armida, which both inspired it, may serve to demonstrate his special power in making actual. In *Orlando Furioso* (Book VII) the episode is brief. Alcina accords a formal welcome to Ruggiero to her castle; she entertains him to a sumptuous feast; he breathlessly waits in his chamber for her to come to him; she comes secretly to his bed, and they couple hastily. In *Gerusalemme Liberata* (Book XVI), from which Spenser drew much detail for the Bower of Bliss sequence, the Armida episode is equally courtly, though it takes place in a garden by a lake. In neither case is there any suggestion of a wicked enchantress, until the conclusion of the episode, when Alcina is revealed in all her real deformity (like Spenser's Duessa), and when Armida, after Rinaldo has come to his senses and departed, destroys her palace (as Britomart destroyed Busirane's palace). Although in these episodes both Ariosto and Tasso had a moralising intention, they described the seduction neutrally from a secret onlooker's viewpoint. They pointed the moral separately after the conclusion of the episode. Characteristically, Spenser intensified the emotional force, by describing and moralising at one and the same time. (In any case, he makes the episode the climax of his book; in Ariosto and Tasso it is but an episode in a larger framework.) Spenser was frankly concerned to move his readers to realise in their own senses the power of the temptation, and so the possibility of their own succumbing to such temptation. We are required to judge at the same time as we are incited to desire Acrasia. Spenser knows, with the classical writers and the Renaissance emblematists and mythographers, that Circe, ancestress of Acrasia and her Italian siblings, is the type of self-indulgence and sensuality, able to make men, despite their angelic potentialities, into lusting beasts. In Ariosto and Tasso the enchantress is distanced and prettified as in a tapestry, and described predominantly in visual terms. She is attractive to the sight, but not arousing; the descriptions are too formal for that. We see her beauty but we do not feel its power. Spenser, brilliantly paradoxical in this, makes Acrasia very real: she sweats and sighs and dotes and devours. But her physical allure is not so much visual and aesthetic as sensual. So Spenser makes a powerful double appeal to the reader. His animal senses (already titillated, as Guyon's by the two provocative girls at the edge of the little lake displaying their naked charms) are aroused and respond to her sexuality, while his moral sense is alerted and must (and does) reject her animal appeal.

Perhaps above all it is Spenser's vividness that is his greatest poetic virtue. Its achievement is due partly to the exaggeration and repetition of image and sound I have already referred to; partly to his use of all the senses, of touch, taste and smell as well as of sight and hearing of which good examples are the description of the Dragon (1, 11, 8), and of Duessa stripped naked (1, 8, 46 ff.).

But there are many other contributory factors. His similes are usually simple. He always keeps the reader in close touch with the things of ordinary life, and is careful to include the minutest detail – blood running from spurs down a horse's sides; a knight walking slowly because of the weight of his armour; a horse trampling 'dockes' or biting his 'yron rowels into frothy fome'; 'the salt brine' springing out of the 'billowes' as a ferryman rows; the shallow sea discoloured and the waves checked thus betraying the existence of a quicksand; Night's horses softly *swim* away through the black sky; the satyrs, like goats, have 'backward bent knees' and cannot kneel to worship Una as they would have wished. Obviously the poet is thinking hard and visualising clearly. It is vital for his purpose that he should make Faerie land, and all its people and actions, totally convincing. . . .

SOURCE: extracts from *Edmund Spenser : Prince of Poets* (London, 1971) pp. 156–61, 172–8.

Alastair Fowler

NEOPLATONIC ORDER IN
THE FAERIE QUEEN (1973)

. . . One of the most rigorous yet also poetically satisfying of the
poem's Neoplatonic exercises [is] the dance of the Graces, mythic
paradigm of all triads. Spenser emphasizes the focal value of this
image by the alienation effect, rare with him, of autobiographical
treatment. For Colin's vision at the physical centre of twelve pur-
posed books epitomizes his creator's confrontation of his imagined
world. Significantly, from the present standpoint, the cosmic pattern
Colin beholds is a *choresis,* or metaphysical dance, unfolding in triple
rhythm the entire beauty of Venus the formgiver: (VI, 10, 15)

> Those were the Graces, daughters of delight,
>> Handmaids of Venus, which are wont to haunt
>> Upon this hill, and dance there day and night:
>> Those three to men all gifts of grace do grant,
>> And all, that Venus in her self doth vaunt,
>> Is borrowed of them.

Colin explains the Graces after they have vanished (a chastening
sequence for interpreters to reflect upon), by moralizing them under
the three heads. These are: facial expression, nakedness, and posture.
Under each aspect, characteristically, Spenser discovers triads of
qualities, though these disclose themselves in a variety of ways:
(VI, 10, 24)

> 1 Therefore they always smoothly seem to smile,
>> That we likewise should mild and gentle be,
> 2 And also naked are, that without guile
>> Or false dissemblance all them plain may see,
>> Simple and true from covert malice free:

3   And eek them selves so in their dance they bore,
    That two of them still forward seemed to be,
    But one still towards showed her self afore;
That good should from us go, than come in greater store.

Wind's *Pagan Mysteries in the Renaissance* has set out the philosophical
content of the Graces' iconography, and particularly of their 2 + 1
choreographic figure, with a fullness and subtlety it would be grace-
less to try to repeat. But we may notice the poetic means whereby
Spenser mimes their figure. First, take the grammatical structure.
Each aspect seems to be given a description, then a moralisation
introduced by *that* = 'in order that'. But two descriptions are in terms
of seeming, one in terms of being: the Graces 'seem' to smile so that
we should be similarly mild; they 'are' naked so that we may see
them plainly; and two of them 'seemed' outward turned so that we
may follow their example of generous action. Even the verbs join in
the Graces' dance. Or consider the aspects in turn. The Graces smile
'smoothly' (one quality) to make us 'mild and gentle' (two qualities).
Here three qualities are divided 2 + 1 between mankind and the
Graces. Their nakedness, however, presents triads in a different way.
Its purpose is that all may see them 'plain' (one positive) 'without
guile or false dissemblance' (two negatives): 'simple and true' (two
positives) 'from covert malice free' (one negative). That is, positives
and negatives form the 2 + 1 configuration. Next, the Graces exemplify generosity precisely by the 2 + 1 dance figure: two seem facing
'forward' (i.e., outward), only one inward turned. Finally, taking all
three aspects, we notice that while the first and third display single
triads, the second offers a double triad. Again the 2 + 1 figure, whose
cosmic meaning is generosity, liberality, ultimately the creative
spirit of grace itself. And the outgoing movement may also be seen
in the progression of the beholders' attitudes, from an inner response
of gentle mildness, through a reciprocal phase of looking, to the
outward response of giving.

But is this all? So far we have only treated the most obvious chain
of discourse. But actually the stanza is full of syntactic, semantic, and
schematic ambiguities. Are the Graces naked so that we can see that
they are without guile, or so that we may see them without using
guile? And what of the semantic ambiguity that allows us to take
'simple and true from covert malice free' as the third aspect? There

would then be a progression from seeming (aspect 1) through exposure (aspect 2) to inner moral meaning. This movement, moreover, would be appropriately diastolic: the Graces seem smooth so that we may be gentle; they are outwardly naked (that is, without disguise) so that all may see them openly; and all for their part see the Graces as they inwardly are, simple and true. The third, covert aspect, mimetically, has no introductory physical description, but comprises three simple moral qualities. On this analysis the explanation of the dance in lines 5–9 would be a summary, referring to all three aspects treated symmetrically, a triad of qualities being assigned to each. This ambiguity extends to minor details: 'seemed to be' (line 7) can be regarded as a recapitulatory infolding of seeming and being. In short, ingeniously varied schemes throughout correspond to the triad and its shifting divisions into proceeding and reverting phases. And this emphasis, as we know, characterised Renaissance Neoplatonism, not the earlier Neoplatonism of such authors as Dionysius.

All through Book VI the triad of the Graces undergoes repeated expansion and travesty. Everyone has noticed, for example, that Despetto, Decetto, and Defetto constitute an evil antitype: though fewer, perhaps, have traced the correspondences of individual terms of the antitriad with aspects of the Graces. Timias' attackers are introduced in a stanza whose metaphysical inspiration will by now be readily appreciated: (VI, 5, 13)

> The first of them by name was called Despetto,
> Exceeding all the rest in power and height;
> The second not so strong but wise, Decetto;
> The third nor strong nor wise, but spitefullest Defetto.

The powerful loftiness of Despetto exactly opposes the mild gentle smiling of the Graces. Similarly the Graces' *nuda sinceritas*, their plain guilelessness, contrasts with Decetto's deceitfulness or 'false dissemblance'; and their simple truth with the ungenerous faultfinding ('covert malice') of Defetto. The antitriad even receives an iconographical expression equivalent to that of the Graces in the attack on Timias. For proud Despetto is the only adversary who attacks frontally, while Decetto tries to 'circumvent' Timias, spiteful Defetto to destroy him behind his back.

The qualities of the Graces and anti-Graces alike find expansion in the several episodes of Book VI. Graham Hough's opinion, that 'it would be absurd to look for formal allegorical significance' (*A Preface to 'The Faerie Queene'*, p. 205) in the early episodes of the book, might itself be called absurd, were that not to risk Despetto. Consider Disdain, who walks on tiptoe on brittle legs, who stares with unsmiling 'stern eyebrows' (VI, 8, 26), and who with Scorn abuses Mirabella in 'foul despite' (VI, 8, 6): is he not an expansion of Despetto? And surely the same applies to Mirabella herself, at whose trial for cruelty in love 'fell Despite / Gave evidence' (VI, 7, 34). The Disdain and Scorn she suffers punishment from are her own: they have become habitual, so that even when she takes pity on Timias scornful disdain is punishing to both. Crudor develops Despetto in a less psycho-pathological vein. The reverse of 'mild and gentle', he roughly exacts a service in love for which he makes no return. As Kathleen Williams has remarked, the 'movement of the circle' completed by the Graces is here reversed. In the same way tricky Turpine doubles the deceits of Decetto, contriving to 'cloak' his mischief, until Arthur strips him of his courteous disguise, despoils and 'baffles' him (VI, 7, 4, 26–7). Meanwhile the Blattant Beast nips in from time to time to show up Defetto.

Triad and antitriad also function structurally, with their terms alternating as in a dance, now within a canto, now at greater length. Canto 6, for example, unfolds all three terms: the hermit explains the Blattant Beast (Defetto); Mirabella in penance exhibits her Despetto; and Arthur deceives Turpine, whose wounded body is concealed by Blandina (Decetto). In the early cantos the development of sophisticated virtue takes forms easily missed or even mistaken for contraries to the Graces. Thus, faced with Despetto's oppression of helpless victims, the virtuous knights at first seem themselves 'despiteous' and crude. Calidore butchers Maleffort, Tristram the Knight of the Summer Barge; until we badly need a reminder that 'Blood is no blemish' (VI, 1, 26). Similarly Calidore is capable of conspiring in deceptions to circumvent the compromising position Priscilla's guileless simplicity has betrayed her into (3, 18), or to restore marital harmony between Matilda and Bruin (4, 34–8). And Arthur twice deceives Turpine, once quite deviously, by getting Enias to lie for him. Looking more closely, however, we see an aspect of the Graces developed in each episode. Calidore remains mild under the nagging reproaches of Briana. His white lies to Priscilla's father, like Arthur's various deceptions, are the 'sweet semblant' of the gracious courtier, which no courteous reader will long confuse with Decetto's malicious falsity. And the knights who are surprised unarmed making love – Aladine with Priscilla, Calepine with Serena – manifest to the charitable eye a complementary quality of the Graces, guileless nakedness.

The last cantos penetrate to the Grace's meaning, liberality and the conception of Grace itself. They are filled with images of generosity: Calidore's kindness to the miserable Coridon, and his repeated readiness to give his life for Pastorella; Meliboe's hospitality to Calidore; and the outgoing love at great cost of Claribell and Bellamour. By contrast most of the evil characters are now thieves, not because the criminal classes are specially impolite, but because they lack the grace of giving. This is so, whether you consider the lustful savage thieves who grudge even to share Serena with their fellow cannibals, or the brigands – so contrary to generous Meliboe that they soon cause his death – who deal in human lives and freedom for the sake of their own security, or even, by slave-trading, for gain, and who kill their own captain as soon as he treats Pastorella personally enough to desire her love; down to the Blattant Beast itself, which, though it includes all those discourtesies classified under Defetto, is in these cantos known by its spoil (12, 22) and its thefts from the clergy (12, 23, 25).

Calidore's own part in Book VI has a triadic rhythm of one proceeding and two reverting phases. For, after a first period of virtuous (reverting) activity, during his so-called truancy he mainly receives benefits, such as Meliboe's hospitality, and seems to forget his mission. Finally, inspired by his glimpse of the Graces (a poetic vision proceeding from the divine), he enters on another reverting phase of activity. His truancy, then, may not be a moral failure quite like those of the other knights patron, but rather a life-stage. Kathleen Williams thinks that he temporarily forgets his responsibility to make return for life's benefits, which in a sense is true. But one almost feels that the 'fault' serves partly as a means of provoking blame and hence an encounter with the Blattant Beast of defamation. After all Calidore could hardly have defeated the Beast if his own culpability had been very great. There is a remarkable alienation effect here, whereby Spenser, in what from some points of view is his most serious book, comes near to questioning with Meliboe the whole validity of the court as an image of glory.

These structural extensions and replications of the triad in multiplicities of dazzlingly intricate forms are constructs of art, not exercises in philosophy. Still Spenser may have found a suggestion for an aim for his artistic endeavours in the Neoplatonic conception, developed by Pico, Ficino, and others, that every part of the universe is a triadic microcosm of the whole, in which the contemplative observer may see vestiges of the Trinity through its very texture: *Divinam trinitatem in rebus cunctis agnosces*. Alternatively, he may have been influenced by the mediaeval tradition, going back to SS Augustine and Bonaventura, that traced a trinitarian pattern in operations of the human mind.

More generally, Platonism informs the relation of personal image to idea throughout *The Faerie Queen*. All the main characters are 'images of virtues, vices', and so imply a system of ideas and images of ideas. By the same Platonic compliment that Drayton paid in *Idea's Mirror* and Sidney in *Astrophil and Stella* xxv, Spenser elevates Queen Elizabeth to the realm of ideas. Consequently he may 'express' her in more than one image – in Una, Medina, Britomart, and Mercilla, as well as in Belphoebe and Gloriana. On the other hand, he usually needs several of the Queen's subjects to make up the particular intention of a single image. Both Leicester and Essex resemble Artegall, as the contemporary Cambridge Marginalian noted. We recall Xenophon's account of the process of idealization by which the artist combines features from many individuals in constructing one ideal figure.

The status of images in *The Faerie Queen* has been treated generally by Lewis in *Spenser's Images of Life*. Here I shall only take up the point that in the lower register of the cosmic scale – farthest from reality – the relation between image and idea is that of false to true. The shibboleth 'appearance and reality', currently a fashionable theme to carve out of almost any Elizabethan work, has here some meaning still. As in the Platonic system, so in *The Faerie Queen*, imitations are less good than originals (though not necessarily evil), so that the reader aspires to ideas of divine beauty and virtue by rejecting, or else by loving and transcending, 'mere' images.

Sometimes this distinction receives narrative enactment. Thus

Spenser more than once portrays an evil perversion of good as the fabrication of a double. Archimago tempts Redcrosse away from Una by abusing his fantasy 'with false shows' of her disloyalty. He (I, I, 45–6)

> Had made a lady of that other sprite,
> And framed of liquid air her tender parts
> So lively, and so like in all men's sight,
> That weaker sense it could have ravished quite . . .
>
> And that new creature born without her due,
> Full of the maker's guile, with usage sly
> He taught to imitate that lady true,
> Whose semblance she did carry under feigned hue.

Later in the same book Redcrosse himself is impersonated to deceive Una, and in Book III Florimell is copied by a witch who constructs Snowy Florimell, a false image that some to their cost prefer. But the most elaborate impersonation is Busyrane's magic conjuring of idols of Cupid. His cruel Cupid easily deceives, for Cupid in the world is always cruel. Thus the Cupid on Scudamour's shield has 'cruel shafts'; that of the Garden has returned from ransacking the world with spoils and cruelty (III, 6, 49). But the true Cupid is cruel not of himself, but only through the world's accidents; whereas Busyrane raises false images, 'a thousand monstrous forms', of a passion that ends in cruelty absolute and unthinkable. Spenser's insistence on the false imagery is psychologically acute. Busyrane has filled his house with tapestries and reliefs showing the tyrannous cruelty of Cupid in triumph; not to mention a statue of Cupid maiming the guardian of chastity – in short, a whole culture of erotic images, which Britomart must contemplate, live with, and be conditioned by, before he can subject her imagination, by his charms, to the masque of Cupid. This at first seems a nuptial performance by the god himself; but it too proves illusory when Britomart passes beyond images of fantasy, through the iron gate of life, to the inner and comparatively real image of sex.

Even where Spenser introduces no outright *Doppelgänger* or false image, a similar opposition of evil imitation to good reality may be implicit. Throughout, moral emblems, mythological entities, and symbolic attributes often appear twice over, in true and in false

forms, which can scarcely be understood separately from one another. For a characteristic *modus operandi* of Spenser's imagination
leads to pairs of iconographically similar passages in close moral
relation, even at wide spatial remove. This may be why *The Faerie
Queen* seems morally obscure to some, who perhaps read it too seldom
to make those connections between disjunct passages on which its
meaning depends. And the same applies to criticisms of disunity and
structural weakness levelled not only at Spenser, but also at such
later authors using a constructive method learned from him, as
Fielding and Defoe.

Everyone has noticed the correspondence and contrast that
Spenser develops between the Bower of Bliss and the Garden of
Adonis. Each place is a Garden of Life, in each a genius keeps the
gate – in the Garden of Adonis the true Agdistes (11, 12, 47)

> that celestial power, to whom the care
> Of life, and generation of all
> That lives, pertains in charge particular,
> Who wondrous things concerning our welfare,
> And strange phantoms doth let us oft foresee,
> And oft of secret ill bids us beware:
> That is our self . . .

but in the Bower a being (11, 12, 48)

> quite contrary,
> The foe of life, that good envies to all,
> That secretly doth us procure to fall,
> Through guileful semblants, which he makes us see.

Over one a lustful *Venus naturalis* presides, over the other a creative
Venus genetrix. The good Venus enjoys an Adonis who has lived
through death, transformation, and rebirth to everlasting joy; the
evil Venus, Acrasia, enjoys a Verdant who sleeps forever in life's
selfish springtime. Finally, both places have a symbol of chaos, or
chaotic sensuality: Grill, declining to be restored from hoglike to
higher form; and the boar, safely imprisoned under the Garden
Mount by Venus the formgiver.[1]

No one could miss these echoes, which sound loudly even in the
ears of Momus. But we must read often to hear the overtones of a

more delicate order. Thus, the Bower of Bliss fountain is built of a
mysterious unnamed substance: (II, 12, 60)

> a fountain stood,
> Of richest substance, that on earth might be,
> So pure and shiny, that the silver flood
> Through every channel running one might see;
> Most goodly it with curious imagery
> Was overwrought,

and with shapes of wanton *putti*. Now Spenser reintroduces the same
transparent material at the Temple of Venus, where Scudamour re-
leases Amoret from maidenhood. But this time it takes the religious
form of an altar, or, by Empsonian ambiguity, of an *idol* of Venus:
(IV, 10, 39–40)

> Right in the midst the goddess' self did stand
>   Upon an altar of some costly mass,
>   Whose substance was uneath to understand:
>   For neither precious stone, nor dureful brass,
>   Nor shining gold, nor mouldering clay it was;
>   But much more rare and precious to esteem,
>   Pure in aspect, and like to crystal glass,
>   Yet glass was not, if one did rightly deem,
> But being fair and brickle, likest glass did seem.

> But it in shape and beauty did excel
>   All other idols . . .

I believe we are to connect these passages and infer that the Bower
dissipates libido from the sexual vessel in a formless stream (the
fountain of will), whereas the Temple offers it in personal form.
True, Acrasia's fountain seems outwardly semi-personal, its exterior
being 'overwrought' with 'curious imagery' of *putti*. But in the better
instance the mysterious substance shapes an altar with an identified
image of Venus, said to be superior to any the pagan world had to
offer. In other words the Temple exists for Christian sacrifice of love,
not merely for expression of will. Taken separately, neither mention
of material is very significant; brought together, they are full of
meaning. Not only do they persuade that self-expression is less personal than love that oblates personal identity; but they also connect

the transparent flesh of the fountain with the brittle glass-like substance of marital loyalty,[2] already introduced in iii, 2.

Generalizing further, we may almost formulate a natural law of Spenser's Fairyland: At least one corresponding evil image precedes a virtuous image. The house of proud Lucifera, where the non-porter Malvenù denies no one, precedes the house of Holiness, where Humilitá warily guards a 'straight and narrow' way. Similarly the bad Venus of the Bower comes earlier than any good Venus, the bad Adonis of Malecasta's tapestry earlier than the Adonis of the Garden, and many cruel or ambivalent Cupids before the 'mild' Cupid of vi, 7, 37, Mirabella's judge: a tetrad of false friends, Ate–Duessa–Blandamour–Paridell, travesties in advance the true tetrad of concord, Triamond–Cambell–Canacee–Cambina: and authority seems evil in the proud, testy, status-conscious Artegall of iv, 4–6, before it is shown virtuous in the reformed co-ruling Artegall of Britomart's dream of state at Isis Church and in the regal Mercilla. It is the same with the two tournaments. The discordant cestus tournament of Book iv degenerates into disorderly strife, with Artegall going off in 'great displeasure' and even Britomart leaving when 'she them saw to discord set' (iv, 5, 29); the tournament of v, 3, however, after the achievement of concord, is characterized by felicitous order, only temporarily disturbed by Braggadocchio's false claim.

Sometimes the approach to an image of virtue goes more ceremoniously through several graduated stages, first of evil, then of neutral or natural images. Thus Spenser leads up to the visionary ring of maidens about the Graces' ring, through descriptions of the concentric circles of friendly or amorous shepherdesses and swains garlanding Pastorella (herself crowned with flowers), from the cluster of greedy robbers surrounding Serena, who lust after her and only grudgingly give her up to their evil god, in dark imitation of the return of graces to the all-giver.

One cannot adequately discuss such correspondences in terms of moral contrast. For that, Spenser had no need to design so elaborate a system of paired images. Where the images are mythological, one can relate them to the astrological and Neoplatonic doctrine that the same deity may exert either an excessive (bad) or a harmoniously modified (good) influence. In general, however, it seems reasonable to construe them as simply Platonic. The movement from false images to true belongs to a larger movement from the world of appearances towards that of reality and ideas.

So regarded, the poem as a whole may be described as an allegorical expansion of Arthur's quest for Gloriana through reflections of her glory on individual ideals or images of virtues. In abstract terms, this is the quest of eros for the heavenly beauty, and as such it can find no fulfilment in any good short of the highest of all, good itself. By apparent goods it is betrayed. Hence only a vagrant 'fancy' and a 'semblant vain' makes Arthur wish that the Florimell he follows (III, 6, 54)

> mote be
> His Faerie Queen, for whom he did complain:
> Or that his Faerie Queen were such, as she . . .

Nevertheless his error hardly seems ignoble: Florimell's shortcoming is simply that of necessity she can only image the one true fair. Thus Arthur's pursuit corresponds on a loftier plane to pursuit of false Florimell by baser characters: as the false Florimell is to the true, so is the true to Gloriana. From this proportional relation large inferences can be drawn. For example, adopting Angus Fletcher's terminology we may say that the heroes of *The Faerie Queen*, especially the titular knights patron, function as subcharacters generated by Arthur.[3] A passage in Toscanella, cited by William Nelson in another connection, is very relevant here. Ariosto's commentator says that his author 'placed several virtues in several individuals, one virtue in one character and another in another character, in order to fashion out of all the characters a well-rounded and perfect man. A well-rounded and perfect man is one adorned with all the virtues.'[4] In Spenser's view the 'well-rounded and perfect man' displays magnificence; 'which virtue,' the Letter to Ralegh tells us, 'is the perfection of all the rest, and containeth in it them all'. And not only does Arthur's magnificence contain the individual virtues, but in each book in turn it issues in 'deeds . . . applicable to that virtue'. Consequently the Legend of Temperance finds Arthur temperate and struggling with Maleger, arch-enemy of the temperate body; the Legend of Friendship finds him intervening between combatants, 'With gentle words persuading them to friendly peace' (IV, 9, 32).

This helps to answer some common criticisms of Spenser's overall narrative structure. We defend the unity of a single book by saying, in effect, that its significant content is allegorical, outwardly symbolized by actions of subcharacters but inwardly attributable to the knight patron. And in the same way we may defend the linking narrative, by saying that Arthur approaches his goal allegorically through the symbolic actions of his subcharacters, the champions of virtues. Like the heroes of individual books, Arthur is morally imperfect. Like them, too, he is not even invariably superior to his subcharacters: Scudamour and Britomart have to restrain him from killing Paridell and his cronies, just as Amoret earlier taught Britomart to spare Busyrane. More dubiously, Mirabella persuades him not to kill Disdain, almost as Mammon persuaded Guyon not to contend with this fault at all (ii, 7, 41–2).

Here Fletcher's theory of the generation of subcharacters requires modification. If one thinks of the allegorical hero as generating other characters, who serve to objectify traits of his personality, one must also think of him as generating a fictive self. For he himself participates in the fiction with the subcharacters. He speaks, struggles, and has dealings with them: he inhabits their world. It is much the same with certain dreams. You generate in them not only symbolic people but also, very often, a dreamer who represents yourself. Represents you, but cannot be wholly identified with you – since you, after all, are having the dream. The relation of dreamer or hero to subcharacters becomes almost explicit in *The Faerie Queen* when Arthur dreams a vision of Gloriana. For Arthur's visitant, who talked throughout the night ('Ne living man like words did ever hear, / As she to me delivered all that night') is a character in his dream. But he is a character in it too. On waking he finds 'pressed grass, where she had lyen'. And from that moment his waking experience extends his dream, as he pursues in life the ego-ideal he dreamt. To change the figure, he goes on to enact the epic Gloriana recited to him in his vision. Significantly this all begins at a time when he is given over to the pleasures of 'looser life'.

Arthur's quest takes him towards Gloriana in a movement that for him must mysteriously take the time of all twelve yearly adventures, though the other heroes seem to attend the court at least annually. Moreover, all the other quests start at court, instead of being directed towards it. This pattern is hardly intelligible, except from a Neoplatonic point of view. In terms of the doctrine of the

triad, however, it makes good sense. For in Arthur's quest through
individual virtues we see a large-scale *choresis* or triadic movement.
The source of the virtues manifested *seriatim* is Gloriana in her
divine general intention, so that Arthur's search for her is the returning phase (*remeatio*) of the cosmic rhythm. Spenser himself puts it
like this, in the Proem to Book VI, where he addresses Queen Elizabeth the 'special intention' of Gloriana:

> Then pardon me, most dreaded sovereign,
>   That from your self I do this virtue bring,
>   And to your self do it return again:
>   So from the ocean all rivers spring,
>   And tribute back repay as to their king.
>   Right so from you all goodly virtues well
>   Into the rest, which round about you ring,
>   Fair lords and ladies, which about you dwell,
> And do adorn your court, where courtesies excel.

This stanza hints broadly enough why the questing knights issue
from Gloriana's court to perform their virtuous deeds. With the
help of a suggestion of Maurice Evans's it is not difficult to work out
that the missions correspond to the Neoplatonic *emanatio*, the quests
themselves to the *raptio* or *conversio*, and the ingathering of the virtues
in the complete person of Arthur to the return or *remeatio*. Or, to
construe the sequence personally, an inner spiritual prompting (the
dream of glory that is the divine offering or *emanatio*) initiates a life-
long *askesis*, or mystical way, through virtues to the inclusive integration of the whole man or divine image. Spenser combines the allegorical mode with a well suited philosophical model, in eloquent expression of the experience of vocation.

Some who accept the idea of an overall movement throughout the
poem will look for development of character, and be disappointed,
even with respect to the allegory symbolized by the generated
narratives. This disappointment is unreasonable: Spenser never
intended *The Faerie Queen* as a *Bildungsroman*. But it is also unreasonable to rush with Nelson (*The Poetry of Edmund Spenser*, p. 122) to the
opposite extreme pedagogically, of expecting the characters to be
completely static, or 'stable'. We are bound to look at least for moral
progression in Arthur and the knights patron. To take the more
difficult case, Arthur's, a progression can legitimately be found in

his manifesting virtues in a logical and organic sequence. Each of his virtues transcends its predecessor. When Britomart meets Guyon she overthrows him through the 'secret virtue' (iii, i, 10) of her enchanted spear, because chaste love is a higher virtue than temperance, presupposing it as a *sine qua non*. Similarly the third knight is able to rescue the first, in the unequal fight before the House of Malecasta. And Guyon in his quest seeks to arrest concupiscence – a mission one might define theologically as mortification of the flesh and destruction of the body of sin, or as sanctification; the next stage after the baptism of repentance Book i was concerned with. Try a transformation, putting Book ii before Book i, and you arrive at an unacceptably Arminian theological argument, not to speak of an incoherent psychological sequence. Moving to Part 2, we find similar evidences of progression: justice in Book v takes for granted the concord, alliances, and social contract established in Book iv; but its rough hero Artegall must suffer the Blattant Beast quelled in Book vi. In short, Arthur's moral or erotic aspiration is not a story manifesting virtues in random order, nor exhibiting facets of a static character; but rather imitating a search for moral glory and complete integration, through the insufficiencies of individual virtues, each of which transcends and includes its predecessor. The well-rounded man turns out to be a little like the concentric moral spheres on the title page of John Case's *De sphaera civitatis*, where the outermost *primum mobile* reaches to the queen herself and therefore contains all virtues.

From the point of view of consistency of structure *The Faerie Queen* is really extraordinarily unified, however strange a description of it that has come to seem. The dispute about unity has been partly semantic: some mean unity in Ariosto's or Milton's or Sterne's or Proust's sense; others the unity of Minturno, Waldock, Addison, and Hough.

If *The Faerie Queen* bodies forth a consistent philosophical vision, the questions next arise whether it is a philosophical poem, and what relation the philosophy bears to the poetry. It seems at least as philosophical as, say, Wordsworth's *Prelude*; though not often philosophical in a systematic sense. I have emphasized structural patterning; but every reader knows that *The Faerie Queen* is free from any unnatural rage for order. It never discloses its form to us, except in

piecemeal fashion, pattern by pattern by apparent pattern; gradually, as if you were learning the laws of a real world. Spenser is seldom doctrinaire like Dante, or Blake, or (in a different way) e. e.
cummings. Nevertheless, his philosophy not only serves a useful
purpose: it also seems true.

Aesthetically considered, a Neoplatonic model was good for *The
Faerie Queen*. It gave intellectual structure, while allowing room for
delicate shades of individual feeling. Spenser's philosophy of moral
aspiration, his love-relation with the one true fair, has an elusive
unifying function not unlike that of the search for personal identity
in Proust; though of course very different substantively. Since his
philosophy was not the poet's own construction, it never distracted
him from his true calling, exploration of the inner universe of
sensibility. That exploration he carried out with an unusual integration of feeling, which gives the poem coherence even when it is not
overtly concerned with unity or reconciliation of opposites. Yet the
latter bulks so large that we must count it a great loss not to have the
parts of *The Faerie Queen* in which its larger contraries would have
been brought to narrative resolution.

But the aesthetic advantages of Spenser's philosophy are far from
being only negative or neutral. The flexible metaphysics of Neoplatonism suited his temperament and art as Scholasticism would
never have done: we need only compare the firm, even rigid,
division of the *Divina Commedia* with the fluid metamorphic movement of *The Faerie Queen* to see that. This is not meant primarily as
a value judgment. However, the two philosophies have come to differ
in status so oddly that their relative value invites attention. And
Spenser's poem is important evidence of Neoplatonism's fertile and
beneficent influence on the arts. In that respect *The Faerie Queen*
ranks with the finest works produced by the Medici circle. To go on
from this claim to say that Neoplatonic forms are only a subset of
the range of structures composing this encyclopedic yet Christian
epic, is to give some idea, perhaps, of its stature.

SOURCE: extract from 'Neoplatonic Order in *The Faerie Queen*',
in *A Theatre for Spenserians*, ed. Judith M. Kennedy and James
A. Reither (Toronto and Manchester, 1973) pp. 62–77.

NOTES

1. For the interpretations of the boar as chaos and as concupiscence, see Pierio Valeriano, *Hieroglyphica* . . . (Frankfurt, 1613) 68D.

2. See A. Fowler, *Spenser and the Numbers of Time* (London, 1964) p. 124 n.

3. Angus Fletcher, *Allegory: The Theory of a Symbolic Mode* (Ithaca, N.Y., 1964) p. 195, and *passim*.

4. W. Nelson, *The Poetry of Edmund Spenser* (New York, 1963) p. 121.

A. Kent Hieatt

A SPENSER TO STRUCTURE OUR MYTHS (1975)

It is a characteristic of a mythic world like Spenser's that one can enter it at any point and allow its complexities to unfold around one. The evidence of the correspondences between the parts of this world is so intricate and arises so casually that the pleasures of mythic discovery meet one freshly at each reading. As with music, however, clear prior recognition of what is happening and of what is about to happen only increases our pleasure. The physical locales of *The Faerie Queene* correspond naturally to the parts of a mental and moral country, sometimes in terms of chivalric and romantic adventure, and at other times in symbolically more concentrated allegorical landscapes or dwellings – *paysage moralisé*. Spenser's favored device in *The Faerie Queene* is the multilayered allegorical conceit or metaphor, in which he brings together thematically a group of symbolic meanings in what musically might be called a chord, without much concern for the onward movement of his narrative. . . .

In the island of Acrasia, mistress of Phaedria and Cymochles, the most powerful technical means of a sense-deceiving art . . . strive to create an appearance of the natural. The best available practitioners have been retained: 'A place pickt out by choice of best alive, / That natures work by art can imitate' (11, 12, 42). . . . Acrasia and her new lover Verdant recline in the center of the seagirt island on a bed of roses, and a song about a rose is sung in their presence. As to Cymochles in his earlier visit, two girls have exposed their attractions to Guyon by turns, this time while they are bathing in the overflow from a central fountain. Upon this fountain itself is found ivy, like that previously found in the arbor over Cymochles's head, but the imitation of nature by a competitive and deceptive art is now made more explicit. The prurient tendrils of the plant are made of hard, mineral gold, colored expertly so as to suggest the most palpitantly living organic matter:

> And over all, of purest gold was spred,
>   A trayle of yvie in his native hew:
>   For the rich mettall was so coloured,
>   That wight, who did not well avis'd it vew,
>   Would surely deeme it to be yvie trew:
>   Low his lascivious armes adown did creepe,
>   That themselves dipping in the silver dew,
>   Their fleecy flowres they tenderly did steepe,
> Which drops of Christall seemd for wantones to weepe.
>
> (12, 61)

So it is, as well, with some of the grapes on the vine from which the porter Excesse prepares a cup that she offers to all comers; and the weight of this gold is such as perilously to overburden the boughs provided by nature:

> And them amongst, some were of burnisht gold,
>   So made by art, to beautifie the rest,
>   Which did themselves emongst the leaves enfold,
>   As lurking from the vew of covetous guest,
>   That the weake bowes, with so rich load opprest,
>   Did bow adowne, as over-burdened.   (12, 55: 1-6)

The principle on which the Bower is made attractive is that all stimuli should be intensified up to the breaking point, as though 'With all the ornaments of *Floraes* pride, / Wherewith her mother Art, as halfe in scorne / Of niggard Nature, like a pompous bride / Did decke her, and too lavishly adorne' . . . .

The great preoccupation of the artful supporters of this symbolic landscape is the evanescence of time, and the need to grasp sensual pleasure, as already defined by Phaedria, with an opportunism which in the event turns out to be murderously callous towards others. At the entry to the Bower of Bliss, as in so many other places in it, Spenser at first follows the description of Armida's garden in Tasso's *Gerusalemme liberata*, xvi. For the symbolic figures represented on the gate of the Bower, however, he discards Tasso's instances of man deserting honor for voluptuousness, and substitutes the enormities

committed by the lover Medea in order to get and keep her sensual
bliss. First, Medea drops the gobbets of the flesh of her dismembered
younger brother from her ship to deflect her father's pursuit of her
and her lover Jason; then, at a later point, she employs a stratagem
to burn to death Jason's new love and affianced bride (12, 45). By
a similar stratagem, as recorded in the first canto of Book 11, Acrasia
has caused the death of her former lover Mordant when his wife had
temporarily recovered him, and sorrow for this bloody deed has
provoked the suicide of this wife. The 'death' which stands written
in his name is replaced in the name of Acrasia's new lover by a
signification of youthful growth and new hope – 'Verdant'. He, too,
at the time of Guyon's arrival, is being blighted in this garden of
only artfully simulated natural delight, as Cymochles, son of 'Acrates'
(11, 4, 41:6); cf. 'Acrasia'), had previously been shown to be wholly
blighted (cf. 5, 28):

> His warlike armes, the idle instruments
>   Of sleeping praise, were hong upon a tree,
>   And his brave shield, full of old moniments,
>   Was fowly ra'st, that none the signes might see;
>   Ne for them, ne for honour cared hee,
>   Ne ought, that did to his advancement tend,
>   But in lewd loves, and wastfull luxuree,
>   His dayes, his goods, his bodie he did spend:
> O horrible enchantment, that him so did blend. (12, 80)

In Western culture the lyrical reminder of the moral brevity of
beauty has probably been more frequently expressed by the symbol
of the rose than by any other, but what the rose is meant logically to
support in Acrasia's garden is a culpable lie: so short is our time to
love, says her sect, that by implication the fatal accompaniments of
desire here, murder and the reduction of man's reason to beastliness,
are justified if only we may prolong the one moment of bliss. As in
the lily-song, we hear of the furnishing forth of a bedchamber, and
of the physical act of sex itself with a paramour:

> So passeth, in the passing of a day,
>   Of mortall life the leafe, the bud, the flowre,
>   Ne more doth flourish after first decay,
>   That earst was sought to decke both bed and bowre,

> Of many a Ladie, and many a Paramowre:
> Gather therefore the Rose, whilest yet is prime,
> For soone comes age, that will her pride deflowre:
> Gather the Rose of love, whilest yet is time,
> Whilest loving thou mayst loved be with equall crime.
>
> (12, 75)

True Nature, as against the false artifices of a lying pornography, denies the premise. It is indeed true that each of us is bounded within his mortal prison and can live and love only briefly, yet the act of love itself is bound up with a circumstance that mitigates this hard fate and justifies (not only for dupes but also for the wise) a large-minded generosity towards others, not Acrasia's single-minded, murderous defense of her prey. In love we may beget copies of ourselves who engage our profound affection and in a sense continue us. They, too, will love and beget others, and each life bound by time may, for man's existence and throughout organic nature, become timeless. Of this timelessness the chief organic witness around us is the return of vegetation . . . after their deaths, with the revolving year. The primeval tragedy of the descent of the Idea from the eternal and infinite into the bounded universe of temporal mutability and finite extension receives its classic mitigation in similar terms in the theory recorded in Plato's *Timaeus*. The Demiurge there arranges that the phenomenon of change in the universe should be circular and cyclical, so that all things, pitifully declining and perishable though they are, should by changing return upon themselves and continue the cycle afresh. Having lost the primeval true eternity of divine perfection, they yet are dowered with an eternity of recurrence, and the accomplishment of that eternity is through love.

It is in Mutabilitie, the incomplete seventh book of *The Faerie Queene*, that Spenser mounts his chief celebration of this circumstance for the heavens above and the earth below; but for the life of our species and its mirroring in the organic life of the animal and particularly of the vegetable kingdoms, the chief celebration in *The Faerie Queene* takes place in the . . . Garden of Adonis in III. 6.

Here all is truly in accord with Nature, and a lying artifice has no place. In 'so faire a place as Nature can devize', 'all the goodly flowres, / Wherewith dame Nature doth her beautifie, / And decks the girlonds of her paramoures / Are fetcht'. 'Franckly each paramour his leman knowes', with emphasis on 'franckly' and on the natural, uninstitutionalized, physically sexual meanings of 'leman' and 'knowes' . . . the arbor over Cymochles had been of artfully arranged ivy with eglantine woven through it; the same image of licentious ivy, artfully fabricated of gold, reappeared on the fountain of the Bower of Bliss, and the vines were painfully bowed down by the weight of seeming grapes fashioned of the heaviest metal. All of this now appears in a new guise:

> And in the thickest covert of that shade,
>   There was a pleasant arbour, not by art,
>   But of the trees owne inclination made,
>   Which knitting their rancke braunches part to part,
>   With wanton yvie twyne entrayld athwart,
>   And Eglantine, and Caprifole emong,
>   Fashioned above within their inmost part.   (III, 6, 44:1–7)

The generalization affirmed by Acrasia's song is here reaffirmed up to a point, for Time cannot be denied:

> For formes are variable and decay,
>   By course of kind, and by occasion;
>   And that faire flowre of beautie fades away,
> As doth the lilly fresh before the sunny ray.
>
> (6, 38:6–9)

Yet Nature through her traditional helper and priest Genius sees to it that the supplies are constantly replenished, both of plants and of human beings. Correspondingly, beneath that arbor just described, on a hill in the center of the Garden (and of Book III) lies a cave in which Venus preserves her lover and can, unlike Acrasia, enjoy him eternally. He is Adonis, the dying and reborn god, one of the chief symbols of pagan antiquity for the rebirth of vegetation in the spring-time. A Garden of Adonis is in the first instance a bowl of earth in which grass-seed is ritually allowed to spring up as an earnest of the return of the year after the desolation of winter. Adonis is described as the 'Father of all formes',

> And sooth it seemes they say: for he may not
>   For ever die, and ever buried bee
>   In balefull night, where all things are forgot;

> All be he subject to mortalitie,
> Yet is eterne in mutabilitie,
> And by succession made perpetuall.   (6, 47:1–6)

New shapes are continually imposed in the Garden upon the same enduring matter, of which the old shapes have had continually to pass away (6, 38). The myth here is the same as in the earlier part of this canto, where the annual encourager of plant life, the sun, is described as the 'Great father' 'of generation' to whom his sister the moon provides fit matter for the new living shapes (6, 9). In v, 7 (Isis Church) there appears a similar image of sun and moon in cooperation, there equated with Osiris and Isis, who are both brother and sister and man and wife: Phoebus, correspondingly, is Phoebe's brother in III, 6, and Adonis is Venus's leman. The place where he knows her, in the central mount, is the hill of Venus, the *mons Veneris*, the central point of the female anatomy and the seat of pleasure. . . .

The next of the moralized landscapes to be considered here is a further rendition of the story of Venus and Adonis, this time in its picturesquely pretty Ovidian form. This appears on a tapestry (III, 1, 34–8) of Castle Joyeous, the abode of Malecasta. Suitably, it is a reversion to the egotistical and shallow formulae of Phaedria and Acrasia. The 'joy' in the castle's name is a synonym for the 'bliss' of Acrasia's Bower and the 'joyfulness' to be found in the name 'Phaedria' and the fanciful etymology *Flos deliciae*. 'Malecasta' signifies 'badly chaste', 'unchaste'. In the tapestry Venus woos Adonis to be 'her Paramoure', 'making girlonds of each flowre that grew', and leading him away from the sunlight and from 'heavens vew' and his companions into secret and un-frank darkness. When he bathes, she, like Cymochles, craftily spies on 'each dainty lim', and then throws 'sweet Rosemaryes, / And fragrant violets, and Pances trim' into the water that holds him. Finally he is killed by the boar and transmuted 'to a dainty flowre'. She 'Makes for him endlesse mone'. *Finita la stòria*: there is no trace of the shackled boar and of the eternity in mutability of the classic rendition of Nature's truth in the Garden of Adonis. The flower here, like the other components of the story, and like the contents of the Bower, only appears to possess the lineaments of living nature, and is in truth a lying artifact, 'Which in that cloth was wrought, as if it lively grew'.

The great strength of the ingenuous, straightforward sex of the

Garden of Adonis, as against all the other instances which we have
discussed so far, is that it belongs to Nature; no sophistications of a
feigning art pervert it. Yet it remains true that an acquired art of
another kind in the management of personal relationships is universally acknowledged (although not universally practiced) as a necessary civilized complement to the stubbornly insistent libidinal urge
with which we are naturally endowed. This art, in accordance with
which natural affection is sublimated and amplified into a wise and
friendly respect for the freedom and independence of those whom we
love, is not a denial of nature but its perfecting. This desirable added
dimension in our lives together is Spenser's concern in yet another
allegorical locale, the Isle and Temple of Venus in Canto 10 of
Book IV, Of Friendship. In the other parts of this book, a number of
the components of this moralized landscape are covertly supplied or
reinforced in the course of chivalric adventure, which forms the other
great category of narrative in *The Faerie Queene* in addition to
paysage moralisé. . . .

SOURCE: extracts from 'A Spenser to Structure Our Myths',
in *Contemporary Thought on Edmund Spenser*, ed. R. C. Frushell
and B. J. Vondersmith (Carbondale, Ill., 1975) pp. 100, 106–11.

SELECT BIBLIOGRAPHY

TEXTS

The best one-volume edition of the complete works of Spenser is the Oxford Standard Authors edition, originally published in 1912, and now also in paperback, edited by J. C. Smith and E. de Selincourt. A lightly annotated one-volume edition is that by R. E. N. Dodge (Boston, 1908). The best edition of the poem, but again not annotated, is that in the Oxford English Texts series, in 2 volumes, edited by J. C. Smith (1909). The Variorum edition of the complete works, edited by E. Greenlaw, C. G. Osgood, F. M. Padelford *et al.* (Baltimore, completed 1949, revised 1958), has a volume for each book of *The Faerie Queene*, is fully annotated, includes extensive quotations from articles and books, and from sources, and has textual appendices. (In this edition there is a detailed *Life* by A. C. Judson.) There are good one-volume editions, comprehensively annotated for school and university students, of some individual books: Book I (Oxford, 1965) and Book II (Oxford, 1966) by P. C. Bayley; Books I and II by R. Kellogg and O. Steele (New York, 1965); Book VI by T. Wolff (London, 1959).

BOOKS

The books from which extracts have been taken are all strongly recommended. Publishing details will be found at the end of extracts, and in Acknowledgements, pp. 7–8. Other books from which I would like to have printed extracts are:

L. Bradner, *Edmund Spenser and 'The Faerie Queene'* (Chicago and London, 1948).
D. Cheney, *Spenser's Image of Nature* (New Haven, Conn., 1966).
R. Ellrodt, *Neoplatonism in the Poetry of Spenser* (Geneva, 1960).
Alastair Fowler, *Spenser and the Numbers of Time* (London, 1964).
A. Bartlett Giamatti, *Play of Double Senses* (New Jersey, 1975).
E. A. Greenlaw, *Studies in Spenser's Historical Allegory* (Baltimore and London, 1932).
J. E. Hankins, *Source and Meaning in Spenser's Allegory* (Oxford, 1971).
C. S. Lewis, *Spenser's Images of Life*, ed. Alastair Fowler (Cambridge, 1967).
Isabel G. MacCaffrey, *Spenser's Allegory: The Anatomy of Imagination* (Princeton, 1976).
M. P. Parker, *The Allegory of 'The Faerie Queene'* (Oxford, 1960).
W. L. Renwick, *Edmund Spenser* (London, 1925).
Thomas P. Roche, Jr, *The Kindly Flame* (Princeton, 1964).
H. Tonkin, *Spenser's Courteous Pastoral* (Oxford, 1972).
K. Williams, *Spenser's 'Faerie Queene': The World of Glass* (London, 1966).

ARTICLES

There is a surprising number of collections of essays (whether new or re-printed). They include:

P. J. Alpers (ed.), *Elizabethan Poetry: Modern Essays in Criticism* (London and New York, 1967).

P. J. Alpers, (ed.), *Edmund Spenser*, in Penguin Critical Anthologies series (Harmondsworth, 1969).

K. J. Atchity (ed.), *Eterne in Mutabilitie: The Unity of 'The Faerie Queene'* (Hamden, 1972).

Harry Berger Jr, *Spenser, A Collection of Critical Essays* (Englewood Cliffs, 1968).

R. M. Cummings (ed.), *Spenser, The Critical Heritage* (from 1579–1715) (London, 1971).

J. R. Elliott (ed.), *The Prince of Poets: Essays on Edmund Spenser* (New York and London, 1968).

R. C. Frushell and B. J. Vondersmith (eds), *Contemporary Thought on Edmund Spenser* (Carbondale, Ill., 1975).

A. C. Hamilton (ed.), *Essential Articles for The Study of Edmund Spenser* (Hamden, 1972).

Judith M. Kennedy and James A. Reither (eds), *A Theatre for Spenserians* (Toronto, Buffalo and Manchester, 1973).

W. R. Mueller and D. C. Allen (eds), *That Soueraine Light* (Baltimore, 1952).

W. R. Mueller (ed.), *Spenser's Critics* (from 1715–1949) (Syracuse, 1959).

W. Nelson (ed.), *Form and Convention in the Poetry of Edmund Spenser* (New York and London, 1961).

Critical Essays on Spenser from The Journal of English Literary History (Baltimore and London, 1970).

NOTES ON CONTRIBUTORS TO
PARTS TWO AND THREE

P. J. ALPERS is Professor of English in the University of California at Berkeley. His publications include *The Poetry of 'The Faerie Queene'* (1967) and he has edited *Elizabethan Poetry: Modern Essays in Criticism* (1967) and the Penguin *Critical Anthology* on Spenser (1969).

PETER BAYLEY, formerly English Fellow of University College, Oxford, is now Master of Collingwood College, Durham. His publications include *Edmund Spenser: Prince of Poets* (1971) and he has edited the Oxford University Press editions of Book I and Book II of *The Faerie Queene*.

HARRY S. BERGER Jr, is Professor of English Literature in the University of California at Santa Cruz. His publications include *The Allegorical Temper: Vision and Reality in Book II of Spenser's 'Faerie Queene'* (1957).

H. H. BLANCHARD (died 1971): the main part of his academic career was as Professor of English at Tufts University (formerly Tufts College) in Medford, Massachusetts; after his retirement from Tufts he taught English Literature at Franconia College, New Hampshire.

MARTHA CRAIG teaches in the Department of English at Wellesley College, Massachusetts.

R. E. NEIL DODGE edited the *Complete Poetical Works* of Edmund Spenser (1908).

WILLIAM EMPSON, Professor of English Literature in the University of Sheffield from 1953 to 1971 and subsequently Emeritus Professor there, is the author of *Seven Types of Ambiguity* (1930), *Some Versions of Pastoral* (1935), *The Structure of Complex Words* (1951), *Milton's God* (1961) and several collections of poems.

MAURICE EVANS is Professor of English in the University of Exeter. His publications include *English Poetry in the Sixteenth Century* (1955; revised edition, 1967) and *Spenser's Anatomy of Heroism* (1970).

ALASTAIR FOWLER is Regius Professor of Rhetoric and English Literature in the University of Edinburgh. He is the author of *Spenser and the Numbers of Time* (1964), *Triumphal Forms* (1970) and *Silent Poetry* (1970); and he has edited *The Poems of John Milton*, with John Carey (1968), *Topics in Criticism*, with Christopher Butler (1971), and C. S. Lewis's study, *Spenser's Images of Life* (1967).

NORTHROP FRYE is Professor of English in the University of Toronto. His publications include *Fearful Symmetry* (1947) and *The Anatomy of Criticism* (1957).

A. C. HAMILTON is Professor of English in Queen's University at Kingston, Ontario. His publications include *The Structure of Allegory in 'The Faerie Queene'* (1961), and he is preparing an annotated edition of the poem.

A. KENT HIEATT is Professor of English in the University of Western Ontario. He is the author of *Short Time's Endless Monument: The Symbolism of the Numbers in Spenser's 'Epithalamion'* (1972), and of several articles on number symbolism. He has in the press a study of Chaucer, Spenser and Milton. He is a founder of the *Spenser Newsletter*.

GRAHAM HOUGH, formerly Professor of English in the University of Cambridge, is the author of *The Last Romantics* (1949), *The Dark Sun* (1957), and of *A Preface to 'The Faerie Queene'* (1962), and also of *An Essay on Criticism* (1966) and *Style and Stylistics* (1969).

FRANK KERMODE is King Edward VII Professor of English Literature in the University of Cambridge. His publications include *Romantic Image* (1957) *John Donne* (1957), *The Sense of an Ending* (1967), *Continuities* (1968), *Shakespeare, Spenser, Donne* (1971) and *Renaissance Essays* (1973).

C. S. LEWIS at the time of his death (1963) was Professor of Medieval and Renaissance Studies in the University of Cambridge. His critical studies include *The Allegory of Love, Preface to 'Paradise Lost', English Literature in the Sixteenth Century, Studies in Words, An Experiment in Criticism* and *The Discarded Image*. His study on *Spenser's Images of Life* was edited by Alastair Fowler (1967).

WILLIAM NELSON is Professor of English in Columbia University, New York. He has edited *Form and Convention in the Poetry of Edmund Spenser* (1961) and is the author of *The Poetry of Edmund Spenser* (1963).

ROSEMOND TUVE at the time of her death (1964) was Professor of English in the University of Pennsylvania. Her publications include *Seasons and Months: Studies in a Tradition of Middle English Poetry* (1933), *Elizabethan and Metaphysical Poets* (1947) and *A Reading of George Herbert* (1952). Thomas P. Roche edited her *Allegorical Imagery* (1966) and *Essays on Spenser, Herbert and Milton* (1970).

INDEX

Note. Citations are of the most important references only, but no citation is given where a contribution is devoted to a specific named topic: e.g. Dodge on 'Ariosto', Kermode on 'historical reference', Fowler on 'Neoplatonism'.

ACRASIA 70, 141, 176, 177, 221, 222, 231, 240ff.
Aeneas 54, 180, 194
Aeneid 25–6, 151–2, 180, 183, 194
Alciati 220
Alcina (in Ariosto) 70, 221
allegory 18, 23ff., 36, 41, 147, 148, 158, 185ff., 219
AMORET 71, 104, 105, 122ff.
Angelica (in Ariosto) 69ff.
archaism 128–9
ARCHIMAGO 71, 72, 134, 206, 208
Ariosto 33, 94ff., 161ff., 181, 211
Aristotle 57, 85, 147, 183
Armida (in Tasso) 102, 221–2
ARTEGALL 67ff.
ARTHUR, Prince 79ff., 97, 109, 137–8, 180, 184ff., 190, 234
Astolfo (in Ariosto) 70, 162

BELPHOEBE 84, 104, 114, 150ff.
Beves of Hamtoun 60, 163
BLATANT BEAST 71, 227, 228
Bliss, Bower of 56, 102, 106, 112, 127, 139, 176–7, 221, 231, 240ff.

Boccaccio: *Genealogia Deorum* 51ff.
Boiardo 161–2
Bradamante (in Ariosto) 66, 72
BRAGGADOCCHIO 85, 145
BRITOMART 67ff., 71, 102, 123ff., 237
Bryskett, Lodowick 41
Bunyan, John 44–5, 163
BUSIRANE 105, 119, 123, 125ff., 230

CALIDORE 117, 120–1, 227–8
Chaucer 195, 216–17
CIRCE 26, 70, 222
Coleridge 119
'Colin Clout's Come Home Againe' 215
Comes, Natalis: *Mythologiae* 51ff.
courtesy 19, 139
CUPID 123, 124, 230
CYMOCHLES 61–2, 115

DESPAIR 58, 126, 138, 174, 218
Digby, Sir Kenelm 141–2
DRAGON 60, 163, 175
DUESSA 70, 102, 105, 134, 135, 164, 205, 207ff.

Elizabeth, Queen   67, 81, 202ff.
emblems   218ff., 229
entrelacement   81ff.
euhemerism   54–5

FLORIMELL   69ff., 84, 104,
    105, 192
FRADUBIO   70, 135
Freud   101, 103ff.

Garden of Adonis   112–13,
    231, 243ff.
gardens   212–13, 214
Gerusalemme Liberata (Tasso)
    30, 181, 186–7, 221, 241
GRACES, The   120–1, 224ff.
Greenlaw, Edwin   199ff., 203,
    204
Grey, Arthur, Lord Grey de
    Wilton   66
GUYON   61, 90, 100, 106, 114,
    170ff., 237

Harington, Sir John   18,
    187–8
Harvey, Gabriel,   11
Hazlitt, William   13
HELLENORE   188–9
historical reference   78, 101ff.,
    116, 153, 185, 199ff., 215–16
Homer   130, 133
Hunt, Leigh   14
Huon of Bordeaux   60, 77
Hurd, Richard   13

iconography   198, 200, 225
IGNARO   18, 109
Ireland, depicted or implied
    214ff.
IRENA   215
Isabella (in Ariosto)   70
ISIS   66

letter to Raleigh, Spenser's   17,
    80, 106, 180ff., 234
Lowell, James Russell   14

MALBECCO   18, 71, 188–9, 219
MALECASTA   63, 70, 96, 245
MALEGER   174ff.
Malory, Sir Thomas   79, 93,
    94, 105
MAMMON   28, 38–9, 56, 127,
    163, 218
MARINELL   84
MELIBOE   228
MERLIN   66ff., 95–6
metamorphosis   49–50
Milton, John   40, 118, 127,
    207–8
'Mother Hubberd's Tale'   44
Mutabilitie, Cantos of   19,
    117, 215, 217–18
MUTABILITIE   243
myth   50ff., 150, 245

ORGOGLIO   109, 134, 137,
    163, 209
Orlando Furioso (Ariosto)   18,
    33, 161ff., 181, 187–8, 221
Orlando Innamorato (Boiardo)
    67, 161ff.
Ovid   49ff., 52, 150ff., 245

PARIDELL   188–9
PASTORELLA   228
PHAEDRIA   61ff., 108, 140
Piers Plowman (Langland)   99
Pilgrim's Progress (Bunyan)
    44–5, 101, 106
Plato's *Cratylus*   129ff.
Plato's *Timaeus*   243
Pléiade   129
Plutarch   24–5
PRIDE   136, 137

processions, etc. 214
PROSERPINA and her Garden 56
PROTEUS 70

RADIGUND 50
Raleigh, Sir Walter, *see* letter to
RED CROSS KNIGHT 60, 70, 105, 109, 115, 133–8, 139, 163, 170ff., 190ff., 205ff., 230
Ruggiero (in Ariosto) 66
Rymer, Thomas 12

ST GEORGE *see* RED CROSS KNIGHT
SCUDAMOUR 65
Shakespeare 116, 127, 201
Shepheardes Calender, The 208
Sidney, Sir Philip 41, 108, 119, 185
SINS, THE SEVEN DEADLY 136ff.
Spenserian stanza 40, 142ff., 193–4
Strong, Roy C. 203–4

TANTALUS 56
Tasso, Torquato 30, 181, 186–7, 211, 241
TIMIAS 64, 114
Tristran (in Ariosto) 71

UNA 105, 134, 163, 166ff., 205, 208–9
unity (in *The Faerie Queene*) 12–13, 148ff., 235, 237
Upton, John 12, 199

VENUS 231; and ADONIS 245; Temple of 232
View of the Present State of Ireland 215
Virgil 151ff., 179ff.

Warton, Thomas 13, 20
Watkins, W. B. C. 123
Wordsworth 42

Yeats, W. B. 111

Some Brief Critical Cross-references

Alpers on Lewis 118
Craig on Lewis 128
Dowden on Lowell 41
Evans on Alpers 112; on Tuve 115
Fowler on Hough 227; on Fletcher 235; on Nelson 236
Kermode on Greenlaw 199; on Hamilton 199; on Hough 200
Tuve on Berger 100